WHO DECIDES?

The Abortion Rights of Teens

J. Shoshanna Ehrlich

Foreword by Sarah Weddington

Reproductive Rights and Policy
Judith Baer, Series Editor

PRAEGER

Westport, Connecticut
London

Library of Congress Cataloging-in-Publication Data

Ehrlich, Shoshanna.
  Who decides? : the abortion rights of teens / J. Shoshanna Ehrlich.
      p.   cm.—(Reproductive rights and policy)
  Includes bibliographical references and index.
  ISBN 0–275–98321–8
  1. Abortion—Law and legislation—United States.   2. Pregnant school-
girls—Legal status, laws, etc.—United States.   3. Pregnancy, Unwanted—
United States—Decision making.   4. Teenage pregnancy—United States.
I. Title. II. Series.
  KF9315.E36 2006
  342.7308'4—dc22   2005037080

British Library Cataloguing in Publication Data is available.

Library of Congress Catalog Card Number: 2005037080
ISBN: 0–275–98321–8

First published in 2006

Praeger Publishers, 88 Post Road West, Westport, CT 06881
An imprint of Greenwood Publishing Group, Inc.
www.praeger.com

Printed in the United States of America

(∞)™

The paper used in this book complies with the
Permanent Paper Standard issued by the National
Information Standards Organization (Z39.48–1984).

10 9 8 7 6 5 4 3 2 1

This book is lovingly dedicated to my daughter, Emma Stoskopf-Ehrlich, and to the memory of my mother, Shelley Ehrlich.

Contents

Foreword

Professor Shoshanna Ehrlich has written a timely book in "Who Decides?: The Abortion Rights of Teens." It is organized and composed with the skill of a great artist. The book is fresh and thought provoking. It presents the voices of young women recalling why they chose to have an abortion as well as why they chose not to discuss this decision with their parents. Since we, the readers, do not have that opportunity, Professor Ehrlich gives us a rare insight into those deliberations and thought processes. The inconsistencies and uncertainties of the current legal regard for the decisions of minors are startling for those who do not deal with those issues on a day-to-day basis. The book raises valuable questions about what a more appropriate approach would be and offers useful suggestions toward that end.

I recommend this book to anyone interested in abortion law and policy as well as the rights of teens. From the book's beginning pages the reader gains an understanding of "how we got where we are" in the U.S. regarding the law of abortion and then spotlights the struggle to ensure that young women also have a meaningful right of choice. It should be read by anyone who is involved in or wishes to understand more about the current battle to preserve a woman's right to abortion.

We are now experiencing what feel like the early tremors of a coming earth-quake set off by the changing membership of the U.S. Supreme Court. Will *Roe v. Wade* be overturned has become a pressing question. While the tremors are occurring, states are actively engaged in passing increasingly restrictive abortion laws. For example, South Dakota has enacted an anti-abortion law that essentially reinstates the law of Texas prior to the *Roe v. Wade* decision, and legislators in other states are considering the adoption of similar laws. Proponents of these measures have emphasized their intent to give the U.S. Supreme Court an opportunity to overturn Roe.

While the battle over the future of abortion rights for all continues and even escalates, a separate on-going controversy is what hoops should minors be required to jump through to secure an abortion? This book points out the mature approach of many minors and the care with which they make decisions about abortion. It allows them to articulate why they are determined not to become mothers at that young age and why, from their point of view, involving their parents would not facilitate a constructive solution.

Ehrlich presents a compelling argument that while requiring parental involvement initially sounds reasonable, a close examination of the impact of such statutes reveals the ways in which they are unreasonable. For instance, she discusses how they operate to punish teens who lack supportive and caring parents. The book also points out that the laws are supported by anti-choice folks who would like to outlaw abortion and until they can do so are in hot pursuit of barriers to abortion access, and that professional health groups who work with teens oppose law requiring parental consent. Ehrlich in her conclusion presents thoughtful suggestions for better fact-based approaches to abortion laws that involve minors.

On March 31, 2003 *Time* magazine published a special section to celebrate its 80th birthday. The section was appropriately entitled "80 Days That Changed the World". The day selected for 1973 was the *Roe v. Wade* decision, January 22. The right to make their own decisions about continuing or terminating a pregnancy has truly changed the world for U.S. women. But the current conflict about Roe's future tells us that we are beginning a new stage of controversy, and this book points out that young women are particularly vulnerable targets of anti-choice laws. Readers of "Who Decides?: The Abortion Rights of Teens" will come away with a far better understanding of why we must fight to protect the abortion rights of all women, including teens.

Sarah Weddington
Winning Attorney, *Roe v. Wade*
Adjunct Professor, University of Texas—Austin
Founder, The Weddington Center

Series Foreword

Who Decides? The Abortion Rights of Teens is the first volume in the Praeger Series on Reproductive Rights and Policy. The topics subsumed under this heading include some of the hottest "hot button" issues in the United States, though not everywhere in the world. Both the right to have children and the right not to be forced to have them are threatened and vulnerable. Other reproductive issues include the conditions and constraints of parenting: for example, breast-feeding, fetal-protection policies, and employment discrimination against parents and expectant mothers. The vast amount of scholarship that reproductive issues have generated has by no means exhausted either the insights or the arguments that can be made. As series editor, I envisioned a multidisciplinary, multicultural list that would present new research, new angles, and new insights. Shoshanna Ehrlich has ably inaugurated this series.

The controversy over legalized abortion in the United States has intensified in the three decades since *Roe v. Wade*. Public discourse remains passionate and polarized even though a majority of Americans occupy the center. The relatively few Americans who believe either that abortion is murder or that government should facilitate the choice of abortion make up the group of activists, experts, and lawmakers who dominate the debate. But public opinion surveys have consistently shown general support both for a woman's right to choose and for some limitations on this right.

One familiar compromise position is a willingness to accept special restrictions on the abortion rights of teenage women. The Anglo-American legal tradition accepts that the constitutional rights of minors are less extensive than those of adults and that parents have extensive control over their children's lives. The Supreme Court has, for example, upheld laws authorizing schools to search their pupils' property and laws allowing parents to commit their children to mental institutions without a hearing. The Court has not gone quite so far with respect to abortion. It struck down a parental-consent requirement in 1976, in *Planned Parenthood of Central Missouri v. Danforth*. But dissenting Justice John Paul Stevens declared, "Whatever choice a pregnant young woman makes . . . the consequences of her decision may have a profound impact on her future life. A legislative decision that such a choice will be made more wisely if the advice and moral support of a parent play a part in the decision-making process is surely not irrational." Stevens has had the satisfaction of seeing his views enacted into law.

The Court has never sustained an absolute parental-consent requirement. But as the balance of political power shifted to the right and conservative judges replaced liberals, state legislatures went back to the drawing board. New laws requiring either parental notification or a judicial bypass before a teen could obtain an abortion progressed through the appeal process. As these laws survived judicial scrutiny, more states enacted them. In 2005, 45 states required some sort of consent or notification (not always of a parent) for minors or teens below a stipulated age. These laws are influenced by traditional beliefs in youthful immaturity and parental wisdom.

Ehrlich's original and exciting book studies the decision-making of pregnant teenagers about whether or not to involve their parents in their choices. The young women she interviewed agree with Justice Stevens that the choice to end or continue a pregnancy profoundly affects their lives. But their shrewd and intelligent observations vindicate their own capacity for intelligent decision-making. These teens decided to seek or not seek parental input for many complex reasons. Fear of abuse was one reason, but so was solicitude for parents who were ill or overwhelmed by the circumstances of their lives. *Who Decides?* reaffirms the growing realization that, rather than guiding the young or strengthening the family, parental notification laws are part of a concerted effort to deny reproductive choice to women.

Judith Baer
Series Editor

Preface

Abortion is a loaded word that embodies multiple symbolic meanings. For some, the word implies a disregard for the value of life; for others, myself included, it signifies a regard for female agency and self-determination. The differences in understanding run deep and at times seem unbridgeable. Perhaps this is because the debate is not really about when life begins, but is instead about the "meanings of *women's* lives" and the role that reproductive control plays in shaping a woman's sense of her place in the world.[1]

When the woman seeking to abort is under the age of 18, the abortion decision is weighted with even greater symbolic meaning. Issues surrounding a young woman's expressed desire to control her own destiny go well beyond the disputed nature of the decision itself, landing us in the highly contested realm of family relationships, particularly with respect to the tension between the rights of parental control and adolescent claims to self-agency.

It is here that this book enters the public discourse about abortion. At the heart of this work are the voices of 26 young women from Massachusetts who, under state law, elected to seek court authorization for an abortion rather than obtain consent from a parent. Massachusetts law does not present a unique requirement; most states similarly require young women to either involve their parents or obtain the permission of a court before having an abortion.

The young women I interviewed were referred to me by the attorneys who had represented them in court. We met in public places, such as food courts or libraries, and they shared their stories with me. Some lived in the projects; others resided in affluent suburbs. Some had experienced considerable loss and turmoil; others came from close and relatively stable two-parent households. Regardless of their circumstances, they talked openly about why they chose abortion over motherhood and why they did not disclose their situation to a parent. They also talked about how frightening it was to have a judge determine their fate.

As adults continue to debate the wisdom of mandating adult involvement in the reproductive decision-making of young women, it is my hope that the voices of this diverse group of young women will influence the discussion. The complexity of their lives and the seriousness with which they made the necessary decisions challenge the idea that young women lack the ability to make informed decisions about their own reproductive futures.

Acknowledgments

This book grows out of many years of work and would not have been possible without the support and encouragement of many people. It is with great pleasure that I acknowledge the following individuals and organizations.

This book draws on interviews that were conducted with young women as part of the Minors' Abortion Rights Project. I would like to thank the David and Lucille Packard Foundation and the Robert Sterling Clark Foundation for their generous support of this project. I would also like to express my gratitude to Carol Hardy-Fanta and Jamie Ann Sabino, who were the other principal investigators on this project. This was truly a collaborative endeavor that would not have come to fruition without their tireless effort and unwavering commitment to advancing the reproductive rights of young women.

This book also draws upon several articles that I have written over the course of the last six years. Many colleagues reviewed and commented on various drafts of these articles, and this book has been enriched by their involvement. With much appreciation to: Janet Crepps, Jennifer Dalven, Angela Holder, Dara Klassel, Louise Melling, Jamie Ann Sabino, Walter Wadlington, and Catherine Weiss.

As a professor in the College of Public and Community Service at the University of Massachusetts–Boston, I have the honor of working with a wonderfully diverse and dynamic group of students. I would like to thank several of them for their valuable research assistance. They are: Tony Naro, Deborah Sullivan, and Meredith Williams. I would also like to thank Rebecca Cohen-Taub, Sophie Labaree, and Emma Stoskopf-Ehrlich for their valuable research assistance.

Thank you also to Amy Lucid and Nicki Nichols Gamble from the Planned Parenthood League of Massachusetts, to Ismael Ramirez-Soto and Evelyn Wong from the College of Public and Community Service at the University of Massachusetts–Boston, and to Sandra Tavarez for her administrative support.

I would also like to acknowledge the valuable work of the lawyers and the Planned Parenthood counselors in Massachusetts who assist young women through the judicial bypass process and the Steering Committee, which helps ensure that the bypass law is implemented in the least burdensome manner possible. Through these combined efforts, young women in Massachusetts have continued to have a meaningful right of choice.

Finally, many thanks to the family and friends who have seen me through this effort. In particular, I want to thank my husband, Alan Stoskopf, and my daughter, Emma Stoskopf-Ehrlich, for all of their love and encouragement and my father, Fred Ehrlich, for his faith in me.

1

A Crime No Longer: *Roe v. Wade* and the Constitutional Right of Choice

In 1973, in the case of *Roe v. Wade (Roe)*,[1] the United States Supreme Court considered a challenge to a Texas law that made it a crime to procure or perform an abortion unless the abortion was, as determined by medical advice, "for the purpose of saving the life of the mother."[2] At the time *Roe* was decided, most states had similar laws in effect; accordingly, as in Texas, abortion was permitted only when necessary to save the life of a pregnant woman. However, some states had liberalized their laws to permit abortion in other, albeit generally very limited, circumstances, such as in cases of serious fetal anomalies or when the pregnancy posed a threat to the woman's health or was the result of rape or incest.

Although some critics of the decision responded to *Roe* as if the Court had "suddenly and irrationally decided to undermine something basic in American life,"[3] it is important to recognize that, as in other states, the Texas law under consideration had only been on the books for a little more than one hundred years. Thus, at the time Roe was decided, criminal abortion laws were not a fixed and permanent aspect of American life, as they had only been part of our legal landscape since the second half of the nineteenth century. Thus, although *Roe* resulted in a profound reallocation of decisional authority over pregnancy, the Court had only to look back to the colonial period to find a moral and legal understanding of abortion different from the one embodied in the Texas statute.

Therefore, to better understand the significance of *Roe*, we begin this chapter by situating the decision in its historic legal context. We look first to the colonial era, when the law's approach to abortion was quite fluid. We next consider the mid-nineteenth–century criminalization of abortion, focusing on the central role that doctors played in the effort to make abortion a crime across the nation. We then move to the pre-*Roe* era to consider how, once again, shifting views about abortion paved the way for a reconfiguration of legal rights.

Having set the historic stage, we take a careful look at *Roe* and at how the decision established a constitutionally protected space for reproductive decision-making. The legal history of abortion does not, of course, end here. The response to *Roe* was prompt and fierce, and many states sought to contain the impact of the decision by enacting restrictive abortion laws. The Court was soon faced with challenges to these laws, and we will consider some of the key cases in which the Court relied upon *Roe* to strike down limitations on a woman's right of choice. Although the Court invalidated many of the laws that made it more difficult for women to obtain abortions, its approach was quite different when it came to laws that limited public funding for abortion. In examining these cases, one can see the Court's increasing deference to the interest of states in protecting the life of the unborn and can glimpse the potential fragility of the *Roe* decision.

This fragility was more fully revealed in 1992, when the Court in the case of *Planned Parenthood of Southeastern Pennsylvania v. Casey*[4] (*Casey*), decided that the time had come to reexamine *Roe*. Although the *Casey* Court affirmed the core right of choice, it also decided that states should have more freedom than provided under *Roe* to enact laws promoting respect for the unborn. In examining *Casey*, we pay particular attention to the dynamic tension between the Court's protection of the *Roe* right and its solicitude for the rights of the unborn. As they did after *Roe*, states responded to the Court's decision by enacting a new wave of restrictive abortion laws. We end this chapter by examining these laws, with a particular focus on the debate over bans on the procedure known commonly as a partial-birth abortion.

THE COMMON-LAW APPROACH TO ABORTION

In 1821 the General Assembly of Connecticut revised its law regulating crimes and punishment. Inserted between a provision governing the "intent to kill or rob" and one addressing the "secret delivery of a bastard child," a new provision made it a crime to provide a women who was "quick with child" with a "deadly poison" in order to induce a miscarriage.[5] This anti-poisoning measure was the first of its kind in the nation. Until this point, no American legislative body had addressed the issue of abortion. Rather, the legal status of abortion had been based on English common-law principles.[6]

Under the common law, an abortion that was performed prior to "quickening" was not a crime. "Quickening" referred to the moment in pregnancy when a woman first feels fetal movement—typically the end of the fourth or the start of the fifth month of pregnancy. After quickening, abortion could be punished as a crime; however, it was not considered the equivalent of murder and was punishable as a misdemeanor rather than as a more serious felony offense.[7] Under the common law, only the person performing the abortion could be indicted for the act; the woman was not considered a party to the crime.

The quickening doctrine reflected a number of considerations. First, as a practical matter, until a woman first felt fetal movement, she had no way of knowing for certain whether the cessation of her menses was attributable to pregnancy or to some other cause. Thus, a woman might see a doctor or take herbs in order to "restore her menses" and return her body to its normal harmony. This was an important aspect of health care, based on the common understanding of the body as a "delicate system of equilibrium that could easily be thrown out of balance . . . and that then needed to be restored through active intervention."[8] Early abortion was simply a way of returning the body to its normal state.

Second, and perhaps related to the fact that until fetal movement was felt, a woman could not be certain she was pregnant, a pre-quick fetus was not regarded as a life. So even if a woman suspected her blocked menses was due to pregnancy, destruction of the fetus was not an act imbued with moral meaning. Only with movement was the fetus thought to acquire an identity that was separate and apart from the person of the pregnant woman.

Although grounded in the biological reality of pregnancy, the quickening doctrine also had a moral component, signaling the moment in time when the fetus was thought to acquire a distinct existence. Quickening served to cleave pregnancy into two distinct periods. In the first period, roughly coinciding with the first half of pregnancy, the fetus was regarded as part of the pregnant woman; in the second period, the fetus was thought to assume a distinct identity and to have some claim to life.

The quickening doctrine was not the first to treat pregnancy as a dynamic process in which the fetus was thought to gradually assume a more coherent identity. Rather, the quickening principles had roots in the ancient doctrine of "mediate" animation, which located the start of life at a determined point between conception and live birth. This doctrine is traceable back to Aristotle's three-stage theory of human development. According to Aristotle, humans begin as "indistinct, vegetating tissue masses which differentiate into animal forms with certain, basic capacities, and later become human upon the infusion of a rational soul."[9] Aristotle believed that over the course of a pregnancy, the fetus progressed from the vegetable stage, in which it was simply capable of drawing nourishment to itself, to the animal stage, in which "the rudiments of sensation and directed movement" developed, to the human stage, which was marked by the acquisition of the capacity for rational thought. Aristotle believed that the progression from vegetable to animal took place on or after day 40 of growth for males and on or after day 90 for females.[10]

Aristotle's theory of mediate animation influenced the development of Christian doctrine. In the fourth century, St. Augustine distinguished between an "embryo animatus" (an embryo with a soul) and an "embryo inamimatus" (an embryo without a soul) and indicated that animation, also referred to as ensoulment, did not occur until the second month of pregnancy. In 1140, this view of fetal development was made part of Canon Law; consistent with Aristotle's teachings, the time of animation was fixed at 40 days for a male fetus and at 90 days for a female.[11]

Canon law adhered to the doctrine of mediate animation until 1869, when it was repudiated by Pope Pius the IX in favor of the doctrine of immediate animation—which teaches that a fetus is imbued with a human soul from the moment of conception.[12] Different explanations have been proposed for this shift. One possibility is that the change reflected a greater understanding of the process of fertilization and fetal development. Another is that it was a logical consequence of the Catholic Church's declaration in 1854 that the Immaculate Conception of Mary—the teaching that Mary was without original sin from the moment of her conception—was now part of official Catholic dogma. For this doctrine to make sense, Mary would need to have been possessed with a soul at the time she was conceived, a belief that supports the idea of "immediate" as distinct from "mediate" animation.[13]

Over the course of the nineteenth century, the common-law approach to abortion, with its emphasis on quickening, was gradually displaced by criminal antiabortion statutes. Connecticut's 1821 anti-poisoning law was soon followed by other laws, which, as the century progressed, exerted ever-greater authority over a woman's ability to terminate an unwanted pregnancy. Since we tend to think of abortion as a modern practice, this shift may not seem particularly significant in terms of its potential impact on the lives of women. However, the historical evidence informs us otherwise. Women did have abortions during this time period and a "knowledge of various drugs, potions, and techniques was available from home medical guides, from health books for women, from midwives and irregular practitioners, and from trained physicians."[14]

ABORTION BECOMES A STATUTORY CRIME

Starting with Connecticut in 1821, the nineteenth century witnessed a dramatic transformation in the nation's legal approach to abortion. At the start of the century, abortion was strictly a matter of common-law interpretation—no state had enacted a law regulating abortion. However, by the century's end, every state had a law on the books making abortion a crime, without regard for the quickening distinction that had been so important in common law.

The Beginnings of Change

Between 1821 and 1841, nine states and one federal territory followed Connecticut's lead and passed criminal abortion laws. According to historian James Mohr, these early laws were aimed at regulating the *practice* of abortion, which could be quite dangerous; the methods used to induce a miscarriage, such as toxic poisons, often killed the pregnant woman along with the fetus. Aimed at punishing doctors and apothecaries, these laws, unlike the next generation of criminal abortion laws, did not spring from shifting understanding of fetal life and women's place in society and did not signal a repudiation of the common-law approach to abortion. As Mohr suggests, the narrow focus of these early laws most likely "reflected the continued perception of abortion as a fundamentally marginal practice usually resorted to by women who deserved pity and protection."[15]

A Matter of Grave Public Concern

It may surprise contemporary readers to learn that physicians were the driving force behind the nineteenth-century drive to criminalize abortion. More specifically, the elite or "regular" physicians—those who had been formally trained in the medical science—were the ones to lead the way. Given the importance of those physicians' role in the transformation of the legal status of abortion, we take a brief look at the history of the medical profession in this country, since this history sheds significant light on the motivational impulses behind the doctors' antiabortion activism.

The Search for a Professional Identity[16]

At the time of colonization, physicians in England enjoyed a privileged status. They occupied the top rung of a medical hierarchy that was maintained by the ancient guild system that carefully controlled membership in the various medical "estates." Engaged in a gentleman's profession, physicians did not work with their hands; rather, they "observed, speculated, and prescribed." The manual labor was left to the lower order of surgeons and apothecaries.[17] For the most part, these elite physicians did not find their way to the New World. In contrast to medical practice in England, colonial medicine was mainly a domestic art overseen by women who, as part of their household obligations, were responsible for nursing the ill.

Unlike in England, where the practice of medicine was rigidly controlled, anyone in the colonies who was engaged in healing could hold himself or herself out as a doctor. There was no formal system for distinguishing between "quacks," competent lay healers, and the "regular" doctors who either had attended medical school in Europe or had apprenticed to a practicing physician who had. By the mid-eighteenth century, these "regulars" were increasingly engaged in an effort to "create in America a profession with the standards and dignity that physicians in Europe possessed."[18] In pursuit of this goal, they established medical schools, formed medical societies, and pushed for licensing laws to limit who could hold themselves out as physicians.

By the start of the nineteenth century, the "regulars," although still far from enjoying the privileged status of their English counterparts, had made some progress toward their goal of making medicine an exclusive profession. However, during the 1820s, this goal ran smack up against the democratic ideology of the Jacksonian era.[19] During this time, there was an upsurge in the number of lay practitioners and in the kinds of therapies they offered, including botanics and homeopathy. These healers "saw the medical profession as a bulwark of privilege and they adopted a position hostile to both its therapeutic tenets and its social aspirations."[20] The proliferation of healers led to competition for patients. Making matters worse, state legislatures, in the antielitist fervor of the times, began repealing existing licensing laws, which had come to be seen as "an expression of favor rather than competence."[21] To the extent that these laws had given doctors a measure of professional identity, there was now little to prevent lay practitioners from using the title of "doctor," if they so chose.[22]

As the nineteenth century moved into its third decade, regular physicians were further from their European dream than they had been at the start of the century. Therefore, in 1847, in order to advance their flagging professional interests, they founded the American Medical Association (AMA). The goal of the AMA was to "raise and standardize the requirements for medical degrees" and to hold doctors to a code of ethics, which among other provisions "denied fraternal courtesy to 'irregular' physicians."[23]

Within a decade of the association's formation, Horatio R. Storer, a prominent Harvard professor of gynecology and obstetrics, looked to the AMA to take up the issue of abortion. At the professor's urging, the AMA appointed a committee to investigate abortion practices. Chaired by Storer, the committee reported back to the AMA at its 1859 annual convention in Louisville, Kentucky, calling upon the delegates to approve a resolution that condemned abortion and that committed the AMA to lobbying state legislators to make abortion a statutory crime. With the approval of these resolutions, "one of the first and ultimately one of the most successful public policy crusades ever undertaken by the AMA"[24] was launched. Backed by the AMA, doctors across the country began mobilizing against abortion, and in the end, their efforts would prove to be "the single most important factor in altering the legal policies toward abortion in this country."[25] What remains to be considered is why the AMA and its member physicians seized upon the abortion issue with such vigor.

Investing Abortion with Multiple Meanings

When doctors mobilized to persuade state legislators to criminalize abortion, they did not seek an absolute ban on the practice; rather, they sought to make abortion a crime *unless* a physician determined that an abortion was necessary to save the life of a pregnant woman. The word "unless" is key to understanding a primary motivation behind the doctors' antiabortion activism. By seeking to assert authority over when abortions could be performed, doctors had found a way to demonstrate that they were superior to their competitors and were therefore deserving of special status. As Luker writes, "The abortion issue gave them a way of demonstrating that they were both more scientifically knowledgeable and more morally rigorous than their competitors . . . By becoming visible activists on an issue such as abortion, they could claim both *moral stature* . . . and *technical expertise*."[26] With abortion, doctors could set themselves firmly apart from their competitors, which then gave them a basis for claiming that they had a right to licensing laws that would formally encode their unique status in the world of healers.[27]

With respect to technical expertise, doctors contended that their training distinguished them from lay practitioners by giving them a special understanding of the biological truths of pregnancy. They claimed their education enabled them to grasp that pregnancy was a continuous process from the moment of conception, thus making quickening a meaningless marker of when life begins. As explained by Storer in his book *Why Not? A Book for Every Woman* (*Why Not?*),

Abortion . . . is known by every woman to consist of the premature expulsion of the product of conception. It is not as well know, however . . . that this product of conception is in reality endowed with vitality from the moment of conception itself. . . .

Many women suppose that the child is not alive till quickening has occurred, others that it is practically dead until it has breathed. As well one of these suppositions as the other; they are both of them erroneous.[28]

According to Storer, it was up to doctors to lay bare the scientific truths about abortion and reveal to an ignorant public that it involved the taking of a human life from the outset of pregnancy.[29]

Building from this scientific platform, doctors could then claim the moral high ground—that their knowledge about fetal development invested them with the special responsibility of saving women from the folly of committing murder. As the protectors of fetal life, doctors saw themselves as moral crusaders, seeking to uplift themselves as they educated the public about the evils of abortion.

This crusading spirit ran through the doctors' public pronouncements on the subject of abortion. The following passage from an 1854 lecture by a prominent obstetrician captures this animating spirit and also conveys the doctor's claim to moral and scientific superiority:

> Physicians *alone* . . . can rectify public opinion; they *alone* can present the subject in a manner that legislators can exercise their powers aright in the preparation of suitable laws; that moralists and theologians can be furnished with facts to enforce the truth upon the moral sense of the community . . . and that woman in every rank and condition of life may be made sensible of the value of the foetus. . . .
>
> If they were taught by the speech and daily practice of their medical attendants, that a value attaches to the unborn child . . . they also would be persuaded or compelled to a similar belief in its sanctity.[30]

As presented here, only doctors could be trusted with the grave responsibility of educating the public about the evils of abortion. Only they were in possession of the scientific facts upon which moral arguments could be constructed regarding the sanctity of fetal life.

The doctors' unwavering belief in their special calling is also evident in Horatio R. Storer's 1859 report to the AMA on criminal abortion:

> Our *duty* is plain. If, by any act, we can effect aught towards the suppression of this crime, it must be done. . . . We are the physical guardians of women; we, alone, thus far of their offspring in utero. The case is here of life or death—the life or death of thousands—and it depends, almost wholly, upon ourselves. . . .
>
> If to want of knowledge on a medical point, the slaughter of countless children now steadily perpetrated in our midst, is to be attributed, it is our duty, as physicians, and as good and true men, both publicly and privately, and by every means in our power, to enlighten this ignorance.[31]

Seen here, antiabortion activism was not a matter of choice, but a matter of duty. Asserting their authority over women's bodies, doctors had a moral obligation to use their medical knowledge to stem the tide of ignorance and prevent the "slaughter" of the unborn. It is, however, important to recognize that in mobilizing against abortion, not all doctors were simply seeking to advance their own professional interests. Many had a genuine belief in the sanctity of fetal life and were committed to using this knowledge to stop abortion as a wrong unto itself.[32]

In addition to reflecting professional considerations, and, at least for some doctors, concerns about protecting fetal life, the doctors' campaign was also infused with anxiety about the proper role of women and the changing social order. In large measure, these fears can be traced to changes in the sociodemographic characteristics of the women who were seeking abortions. Until mid-century, the practice of abortion had been associated with single women who, in a world of rigid sexual norms, were desperate to avoid social condemnation.[33] However, as the nineteenth century progressed, there was a noticeable drop in the birthrate, which, at least in part, reflected the fact that married women were increasingly turning to abortion to control family size. Of particular concern, it was not simply that married women as a group were turning to abortion to limit fertility; it was that most of these women were from the same social world as the antiabortion physicians. In short, they tended to be white, native-born Protestants from "respectable" households.[34]

Although the doctors had some sympathy for the plight of the desperate single women, often casting her as an innocent victim of male lust (in keeping with Victorian sexual norms), they had no sympathy for married women who, by aborting, were attempting to interfere with the "end for which they are physiologically constituted and for which they are destined by nature."[35] Abortion in these circumstances was characterized as a "physiological sin" that violated the essence of female existence.[36] As Storer so aptly put it, marriages in which the "parties shrink from its highest responsibilities" were simply a form of "legalized prostitution."[37]

Married women who aborted were portrayed as selfish and as so preoccupied with fashion that they were willing to forsake the most sacred obligation of married life. As Riva Siegal explains, "The profession . . . invested the act of abortion with wider social implications, depicting it as an expression of women's resistance to marital and maternal obligations."[38]

The following passage from a lecture by Dr. David Humphrey Storer, father of Horatio Storer, and prominent professor at Harvard Medical School, captures these sentiments:

> The fashionable young bride, accustomed to adulation, is reluctant to forego at once the excitement of society; she is too often unwilling to feel that

she "has taken the veil"—that she has consecrated her affections to one being—and that his approval and his devotion should keep her heart ever full to overflowing; but wishing still to enjoy the immunities of unmarried life—to be free, as unshackled as ever—she will not endure the seclusion and deprivations necessarily connected with the pregnant conditions, but resorts to means . . . to destroy the life within her.[39]

Storer's condemnation was not limited to the new bride. He also chastised mothers who dared to think that they might have been put on the earth for some reason other than to procreate:

The mother, too, while she acknowledges the happiness she enjoys in possession of her children, not infrequently is willing . . . to pursue a similar course . . . perhaps . . . learning from others that woman was born for higher and noble purposes than the propagation of the species, that it is unreasonable that so large a potion of her life should be yielded to its drudgery.[40]

The aborting woman was thus portrayed as seeking to avoid her fate based on a selfish desire to free herself from the constraints of marriage and motherhood.

In investing abortion with broader social meaning, doctors were also responding to the growing influence of the nineteenth-century women's rights movement, which was seeking to improve the status of women within the domestic realm and to provide them with a voice in the public realm through the vote. According to Mohr, "regular physicians were among the most defensive groups in the country on the subject of changing traditional sex roles,"[41] and in their eyes, the aborting wife was a gender rebel who, in controlling her fertility, was seeking to appropriate the rights and privileges of the male sex in derogation of her rightful place in the social order.[42]

Voluntary Motherhood

Given that the doctors' attitudes toward abortion reflected, at least in part, their opposition to the growing women's rights movement, one might well assume that women's rights activists mobilized to oppose the doctors' efforts to criminalize abortion. However, although these women did have a different understanding of the meaning and place of abortion in the lives of women than the doctors did, they did not actively organize to stem the tide of legal change.

To understand why these early feminists did not actively oppose the effort to criminalize abortion, one needs to appreciate that they were influenced by Victorian sexual norms, which saw men as driven by animal impulses and women as sexually pure. Thus, rather than representing female autonomy, abortion was linked to male sexual excess and the lack of control that women had over their own bodies. For them, self-control meant asserting female authority over the timing of pregnancy; seeking to separate sexual expression from procreation is a far more contemporary demand. Instead, under the banner of "voluntary motherhood," this generation of feminists claimed for women the right of control over when they had sexual relations with their husbands.[43]

Although this idea may seem quaint to modern sensibilities, the idea that women could claim "self-ownership" of their bodies and the right to control the sexual access of their husbands was a radical notion, given the near-complete legal supremacy of husbands over their wives. Rather than seeking to liberate female sexuality, these early feminists sought to rewrite the sexual norms of marriage. By empowering women to say "no" to their husbands, they challenged the prevailing view that husbands had an unconstrained right to their wives' bodies.

Like the doctors, these feminists also drew on the metaphor of "legalized prostitution" when discussing the marital relationship, but they saw the husband's sexual demands as the illicit act. For them, it was his right of access, rather than the woman's avoidance of procreation, that degraded the marital relationship. Accordingly, to elevate marriage above the realm of prostitution, women needed to claim self-ownership of their bodies.[44] Their focus was thus on containing male lust rather than on giving expression to a female sexuality that was uncoupled from procreation.

The Crime of Abortion

By the start of the twentieth century, all states had a law making abortion a crime from the outset of pregnancy, although most, if not all, of these laws included a therapeutic exception permitting abortion when a doctor determined it was necessary in order to save a pregnant woman's life. In contrast to the common-law approach, the legality of abortion no longer turned on when during the pregnancy it was performed, but rather on whether a doctor deemed it medically necessary.

Interestingly, these state criminal abortion laws did not define what was meant by "necessary," and there was considerable disagreement among doctors about the scope of this therapeutic exception. In practice, the lack of a clear legal standard meant that doctors had considerable discretion to determine the circumstances under which they would perform abortions. Some doctors interpreted the therapeutic exception very narrowly to only permit abortion when necessary to prevent the imminent death of the pregnant woman. Others read it more liberally to encompass what might be considered quality-of-life considerations rather than strictly life-or-death concerns. As professor Leslie Regan explains, the indeterminacy of the law provided "a space in which doctors and women could negotiate. . . . They could, whether in conscious collusion or unconscious sympathy, use the legal loophole to provide wanted abortions. The medical indications for this procedure left room for social reasons and personal judgment as well as for 'real' reasons."[45]

One certainty is that this legal approach worked to the clear disadvantage of poor women and women of color. Affluent white women had greater access to "legal" abortions, at least in part because they were more likely than other women to have an ongoing relationship with a trusted physician who might be willing to relax the rules a bit. Poor women and women of color were far more likely to resort either to self-abortions, which often resulted in serious complications that required hospitalization, or to what Lawrence Lader has labeled the "underworld" of abortion, in which unskilled practitioners performed abortions under unsanitary conditions.[46] As a tragic reminder of the inequity of this dual system of abortion, most of the women who died due to abortion-related complications during the era in which abortion was a crime were women of color.

THE TIDES OF CHANGE: SETTING THE STAGE FOR *ROE V. WADE*

With criminal laws in effect across the nation by 1900, the basic legal approach to abortion that would remain in place until well into the second half of the century was set. During the first half of the century, abortion did not carry the charge that it had during the years of the doctors' campaign, when the issue had been invested with deep moral and social meaning. At least in part, this lack of charge reflected that the law now entrusted the abortion decision to doctors, to be made based upon their scientific expertise. Thus, at least in a formal sense, abortion belonged in the medical realm, under the authority of the experts.[47]

Abortion Practice

The success of the campaign to criminalize abortion did not, however, mean that women stopped having abortions or stopped seeking them for reasons ranging far beyond the narrow medical indications permitted by law. Hence, at the start of the twentieth century, doctors launched a second antiabortion crusade in order to clamp down on the practice. They sought to educate women whom they criticized for stubbornly refusing to relinquish their ignorant belief in the significance of quickening; they mobilized to drive out midwives whom they regarded as largely responsible for the practice of illegal abortions; and they sought to rid their own ranks of "abortionists."[48]

Despite the doctors' efforts, the demand for abortion grew over the course of the economically grim years of the Great Depression, and many doctors responded to the desperate plight of women seeking to avoid adding another member to their already struggling households:

> As women pressed doctors for help, the medical practice of abortion, legal and illegal expanded ... Physicians granted for the first time, that social conditions were an essential component of medical judgment in therapeutic abortion cases.[49]

Exposure to this quiet desperation led a few lone doctors to begin thinking about legal reform to expand the circumstances under which abortions could be lawfully performed. These doctors were also influenced by a growing awareness of the tragic consequences of illegal abortions, which had become more visible as the locus of medical care shifted from the home to the hospital, thus bringing women with post-abortion complications into the hospital wards. Although the call for legal reform was limited to a handful of doctors, the Depression years did expand access to "legal" abortions, as more doctors extended the borders of the therapeutic-abortion exception to include consideration of a woman's social and economic reality.[50] The controlling concept of "life" was thus imbued with social meaning, rather than simply serving as a biological determinant of when an abortion was justifiable.

The more liberal years of the Depression were followed by a period of increasingly restricted access that ultimately led to a growing drive for change. In large measure, restricted access was a result of the therapeutic-abortion committees that were established in hospitals during the 1940s and 1950s to address the growing disagreements among doctors as to the permissible indications for performing a legal abortion. Once a committee was established, in order to schedule an abortion for a patient, a doctor had to submit the case for review to determine whether it was "necessary" within the meaning of the law. As increasing numbers of hospitals established therapeutic-abortion committees, the concept of a legal abortion became equated with an abortion that had been formally approved by such a committee and performed in a hospital setting, as distinct from an abortion performed in a doctor's office, based on an individual doctor's determination of legality.[51] In effect, these committees served to police the boundaries between legal and illegal procedures.

Despite their initial aim, these committees did not lead to the standardization of the practice of abortion, and, in 1959, the authors of an influential study declared, "The abortion problem exhibits a dramatic variation between legal norm and social fact."[52] Their conclusion about the gap between law and practice was based on a study in which they asked hospitals to respond to hypothetical case studies of women seeking an abortion, using the hospital's own criteria for determining if an abortion request would be granted. Responses showed that there was a wide variation in abortion practice "as performed in respectable hospitals by respectable medical men,"[53] leading the authors to conclude,

> There is considerable diversity of opinion among hospitals as to the appropriate medical standards for the performance of TA's [therapeutic abortions]. Even those indications for the performance of a TA which may be regarded as plainly within the legal justification are not unanimously accepted. And no indication, not even the purely socio-economic, is uniformly rejected.[54]

As a practical matter, this meant that not only was a woman seeking an abortion forced to offer up intimate details to an impersonal committee for review, but also, the results of this review process were highly unpredictable. Moreover, although this system was oppressive to all women, middle-class women with access to a physician who was willing to serve as her advocate through the review process as well as women in more liberal states, such as New York and California, were likely to fare better than other women.

Over time, therapeutic-abortion committees came under increasing pressure to limit the number of abortions they approved, and many began to impose a quota system for how many abortions they would approve in any given time period. Once the limit had been reached, a woman's request for an abortion would most likely be denied, even if the reasons for it fell within the narrow parameters of the law.[55]

Seeking Legal Reform

The gap between law and practice and the increasing strictness of therapeutic-abortion committees prompted some liberal-minded doctors to consider seeking reform of the strict laws for which their predecessors had fought so hard a century earlier. These doctors were motivated by several concerns. One concern, in light of disagreements about when an abortion could legally be performed, was the possibility of prosecution, which was not an idle fear, as the later-discussed prosecution of doctors during the rubella epidemic makes clear. Doctors were also motivated by a concern for the well-being of their patients and a belief that they, rather than the state, were in the better position to determine the terms of acceptable medical practice.[56]

In 1955, in response to this shifting sentiment, Planned Parenthood organized a small, unpublicized national conference for doctors and other health professionals concerned about the legal status of abortion. Following intense discussions, participants issued a joint statement calling for legal reform. This marked the first time in the United States that "a group of elite physicians and other professionals advocated reform of the criminal abortion laws."[57]

This was soon followed by another important development. In 1959 an elite group of lawyers, under the auspices of the American Law Institute (ALI), added their voices to those calling for change. The ALI seeks to bring rationality to the American legal system, and in the 1950s, it was focused on the criminal justice system. Toward this end, the ALI drafted a Model Penal Code, which included a draft abortion provision. This provision essentially codified the liberal interpretation of the therapeutic-abortion exception, thus recommending the legalization of abortion in cases of rape and incest, in cases of fetal anomalies, and in cases when abortion was necessary to safeguard the physical or mental health (as well as the life) of the pregnant woman. This model law would shape subsequent legislative-reform efforts.

Two subsequent events further galvanized these early reform efforts and helped move the abortion issue back into the public arena. In 1962 a woman named Sherri Finkbine, who was pregnant with her fifth child, learned that a sleeping pill she was taking, which her husband had brought home from Europe, caused very serious birth defects. After consulting with her doctor, Sherri decided she wanted to terminate the pregnancy. Her doctor scheduled the abortion, certain that the hospital's review committee would approve it. To alert other women to the potential dangers of this drug, Sherri called the local paper, which printed a story about her situation. As a result of the subsequent publicity, the hospital canceled the scheduled abortion, and although polls showed that most Americans agreed with Sherri Finkbine's decision, many reacted with outrage, and both Sherri and her family were the targets of death threats. Ultimately, Sherri traveled to Sweden for her abortion.

As Luker explains, the Finkbine case brought long-simmering differences about acceptable indications for an abortion to the surface. To doctors who read the law narrowly, Sherri's situation was unambiguous: the pregnancy did not pose a threat to her life and thus could not be legally terminated. To other doctors, however, her situation reflected a complex array of factors, which included fetal indications that were appropriate for a doctor to take into account when deciding whether to perform an abortion.[58] According to Luker, "strict constructionists" who "were willing to turn a blind eye when they thought that [a] not-yet-born person was being sacrificed in a 'good cause,' namely to preserve the life of its mother," were distressed to learn that many of their colleagues did not share their view, but rather, were willing to "sacrifice" the unborn for other—and in their view, far less justifiable—considerations.[59]

When an epidemic of rubella (German Measles) swept the country in 1964, this simmering tension further intensified, since exposure to rubella can result in very serious damage to a developing fetus. During the epidemic, many pregnant women fearing fetal harm sought to terminate their pregnancies. Based on its opposition to the performance of abortions for "fetal indications," the California Board of Medical Examiners brought charges of unprofessional conduct against nine doctors in San Francisco who had performed abortions on women exposed to rubella.

Aware of the professional risk of performing abortions under anything but the narrowest of circumstances, and seeking a more humane approach to the practice of medicine, doctors, along with other health and legal professionals, began to actively seek reform of the criminal abortion laws. As a result, during the second half of the 1960s, state legislatures across the country considered reform proposals, and between 1967 and 1970, twelve states revised their laws along the lines suggested by the ALI Model Penal Code.

Although these reforms were an important step along the way to making abortion legal, it is important to realize that they simply expanded—or perhaps more accurately clarified—the circumstances under which a doctor could lawfully perform an abortion. These laws expanded the formal decisional authority of doctors, without transferring control over the decision to women. It would take another group of reformers to bring the concept of "abortion on demand" to the table.

The Demand for Repeal

In 1970 the legislatures in three states, Alaska, Hawaii, and New York, went well beyond reforming their criminal abortion laws along the ALI lines and instead voted to actually repeal them. This radical reconfiguration of the abortion right reflected the emergence of another constituency with a very different vision of what change should look like. The early 1960s had witnessed the rebirth of the women's rights movement, and unlike during the nineteenth-century movement, abortion soon became a central platform in the demand for legal and social equality. Claiming abortion as a right of women, activists began pushing for the repeal, instead of the reform, of existing criminal laws. Rather than seeking to simply enlarge the scope of professional decision-making authority, they sought to place authority directly into the hands of pregnant women. Abortion was recast as an individual choice that each woman had a right to make for herself. Feminists also recognized the broader role that the criminal antiabortion laws had played in defining and maintaining the proper role of women.

Unwilling to settle for legal reform, which would do little to give women direct control over their own reproductive lives, activists began mobilizing on a number of different fronts. They held speak-outs in order to bring the horrors of illegal abortion to public attention; they organized referral networks to help women find providers who were willing to perform safe, though not necessarily legal, abortions; and they took to the streets in protest. In 1967 the National Organization for Women (NOW), one of the more "mainstream" groups within the feminist movement, included "The Right of Women to Control Their Reproductive Lives" in their Bill of Rights, thus signaling the importance and acceptance of this claim in the drive for full social and legal equality for women.

Central to this effort was a decision to turn to the courts, rather than rely on the legislature, to achieve more sweeping legal changes. Across the country, young lawyers and legal scholars who were committed to using the law for purposes of social change began developing legal theories and looking for test cases to challenge the validity of existing criminal laws.[60] In 1973 this strategy paid off, as the United States Supreme Court, in the seminal case of *Roe v. Wade*, declared that the nation's criminal abortion laws impermissibly interfered with a woman's right to make her own abortion decision. But before we turn to *Roe*, three earlier cases merit specific mention, since they form a direct bridge to this decision.

Griswold v. Connecticut (Griswold)[61]

In 1965 the United States Supreme Court struck down a Connecticut law that made it a crime for married couples to use contraceptives or for anyone to counsel them about or help them to obtain contraceptives. In evaluating the constitutionality of this law, the Court focused on the concept of privacy. The Court stated that although privacy is not specifically mentioned in the Constitution, specific guarantees in the Bill of Rights—including the right of free speech, the protection from unreasonable search and seizure, and the right against self-incrimination—together create a "zone of privacy" that protects individuals from unwarranted governmental intrusion into their lives. The Court went on to explain that specific constitutional guarantees have "penumbras" (or peripheral rights) that give them "life and substance."[62] For example, the Court noted that although the Constitution does not specially mention the right of association, the First Amendment has been construed to include this right in order to make its "express guarantees" of free speech meaningful."[63]

Turning to the Connecticut statute, the Court focused on the concept of marital privacy. Characterizing marriage as a relationship that lies "within the zone of privacy created by several fundamental constitutional guarantees," the Court described marriage as an "association for as noble a purpose as any involved in our prior decisions."[64] Accordingly, the Court held that, in forbidding the use of contraceptives, the Connecticut law represented an unwarranted governmental incursion into the private realm.

People v. Belous[65]

Although not a United States Supreme Court decision, and thus not a formal legal precedent outside of the state of California, the *Belous* case is worth noting because it was the first decision to hold that women have a constitutional right to abortion. The decision also stands as an important reminder of the concerted efforts of legal activists, who were engaged across the country in developing litigation strategies to recast abortion as a right belonging to women.

Leon Belous, a gynecologist from California, was convicted of conspiring to perform an abortion, based on an abortion referral he had made for a young college student. His lawyers appealed his conviction on two constitutional grounds. They argued that the state's criminal antiabortion law violated the right of privacy as articulated in *Griswold* and that the law was unconstitutionally vague, in that it did not provide doctors with a clear understanding of the circumstances under which abortions could be legally performed. The California Supreme Court agreed that the law was vague, since it could not be determined with certainty when an abortion was actually "necessary" to "preserve" the life of the pregnant woman, and the court thus declared the law unconstitutional. However, the California Supreme Court also went beyond this, agreeing with the plaintiffs that the right of privacy discussed in *Griswold* also protects a woman's right to make her own decision about whether or not to carry a pregnancy to term. This landmark decision was a major victory and source of inspiration to activists seeking to repeal, rather than just reform, the nation's criminal abortion laws.

Eisenstadt v. Baird[66]

The groundbreaking United States Supreme Court decision in *Eisenstadt v. Baird* extended the right of privacy articulated in *Griswold* to unmarried persons, thus providing the *Roe* Court with an essential precedent. Bill Baird, a birth-control activist, was convicted for distributing contraceptive foam to college students at Boston University in direct violation of a Massachusetts law, which prohibited the exhibition or distribution of contraceptives to unmarried persons.

When the case was appealed to the Supreme Court, the Court held that the constitutional right of privacy is not limited to married persons:

If under *Griswold* the distribution of contraceptives to married persons cannot be prohibited, a ban on distribution to unmarried persons would be equally impermissible. It is true that in *Griswold* the right of privacy in question inhered in the marital relationship. Yet the married couple is not an independent entity with a mind and heart of its own, but an association of two individuals each with a separate intellectual and emotional makeup. If the right of privacy means anything, it is the right of the *individual,* married or single, to be free from unwarranted governmental intrusion into matters so fundamentally affecting a person as the decision whether to bear or beget a child.[67]

Looking ahead to *Roe,* this passage is important on several levels. First, it sees the individual, rather than the marital unit, as the holder of the right of privacy. Second, it is explicit about the nature of the right, making it clear that what is at stake is the ability of each individual to decide whether to "bear or beget a child." Moreover, by framing the right broadly to encompass decisional authority over reproduction, rather than designating the right simply as one of access to birth control, the Court may have been knowingly laying the foundation for a future decision on the question of abortion.

ABORTION AS A CONSTITUTIONAL RIGHT: FROM *ROE* TO *CASEY* AND BEYOND

Having traced the legal history of abortion from the colonial era's quickening rule through the drive for criminalization and the modern campaigns for the reform and repeal of existing criminal abortion laws, we now enter a new era in this history—abortion as a constitutionally protected right. Two Supreme Court cases—*Roe v. Wade* and *Planned Parenthood of Southeastern Pennsylvania v. Casey*—anchor this discussion as the seminal cases that established the operative constitutional framework for the abortion right. Almost twenty years separate these two decisions, so we also consider some of the critical intervening legal developments that helped pave the way for the *Casey* decision, which both affirms and undercuts *Roe*.[68]

Roe v. Wade

On January 22, 1973, the United States Supreme Court struck down Texas's criminal abortion law, thereby ushering in a new era with respect to the legal configuration of the abortion right. At issue in the case was a state statute dating back to 1854 that made abortion a crime unless "procured or attempted by medical advice for the purpose of saving the life of the mother."[69] At the time, similar laws were in effect in a majority of states, although, as we have seen, by the time the *Roe* case reached the Court, a number of states had liberalized their laws, and three had repealed them altogether.

The plaintiff, a young woman using the pseudonym of Jane Roe, brought a lawsuit challenging the constitutionality of the Texas law when she was unable to obtain a safe and legal abortion because the continuation of her pregnancy did not pose a threat to her life. She argued that the law was unconstitutionally vague and abridged her right of personal privacy. Defending the law, the State of Texas asserted its right to protect the health of a pregnant woman and the life of the fetus by prohibiting an abortion not medically necessary to save the woman's life.

In evaluating these competing claims, the Court agreed with the plaintiff that the Texas law abridged her right of personal privacy. Relying on a line of earlier cases in which the Court had identified a right of privacy in a variety of contexts, including in the use of contraceptives, the Court held that the "right of privacy . . . founded in the Fourteenth Amendment's concept of personal liberty and restrictions upon state action . . . is broad enough to encompass a woman's decision whether or not to terminate a pregnancy."[70] In so holding, the Court recognized "the detriment that the State would impose upon the pregnant woman by denying this choice,"[71] including psychological harm, the distress of bringing a child who is unwanted into the world, and the possible stigma of unwed motherhood.

This, however, was not the end of the Court's analysis. While making clear that abortion is a fundamental right, the Court rejected the plaintiff's argument that the right is absolute and instead held that a woman's right must be balanced against the interests of the state. In considering the asserted interests of the State of Texas, the Court disagreed with the state's claim that the fetus is a person within the meaning of the Constitution and that the fetus is thus deserving of full legal protection. In rejecting the idea of fetal personhood, the Court reviewed the term "person" as it appears in the Constitution and determined that the legal definition of "person" does not include the unborn. The Court also pointed out that if the fetus were a legal person, the therapeutic-abortion exception would, in effect, be an authorization to save one life through the intentional destruction of another—an act the law would not sanction. The Court also declined to fix the start of life at the moment of conception, as it was urged to do by the State of Texas, stating, "We need not resolve the difficult question of when life begins. When those trained in the respective disciplines of medicine, philosophy, and theology are unable to arrive at any consensus, the judiciary, at this point in the development of man's knowledge, is not in a position to speculate as to the answer."[72]

Although declining to vest the fetus with a formal legal status or declare when life begins, the Court did find that states have an interest in protecting both the health of pregnant women and the potentiality of life and that these interests can be taken into account in shaping the contours of the abortion right. Recognizing both the fundamental nature of the abortion right and the fact that pregnancy is a dynamic, rather than a static, process, the Court held that these state interests are not of sufficient magnitude throughout pregnancy to support state regulation of abortion. Rather, these interests grow in significance over the course of pregnancy and become "compelling" at distinct stages of pregnancy, so as to support regulation of the abortion right.

To accommodate the tension between a woman's constitutional right of choice and the interests of the state, the Court constructed its now famous trimester approach to abortion: in the first trimester, the interests of the state are not of sufficient weight to justify intrusions on a woman's right of choice; in the second trimester, when the procedure potentially increases in risk, the state's interest in the health of the pregnant woman becomes compelling and justifies regulations that are intended to protect her well-being; finally, as a pregnancy enters the third trimester, and the fetus become viable (defined by the Court as being capable of "meaningful life outside the mother's womb"),[73] the state's interest in the potentiality of life becomes compelling, and it may prohibit abortion. However, the Court also made clear that the life and health of the pregnant woman always takes precedence over potential life, and a state must therefore permit third-trimester abortions that are necessary to protect the life or health of the woman.

The Reaction to Roe

Although there was some disappointment that the Court did not recognize abortion as an absolute right, abortion-rights supporters were elated by the Roe decision. Notably, Roe vindicated the approach of the women's rights movement, since it effectively repealed existing abortion laws, thus shifting decisional authority to pregnant women, rather than simply expanding the circumstances under which abortions could lawfully be performed.

Although recognizing the monumental importance of Roe, abortion-rights supporters were also aware that the decision was not self-actualizing and that without working to ensure that women actually had access to safe and affordable abortions, the victory would be hollow. They recognized that the challenge lying ahead would be to translate the promise of Roe into a reality for all women. Reflecting the principle that reproduction is a matter of choice rather than a biological imperative and addressing the closely related idea that women must be free to make choices about their lives without the constraints of gender stereotypes, supporters began referring to themselves as "pro-choice" instead of "pro-abortion."

Clearly, opponents of abortion had a very different response to the decision. To them, Roe was an outrage—in a single fell swoop, the Court had invalidated the laws that they had been fighting to preserve. Much as the campaign for abortion rights had energized the women's rights movement in the years leading up to 1973, the *Roe* decision served to galvanize the antiabortion, or "pro-life," movement. Characterizing abortion as murder, they quickly mobilized on multiple fronts.[74]

Antiabortion activists developed a two-pronged legal strategy. They sought to overturn *Roe* by way of an amendment to the United States Constitution that either would declare abortion a matter over which states have complete authority or would vest the fetus with legal personhood; they simultaneously began seeking to enact laws at the state level to restrict a woman's right of choice, which ultimately proved to be the more successful strategy. Taking the long view, abortion opponents also hoped that if these laws were challenged in court—an almost certain occurrence—the abortion battle would eventually be replayed before a differently constituted Supreme Court that might be willing to either overturn *Roe* or significantly narrow the scope of the decision.

This legislative strategy resulted in a flurry of activity at the state level, and within a year of *Roe*, states across the country had enacted a wide variety of restrictive laws designed to make it more difficult for women to obtain abortions. Examples of common restrictions included spousal- and parental-consent requirements; informed-consent requirements, which were often intended to encourage women to change their minds about abortion; waiting periods; the elimination of public funding for abortion; fetal-protection requirements; and performance requirements, such as mandates that all abortions be performed in a hospital.

Not surprisingly, these laws were promptly challenged on the grounds that they interfered with a woman's fundamental right of privacy to decide for herself whether or not to carry a pregnancy to term. Over the course of the next 18 or so years, the Court remained essentially true to the *Roe* framework, and it invalidated most of these restrictive laws as violations of a woman's constitutionally protected right of choice. However, as discussed later in this chapter, as well as in the next chapter, cracks in the Court's support of *Roe* had appeared well before 1992, when the Court, in the case of *Planned Parenthood of Southeastern Pennsylvania v. Casey* reconfigured the abortion right. We now turn to consider the basic contours of the Court's approach to abortion in the post-*Roe* era.

Reaffirmation of the *Roe* Right

From 1976, when the first post-*Roe* abortion case reached the Supreme Court, until the Court's 1992 *Casey* decision, the Court adhered to *Roe*'s trimester framework to assess the constitutionality of restrictive abortion laws. As exemplified by the following three cases, more often than not, this resulted in the invalidation of these restrictive laws.

In the 1976 case of *Planned Parenthood of Central Missouri v. Danforth (Danforth)*, the Court invalidated key provisions of Missouri's antiabortion law, including a spousal-consent requirement and a prohibition on the use of saline amniocentesis as an abortion method after the first trimester.[75] Striking down the spousal-consent provision, the Court acknowledged the potential interests of a husband in his wife's pregnancy and recognized that in a well-functioning marriage, the decision to abort would most likely be a shared decision, but made clear that little would be gained in terms of marital harmony by giving a husband what would be tantamount to veto power over his wife's abortion decision. The Court also made clear that the State of Missouri could not delegate to a husband authority that, under *Roe*, the state did not possess.[76]

With respect to the use of saline amniocentesis after the first trimester,[77] the Court rejected the state's argument that the prohibition was a valid health measure. Although acknowledging the potential risks of this procedure, the Court pointed out that, although other safer approaches to inducing abortion may have existed, saline amniocentesis was the safest method that was actually available to women in the state of Missouri; moreover, Missouri had not banned far less common, but more dangerous methods of post–first-trimester abortions. Additionally, in terms of relative risks, the Court noted that "the maternal mortality rate in childbirth does, indeed, exceed the mortality rate where saline amniocentesis is used."[78] Accordingly, the Court concluded that the restriction was actually an attempt to limit women's access to abortion rather than a measure to protect their health.

Several years latter, in the case of *City of Akron v. Akron Center for Reproductive Health, Inc. (Akron)*,[79] the Court invalidated several provisions of a restrictive municipal ordinance enacted by the City of Akron. Specifically, the Court invalidated an abortion-consent provision, together with a closely related waiting-period requirement. As in *Danforth*, it also invalidated an abortion-performance restriction.

In *Akron* the consent provision, rather than involving a third party, was ostensibly aimed at ensuring that a woman's own consent was fully informed and freely given; the provision required that physicians provide women with state-scripted information at least 24 hours before performing an abortion, information including the statement that "the unborn child is a human life from the moment of conception."[80] Although the Court made clear that, like with other medical procedures, a state can impose an informed-consent requirement, this ordinance exceeded permissible limits. The Court explained:

Akron has gone far beyond merely describing the general subject matter relevant to informed consent. By insisting upon recitation of a lengthy and inflexible list of information, Akron has unreasonably placed "obstacles in the path of the doctor upon whom [the woman is] entitled to rely for advise in connection with her decision."[81]

In addition to straitjacketing doctors and interfering in the doctor-patient relationship, "much of the information required," the Court found, "is designed not to inform the women's consent but rather to persuade her to withhold it altogether"[82]—a clearly unconstitutional objective under *Roe*. The Court also invalidated the closely related waiting period, on the grounds that it did not serve to enhance either the safety of the abortion procedure or the quality of a woman's decision-making and thus did not advance any legitimate state interest.

The Court further invalidated the requirement that all second-trimester abortions be performed in a hospital. Although it acknowledged that this requirement made abortions more expensive and generally less available, the city of Akron asserted it was a valid health measure that was intended to ensure that abortions were performed in appropriate settings that minimized potential risks to a woman's health. Noting that the safety of second-trimester abortions had improved dramatically since the ordinance had gone into effect, the Court held that the requirement, at least as applied to early second-trimester abortions, imposed a "heavy and unnecessary burden . . . on women's access to a relatively inexpensive, otherwise accessible, and safe abortion procedure,"[83] without providing a discernible health benefit.

Three years later, in the case of *Thornburgh v. American College of Obstetricians and Gynecologists (Thornburgh)*,[84] the Court recognized that the cumulative intent behind Pennsylvania's Abortion Control Act was to impose significant burdens on the abortion right. The Supreme Court therefore struck down multiple of the act's provisions, including "extreme" record-keeping and reporting requirements, which asked for detailed information without adequate confidentiality safeguards, and a requirement that when performing a late-term abortion, the physician use a method that would give the fetus the best chance to be born alive, without adequate considerations for the health of the pregnant woman. The Court also struck down an informed-consent and waiting-period provision that, according to the justices, served to "confuse and punish [the pregnant woman] and to heighten her anxiety, contrary to accepted medical practice."[85]

Having seen the act for what it was, the Court concluded the opinion by reaffirming its continued support for *Roe*:

We recognized at the very beginning of our opinion in *Roe*, that abortion raises moral and spiritual questions over which honorable persons can disagree sincerely and profoundly. . . . Few decisions are more personal and intimate, more properly private, or more basic to individual dignity and autonomy, than a woman's decision . . . whether to end her pregnancy. A woman's right to make that choice *freely* is fundamental. Any other result, in our view, would protect inadequately a central part of liberty that our law guarantees equally to all.[86]

However, the reality was, in fact, a bit more complex than suggested by this passage. Although a majority of the *Thornburgh* Court reiterated its support for *Roe*, the integrity of the *Roe* decision had already been undercut by a series of decisions upholding restrictions on the abortion rights of poor women (discussed next) and teens (discussed in chapter 2.)

Unless You Are Poor: The Creeping Pronatalism of the Court

Following *Roe*, as states enacted restrictive abortion laws, a popular choice was to pass laws eliminating Medicaid funding for all non–medically necessary abortions for low-income women.[87] These bans were challenged in court by low-income women (as well as by some abortion providers), on the basis that the denial of funding interfered with their fundamental right to abortion, especially since Medicaid funded the cost of childbirth, thus injecting financial incentives into the decision-making process.

The Court agreed that this disparity in funding would make childbirth a "more attractive alternative";[88] however, because of the state's interest in the potentiality of life, the Court did not think this was a problem. In reaching this conclusion, the Court distinguished the denial of funds from other types of restrictions, maintaining that there is a "difference between direct state interference with a protected activity and state encouragement of an alternative activity."[89] It asserted that unlike a requirement, such as that a woman obtain the consent of her husband, which is a state-imposed obstacle, the denial of funds "place[s] no obstacles in the pregnant woman's path to abortion. The State may have made childbirth a more attractive alternative, thereby influencing the woman's decision, but it has imposed no restriction on access to abortions that was not already there."[90]

By identifying the barrier as the woman's own poverty, as distinct from a state-imposed obstacle, the Court was able to claim that its acceptance of a ban on public funding for abortion did not signal a "retreat" from *Roe* and its progeny. Seeking to locate the funding cases within the existing jurisprudential framework, the Court asserted that protecting a woman's right of choice does not "translate into a constitutional obligation . . . to subsidize abortions."[91]

The funding-ban decisions drew scathing dissents from the more liberal justices on the Court, who saw the issue quite differently. Rather than seeing the problem as the woman's own poverty, these justices recognized that the funding and access disparities between abortion and childbirth injected a coercive element into the decision-making process, thus making the exercise of the right of choice more difficult. The dissenting justices wrote,

> A distressing insensitivity to the plight of impoverished pregnant women is inherent in the Court's analysis. . . . many indigent women will feel they have no choice but to carry their pregnancies to term because the State will pay for the associated costs of medical services, even though they would have chosen to have abortions if the State had also provided funds for that procedure . . . This disparity in funding by the State clearly operates to coerce indigent pregnant women to bear children they would not otherwise choose to have. [92]

Viewed from this perspective, the obstacle is not a woman's poverty, but is instead the uneven handed approach of the state.

The Reconfiguration of the Abortion Right: *Planned Parenthood of Southeastern Pennsylvania v. Casey*

As we have seen, the Court sought to reconcile its approval of the ban on publicly funded abortions with its decision in *Roe* by claiming that the prohibition simply operated to encourage childbirth without imposing a direct burden on the abortion right. However, a mere three years after the *Thornburgh* ruling, the Court's conservative justices openly proclaimed their hostility to *Roe*.

In *Webster v. Reproductive Health Services (Webster)*,[93] a case involving a challenge to a Missouri law that made it unlawful to use public facilities for the performance of abortions or for public employees to perform abortions, unless necessary to save the life of the pregnant woman, four Supreme Court justices (one shy of a majority) openly expressed their dislike of *Roe*'s trimester formula. Stopping short of actually calling for an overturn of the decision, three of these justices asserted that the "rigid *Roe* framework is hardly consistent with the notion of a Constitution cast in general terms, as ours is" and questioned why "the State's interest in protecting life should come into existence only at the point of viability,"[94] rather than at an earlier point in pregnancy. The fourth justice criticized his colleagues for their overly cautious approach, complaining, "It appears that the mansion of constitutionalized abortion law, constructed overnight in *Roe v. Wade*, must be disassembled doorjamb by doorjamb, and never entirely brought down, no matter how wrong it may be."[95]

Deeply troubled by these sentiments, Justice Blackmun, author of the *Roe* decision, gave voice to his worries for the future in his dissenting opinion in *Webster:* "I fear for the future. I fear for the liberty and equality of the millions of women who have lived and come of age in the 16 years since *Roe* was decided. I fear for the integrity of, and public esteem for, this Court."[96] Thus, by the time *Casey* reached the Court, it was clear that the jurisprudential winds were shifting and that the foundation of *Roe* had been strongly shaken.

Three years after *Webster,* in the case of *Planned Parenthood of Southeastern Pennsylvania v. Casey,*[97] the Court announced its intention to "review once more the principles that define the rights of the woman and the legitimate authority of the State respecting the termination of pregnancies by abortion procedures."[98] Justice Blackmun's fears for the future were not fully realized, since *Casey* did not overturn *Roe;* however, in deciding that the interests of the unborn should be given greater weight, the Court did significantly undercut the abortion right.

In reviewing *Roe,* the Court indicated that if the abortion question was before it for the first time, it might have decided the matter differently. However, any reservations that some of the justices may have had about reaffirming what they regarded as the "central holding" of *Roe* were outweighed by their respect for the concept of individual liberty in combination "with the force of stare decisis" (literally meaning "to stand by that which is decided"), which limits the ability of a court to overrule prior decisions.[99] The Court thus upheld what it characterized as the "central principle" of *Roe*—the right of a woman to terminate her pregnancy before viability.[100] Focusing on this aspect of the decision, *Casey* was clearly an important victory for supporters of abortion rights, with the decision leaving no doubt that abortion was still a fundamental constitutional right. Likewise, the reaffirmation of the core *Roe* right was a major defeat for abortion opponents.

This, however, was not the end of the Court's analysis. Having first focused on the abortion issue from the perspective of the pregnant woman, the Court then shifted perspectives to consider the state's interest in the potentiality of life. It is with this shift that the decision undercuts the integrity of *Roe.* As discussed, under *Roe* the state's interest in the potentiality of life is not considered of sufficient magnitude to justify incursions into a woman's right of choice until the third trimester. The trimester framework thus serves to contain the state's interest in life until late in pregnancy, as the state's interest lies dormant until the point of fetal viability.[101]

But according to the *Casey* Court, the trimester framework was not part of "the essential holding" of *Roe.* Instead, it asserted that it was a rigid constraint on the ability of states to promote their legitimate interest in the potentiality of life:

The trimester framework, however, does not fulfill *Roe*'s own promise that the State has an interest in protecting fetal life or potential life. *Roe* began the contradiction by using the trimester framework to forbid any regulation of abortion designed to advance that interest before viability.[102]

Dramatically reconfiguring the role of the state vis-à-vis the unborn, the Court decided to abandon *Roe*'s trimester framework in favor of the "undue burden standard," declaring that it is the "appropriate means of reconciling the State's interest with the woman's constitutionally protected liberty."[103]

Under this newly enunciated standard, laws that are designed to promote the state's interest in the unborn from the outset of pregnancy are constitutionally acceptable so long as they do not impose an undue burden, or "substantial obstacle," in the path of a woman seeking to terminate a pregnancy. Highlighting the new place of the unborn in abortion jurisprudence, the *Casey* Court concluded its reconsideration of *Roe* as follows:

> What is at stake is the woman's right to make the ultimate decision. . . . Regulations which do no more than create a structural mechanism by which the State, or the parent or guardian of a minor, may express profound respect for the life of the unborn are permitted, if they are not a substantial obstacle to the woman's exercise of the right to choose. Unless it has that effect on her right of choice, a state measure designed to persuade her to choose childbirth over abortion will be upheld if reasonably related to that goal.[104]

Using the undue-burden standard, the Court then considered the constitutionality of Pennsylvania's Abortion Control Act. We take a look at the Court's approach to the act's spousal-notification and informed-consent provisions, which best elucidate the application of this new standard.

In considering the spousal-notification requirement, the Court displayed a commendable sensitivity to the plight of battered women. Invalidating the requirement because it imposed an undue burden on women who suffer or fear abuse at the hands of their spouses, the Court stated,

> The spousal notification requirement is thus likely to prevent a significant number of women from obtaining an abortion. It does not merely make abortions a little more difficult or expensive to obtain; for many women it will impose a substantial obstacle. We must not blind ourselves to the fact that the significant number of women who fear for their safety and the safety of their children are likely to be deterred from procuring an abortion as surely as if the Commonwealth had outlawed abortion in all cases.[105]

The Court, however, treated the requirement of informed consent with a 24-hour waiting period quite differently. As discussed earlier, the Court had previously invalidated such requirements as inconsistent with the trimester formula, but now the Court concluded that these provisions are a valid expression of the state's interest in the unborn. The Court explained,

> We depart from the holdings of *Akron I* and *Thornburgh* to the extent that we permit a State to further its legitimate goal of protecting the life of the unborn by enacting legislation aimed at ensuring a decision that is mature and informed, even when in so doing *the State expresses a preference for childbirth over abortion.* . . . Requiring that the woman be informed of the availability of information relating to fetal development and the assistance available should she decide to carry the pregnancy to full term is a reasonable measure to ensure an informed choice, one which might cause a woman to choose childbirth over abortion. This requirement cannot be considered a substantial obstacle to obtaining an abortion, and it follows, there is no undue burden.[106]

Similarly, although the Court recognized that the related 24-hour waiting period increased both the "cost and risk of delay of abortions" as well as the risk of exposure "to the harassment and hostility of antiabortion protestors," since women had to negotiate two trips to the clinic, it concluded that these obstacles were not significant enough to be an undue burden on the abortion right. Moreover, the delay was a reasonable expression of the state's interest in the unborn, giving women time to reflect upon their decision and to possibly change their minds about abortion.[107]

It is readily apparent that with the undue-burden standard, the tables have been turned. The first section of *Casey* was a clear victory for abortion supporters and a defeat for abortion opponents who had hoped the Court would overrule *Roe*. However, when it comes to the place of the unborn, the decision was a major setback for abortion-rights supporters, in that the decision gives states the go-ahead to enact laws to discourage women from having abortions, and it was an important victory for abortion opponents since the unborn now have a far more prominent place in the abortion jurisprudence of the Court.

Taking Up the Cause of the Unborn: The States Respond to *Casey*

No longer fenced in by the trimester formula, states across the nation wasted no time responding to *Casey* by once again passing restrictive abortion laws, including mandatory waiting periods, state-scripted informed-consent requirements, and what are known as TRAP (Targeted Regulation of Abortion Providers) laws; the latter laws impose obligations on abortion providers that are not imposed on comparable medical providers, such as minimum square-footage requirements in hallways and waiting areas. In 2003 legislators in Georgia filed a bill that would require any woman who wanted to terminate a pregnancy to first obtain a "death warrant" from court. A guardian would be appointed for the fetus, and a jury trial would be conducted in which the "rights of the person seeking to have the execution performed" would be balanced against the interests of the fetus. A doctor who performed an "execution" without a valid court-issued death warrant would be subject to criminal sanctions.[108] Although not enacted into law, this bill exemplifies the intensity of antiabortion sentiment and heightened concern for the fetus.

Also critical to this effort has been the popular campaign to ban abortions known as "partial-birth" abortions, in which the fetus is removed through the cervix intact, rather than in segments. In medical terms, this procedure is referred to as either a dilation-and-extraction (D & X) abortion or an intact dilation-and-evacuation (D & E) abortion, and is usually only used in late second terms abortions. Using graphic descriptions and visual aids, including the dismantling of dolls, proponents of the ban on partial-birth abortions met with considerable legislative success, and by 2000 a majority of states had laws on the books banning these procedures. Although most of these new laws included an exception for cases in which the pregnant woman's life is in danger, most did not include a health exception.

In opposing these laws, abortion-rights supporters drew attention to the fact that late abortions are extremely rare (about 90 percent of all abortions are performed during the first trimester; of those performed in the second trimester, only about 2 percent are performed after the 20th week[109]) and are usually only done because something has gone terribly wrong in the pregnancy. Other concerns are that an intact abortion may be the best medical choice for a woman in a given situation and that because of definitional vagueness, these laws will be interpreted to include other abortion procedures in their sweep.

In a challenge to Nebraska's law regarding partial-birth abortions, the Supreme Court, relying upon *Casey*, struck down the law because it failed to include a health exception, stating,

> Where substantial medical authority supports the proposition that banning a particular abortion procedure could endanger women's health, *Casey* requires the statute to include a health exception. . . . Requiring such an exception in this case is no departure from *Casey*, but simply a straightforward application of its holding.[110]

The other important consideration was that the law could potentially have been interpreted to have included other types of abortion, thus imposing an undue burden on a woman's right of choice.

Last, although not on the surface aimed specifically at abortion, fetal-rights laws have become an increasingly popular option for those seeking to restrict a woman's right of choice. These laws seek to enhance the status of the fetus (or embryo) by vesting it with legal personhood for a variety of purposes, such as treating it as an independent victim of a violent crime perpetrated against a pregnant woman, rather than considering any harm to the fetus as part of the harm to the woman. By diminishing the moral and legal distance between a pregnant woman and her unborn child, proponents of fetal-rights legislation hope to create a culture that is increasingly hostile toward abortion.

In tracing the legal history of abortion rights from the colonial era through the present, one can readily see how layered with meaning the issue has been and continues to be. Once regarded holistically as an integrated aspect of a woman's domestic-health regime, abortion has been vilified as "physiological sin" and also has been seen as an essential element of women's full participation in society. It has been criminalized in all but the narrowest of circumstances, has been elevated to a fundamental constitutional right, and has then been limited in deference to fetal interests. However, abortion is vested with yet other layers of meaning when the person seeking to abort is a teen. Not only does the abortion debate embody considerations of when life begins as well as the weight and meaning of women's lives, but considerations of adolescent sexuality and the parent-child relationship are also woven into the tapestry of the debate over whether and under what conditions a young woman is entitled to control her reproductive outcomes.

these understandings, we then take a close look at the landmark cases of *Planned Parenthood of Central Missouri v. Danforth*[1] and *Bellotti v. Baird*[2] and examine how the resulting judicial-bypass compromise reflects competing legal understandings of youth. Completing this legal picture, chapter 2 concludes with an overview of the status of parental-involvement laws, which are currently in effect in a majority of states. The task of critiquing the Court's approach to the abortion rights of minors is reserved for subsequent chapters.

A HISTORICAL OVERVIEW OF THE LEGAL STATUS OF CHILDREN AND ADOLESCENTS

In this section, we look at different approaches the law has taken with respect to the rights, needs, and status of children and adolescents. Each approach is rooted in a specific time period and reflects that period's understanding of the weight and meaning of childhood. You should keep several things in mind while reading this section. First, the dominant representation of youth in any given era is never all encompassing. For example, as our nation moved from an agrarian to an industrial society, children began to be seen as innocent and in need of gentle nurture and protection; however, this vision did not include slave children, who remained subject to brutalizing and inhumane conditions. Second, although particular legal approaches are linked with specific time periods, reality is never this tidy, since competing representations of and legal responses to youth frequently coexist at the same moment in time. Last, this presentation is intended to provide a historical anchor for the *Bellotti* decision rather than comprehensive historical coverage. Accordingly, time periods are greatly compressed and historical approaches described by way of global, overarching themes.[3]

The Child in the Colonial Era: Obedience and Authority

The colonial family was hierarchical in nature, and each member had a defined place in the family's internal structure. The husband and father was the "governor" of the household. His wife and children occupied well-defined subordinate positions and were subject to his unquestioned authority and control. The well-ordered family was the foundation of community life, and it served as a "model for all other social relations."[4]

In this preindustrial agrarian world, the realms of home and work were essentially one and the same. As historian Michael Grossberg explains,

> Most colonists conceived of the family as part of a hierarchically organized, interdependent society, rather than as a separate and distinct sphere of

experience. Households were tightly bound by taught strings of reciproc-
ity . . . the family's status as a vital link in the colonial chain of authority,
provided the major rationale for its internal organization.[5]

Given this reciprocal relationship, family disorder was a threat to social harmony
and stability, and the community had a direct stake in ensuring that families were
well run and that individual members fulfilled their familial obligations

By and large, families were self-sufficient units of production, and all members,
except for the very youngest children, were responsible for contributing to the
family economy. Work was a normal part of childhood, often taking priority over
education and certainly taking precedent over leisure time. Harsh physical punishment was also a defining aspect of colonial life, since a widespread belief held
that children were born with the taint of original sin, which had to be beaten out
of them if they were to grow up properly.

The legal position of minors in this time period is best expressed by the terms
"authority" and "obedience." Rooted in the ancient Roman doctrine of *patria
potestas,* which gave Roman fathers the right of absolute control over their children, the colonial father enjoyed substantial legal authority over his children.
Responsible for controlling their behavior, he had the corresponding authority to
punish them in order to command their obedience.

A father was in charge of the education and training of his children. He also
"owned" their labor—a valuable right in an agrarian society where children were
an integral component of the family economy. This gave him the authority to
apprentice his children to another family without any consideration for the
child's wishes or needs, and he was entitled to any wages a child earned working
for someone else. As a natural outgrowth of this patriarchal control, a father was
entitled to custody of the children in the unlikely event of divorce, and even
after he died, a father could continue to assert authority over his children (and
his wife) by assigning the children's care to someone other than their mother in
his will.[6]

Children had a corresponding legal duty to obey their parents, particularly
their father, since mothers, as succinctly stated by the famous English legal com-
mentator William Blackstone, were "entitled to no power, but only reverence
and respect."[7] The New England colonies took this obligation particularly seriously. Children who did not obey their parent could be whipped publicly,[8] and
the stubborn-child laws allowed a court to order a son put to death (although no
court ever did) based upon the testimony of his parents that "their son is stubborn
and rebellious and will not obey their voice and chastisement."[9]

The colonial patriarchal family structure began to break down as America
transitioned from an agrarian to an industrial society. As work moved out of the

home and into factories, a new child-centered domestic realm began to emerge in which children were reconceptualized as "economically useless, but emotionally 'priceless.' "[10] In turn, the law began moving away from its virtually singular emphasis on authority and obedience.

The Child in the Industrial and Progressive Eras: Vulnerability and Protection

The industrial revolution, which began taking hold in the early 1800s, did not simply alter the economic means of production; it also reshaped society, including the structure and meaning of family life. In the wake of change, domestic roles were reconstituted and family relationships redefined. Over time, these shifts contributed to a revised legal approach toward youth.

As production moved from the farm to the factory, the previously interconnected realms of work and home were uncoupled. Losing its identification with productive labor, the home was recast as a refuge from the harsh realities of the industrial world. Home became a female space, where the presiding "angel of the hearth" infused the space with her domestic glow.[11]

These changes both contributed to and were influenced by important shifts in cultural understandings of childhood. As work took fathers out of the home, the domestic authority they had previously enjoyed over their children was naturally eroded. At the same time, due in part to the influence of Enlightenment thinkers, such as John Locke, the earlier understanding of children as innately depraved beings gradually gave way to a view that children were innocent and malleable and potentially capable of rational thought. Consequently, "less emphasis was placed on physical punishment, while correspondingly more importance was given to psychological methods of discipline."[12] A logical consequence of these structural changes in conjunction with the reconceptualization of childhood was that mothers replaced fathers as "the most powerful agent in developing a child's character."[13] As eloquently expressed by family historian Carl Degler, "Exalting the child went hand in hand with exalting the domestic role of women; each reinforced the other while together they raised domesticity within the family to a new and higher level of respectability."[14]

Also important was that unlike in earlier times when there was no clearly defined concept of adolescence, and "youth was seen as a long period of gradual preparation for adult responsibilities,"[15] increasing attention was now being paid to the teen years. Over time, the boundaries of childhood were extended outward to embrace these transitional years, and like younger children, teens were seen as needing protective guidance to ensure their safe passage into adulthood.

As the prevailing understandings of youth changed, the dominant motif of authority and obedience lost its firm grip on the legal construction of childhood. Responding to the emerging view of children as innocent and vulnerable, the law began paying greater attention to their needs. Exemplifying these changes, in 1874 the first Society for the Prevention of Cruelty to Children was established in order to protect children from parental abuse and neglect. Also reflecting the new cultural understanding of childhood, courts began moving away from automatic awards of custody based upon paternal authority, in favor of a more child-centered best-interest standard, which over time was increasingly equated with maternal custody, especially with respect to young children. But as children, particularly sons, approached the adolescent years, some judges continued to evince a preference for the father, believing he could best prepare his sons for the adult world.

At the turn of the century, Progressive Era reformers sought to carve out a separate legal realm for children in order to shield them from the harsh realities of the adult world.[16] Placing their faith in the combined ability of the state and a host of well-trained experts, "progressive programs were intended to structure child development and to control and mold children while protecting them from exploitation."[17]

As part of their "child-saving" efforts, reformers fought for the passage of compulsory school attendance and child labor laws. These measures combined to create a separate social space for youth, reflecting the dominant middle-class view that parents who allowed their children to work were exploiting them and depriving them of their right to enjoy childhood unencumbered by adult responsibilities. As Zelizer explains, "For reformers, true parental love could only exist if the child was defined exclusively as an object of sentiment and not as an agent of production."[18] These laws thus embodied the dominant cultural view of children as "economically 'worthless' but emotionally 'priceless.' "[19]

Also central to Progressive Era reform efforts was the creation of the juvenile court system. Reformers argued that children did not belong in the adult criminal justice system because they lacked the ability to fully comprehend the significance of their deeds and were thus less responsible for their misdeeds than were adults. Reformers also believed that children were more amenable to rehabilitation than adults and that the focus should be not on whether the youth had committed a wrongful act, but on "what he is, how he has become what he is, and what had best be done in his interest and in the interest of the state to save him from a downward career."[20]

Beginning with Illinois in 1899, states began to establish separate courts for youthful offenders in which, in accordance with the reformers' vision, children were to be provided with a "special kind of justice uniquely suited to their needs."[21] Children were to be "treated" and "rehabilitated" rather than found guilty and punished.[22] To carry out this responsibility, judges were given almost limitless discretion to fashion particularized responses that were designed to meet the "real" needs of the individual child who was before the court.[23]

Based on an understanding of youth as more vulnerable and in need of greater protection than adults, these reforms, when taken as a whole, reinforced the social and legal divide between children and adults. Although this protective legal approach was certainly kinder than the authoritarian approach identified with the Colonial Era, it too had its limitations. As developed in the following section, the modern children's rights movement challenged the inherent paternalism of this protective approach, arguing that it failed to acknowledge the legal personhood of youth.

The Child in the Modern Era: Autonomy and Rights

The 1960s were a time of social activism and change. An active antiwar movement was launched in opposition to the war in Vietnam, and historically disempowered groups, most notably blacks and women, began mobilizing to challenge their subordinate social status, thus giving rise to a powerful civil rights movement. In seeking to dismantle entrenched hierarchies, reformers realized that the law had contributed to historic inequalities by encoding stereotypic assumptions about "innate" abilities and appropriate roles. Committed to a vision of equality, reformers turned to the courts to challenge discriminatory laws, arguing that each individual has the right to structure his or her own life free from imposed stereotypes about assumed group characteristics (such as the stereotype that women are less rational than men) and to make life-shaping decisions free from governmental dictates about what is appropriate and natural (such as the dictate that whites should not marry persons of color).

Inspired by this activism, a diffuse network of activists, academics, and others concerned about the welfare of children began rethinking the legal position of children. Although recognizing the undeniable differences between children and adults, they drew parallels between the legal subordination of blacks and women and the systematic denial of legal personhood to children:

> The assignment of children to a protected private space where they can exist as innocent [and] carefree is reminiscent of the separate spheres ideology that disempowered women. . . . the ideology insisted that there were natural differences between women and men that authorized women's

confinement to a separate domestic sphere. . . . [and the ideology] had tremendous consequences for women. . . .

Similarly, the ideology of the carefree, happy slave was used as justification for the denial of citizen rights to black Americans.[24]

In a similar vein, comparisons also drew upon the concept of the individual as property:

Historically, the law justified treating people of color and white women as property. . . . Our perception of children's inferiority likewise permits us to ignore children's legal claims. . . . By denying children legal personhood and standing we refuse to entertain and hear their claims. We thus continue to exclude children from redress for injustice just as historically we excluded white women and people of color.[25]

As the children's rights movement emerged, the Supreme Court handed down two cases that both reflected and further consolidated new understandings of children as individuals. Giving concrete expression to this transformative view, in the late 1960s the Court made clear for the first time that minors are individuals with enforceable constitutional rights that are neither wholly derived from nor dependent upon their place within the family hierarchy.

The first of these two cases, *In re Gault (Gault)*,[26] involved a 15-year-old boy who was adjudged delinquent for making lewd telephone calls to a neighbor and committed to the State Industrial School until his 21st birthday—a far greater punishment than he would have received had he been tried as an adult. Disturbed by both this outcome and the informality of the juvenile-court process, the Supreme Court addressed the shortcomings of the juvenile system:

Juvenile Court history has again demonstrated that unbridled discretion, however benevolently motivated, is frequently a poor substitute for principle and procedure. . . . The absence of substantive standards has not necessarily meant that children receive careful, compassionate, individualized treatment. The absence of procedural rules based upon constitutional principle has not always produced fair, efficient, and effective procedures. Departures from established principles of due process have frequently resulted . . . in arbitrariness.[27]

To correct these inequities, the Court held that the "fundamental fairness" requirement of the due process clause applies to juvenile proceedings, stating explicitly for the first time that "neither the Fourteenth Amendment nor the Bill of Rights is for adults alone."[28]

Two years later in the case of *Tinker v. Des Moines Independent School District (Tinker)*,[29] the Court ruled that school officials could not expel students for wearing black armbands to protest U.S. involvement in Vietnam without proven disruption to the school's functioning. In even stronger language than in *Gault,* the Court reiterated that minors are holders of constitutional rights, stating that "students in school as well as out of school are '*persons*' under our Constitution. They are possessed of fundamental rights which the state must respect."[30]

In recognizing children as rights-bearing individuals whose legal identity is not wholly subsumed by the family as an organic unit, these cases represent a fundamental shift in the Court's thinking about minors. It would, however, be a mistake to read them as signifying a wholesale repudiation of the legal distinction between childhood and adulthood.

To begin with, the historic configuration of the parent-child relationship continued to operate as a powerful constraint upon the extension of legal rights to children. In seeking to bring order to the law's "contradictory and uncertain" response to cases involving the rights of children, Professor Janet Dolgin astutely points out, as we have seen in both *Gault* and *Tinker*, that although the Supreme Court "has been willing the redefine children outside the domestic sphere," it has

been more cautious with regard to redefining children within families, reaffirming a traditional model of the family more often than disparaging or replacing that model.

Because the Supreme Court has not expressly and clearly applied the Individualist Model to cases involving disputes between children and their parents, it can be argued that the Court, in redefining children as autonomous individuals, has hoped . . . to preserve traditional understandings of childhood within the family context as it redefines children in the other contexts.[31]

Shying away from the "Individualistic Model" when faced with cases involving actual or potential disputes between parents and children, the Court has instead continued to rely upon earlier cases in which the virtue of parental control over the "upbringing and education" of their children has been extolled. This approach reinforces "traditional understandings of the parent-child relationship"[32] that, rather than seeing children as rights-bearing individuals, define them "through their status within families,"[33] thus perpetuating their subordinate legal status.

Second, moving beyond the family context, it is clear that there are legally significant differences between adults and children, and even staunch supporters of the individual-rights approach would agree that it would be absurd to treat six-year-olds as legal adults or give them the opportunity to demonstrate qualifying maturity on a case-by-case basis. Although other factors may also be at work, at least some of the legal distinctions between adults and children clearly reflect real, as distinct from fictional, differences across developmental domains. In turn, many of these differences mean that children, by virtue of developmental necessity, are dependent upon adults. Accordingly, to simply speak of children as autonomous legal persons, who in the classical liberal formulation are entitled to freedom *from* governmental interference, is to lose sight of their need *for care*, which at a bare minimum includes access to essentials, such as food, shelter, and education.

Complicating the matter, when one speaks of "children's rights," the meaning of the term is not always clear. As child expert Gary B. Melton explains, "Some who consider themselves 'child advocates' seek to 'liberate' children and increase their self-determination" while "others strive to protect children and to increase community responsibilities for their nurturance."[34] Framed slightly differently, the salient issue is whether the rights of children are best advanced through the erasure of formal distinctions between children and adults, with a corresponding focus on equality and choice at the expense of protection, or, alternatively, through an emphasis upon difference, with a corresponding focus on protection at the expense of equality and choice. Thus, the language of rights can be used to argue either for "more protection" or for "more independence."[35]

In addition to these constraints upon the full-blossoming of an individual-rights jurisprudence for children, not all members of the Court agreed with the view that children should have rights, and they began to push back. Warning of the "conflicts and disorder that rights for children could engender,"[36] these justices sought to preserve the authority that adults have traditionally had over children, both within and outside of families.

By the late 1970s, these voices had grown strong enough to command a majority in a number of cases involving the rights of children. Although the Court did not repudiate its prior characterization of minors as constitutional persons, it drew upon more traditional understandings of the allocation of power between adults and children to justify the curtailment of their rights. Thus, for example, in the case of *Ingraham v. Wright* in 1977,[37] the Court, citing the importance of maintaining order in the schools, upheld the right of teachers to use corporal punishment against errant students. Subsequently, in *New Jersey v. T.L.O.*,[38] the Court held that although the Fourth Amendment applies to searches conducted by school officials, the need, again, to preserve order in the schools frees teachers and administrators from the usual requirement that a search be based on probable cause that a crime has been or is in the process of being committed; the Court held that searches of students are allowed based simply upon a reasonable suspicion of wrongdoing—a far lower standard than the one presented in the Fourth Amendment. Grounded in these competing understandings of the legal status of youth, we now turn to the minors' abortion-rights cases. As we will see, in evaluating the constitutionality of parental-involvement laws, the Court struggled to reconcile a contemporary vision of youth as autonomous individuals possessed of fundamental constitutional rights[39] with a historic, but not moribund, understanding of them as dependent persons lacking legal agency.

MINORS AND THE CONSTITUTIONAL RIGHT TO ABORTION

The Constitutional Foundation: *Planned Parenthood of Central Missouri v. Danforth*

Missouri and Massachusetts were two of the first states in the nation to pass laws requiring minors to obtain the consent of their parents before having an abortion. These laws were promptly challenged, and three years after *Roe*, the Court faced what has become one of the most contentious issues in the abortion struggle, which is whether minors have a constitutional right to make their own abortion decisions, or whether they can be required to obtain the prior permission of a parent. We begin with the Court's decision in *Planned Parenthood of Central Missouri v. Danforth*[40] (*Danforth*), which set the stage for the landmark *Bellotti v. Baird* decision.[41]

In considering the validity of Missouri's requirement that minors obtain the consent of a parent before having an abortion, the Court began its analysis within the individual-rights framework. Relying upon *Gault* and *Tinker* (as well as upon more recent decisions), the Court reiterated, "Constitutional rights do not mature and come into being magically only when one attains the state-defined age of majority. Minors, as well as adults, are protected by the Constitution and possess constitutional rights."[42] Having implicitly extended the right of choice to young women, the Court then sought to determine whether a state could mandate a decision-making role for parents.

Writing for the majority, Justice Blackmun made clear that by giving parents the final say over their daughter's abortion decision, the state of Missouri had gone too far—that this degree of intrusion into a young woman's right of choice could not be justified by either the state's interest in protecting the integrity of the family unit or the authority of parents over their children. As Blackmun explains:

> It is difficult, however, to conclude that providing a parent with absolute power to overrule a determination, made by the physician and his minor patient, to terminate the patient's pregnancy will serve to strengthen the family unit. Neither is it likely that such veto power will enhance parental authority or control where the minor and the nonconsenting parent are so fundamentally in conflict and the very existence of the pregnancy already has fractured the family structure.[43]

As this passage makes clear, the majority's primary concern was that the Missouri law vested parents with veto power over their daughter's decision, thus potentially giving them the ability to divest her of her constitutional right of choice. In contrast, the dissenting judges did not seem in the least troubled by this. In fact, they saw parental involvement as a necessary prerequisite to the exercise of the right, since a young woman might otherwise mistakenly believe that abortion was the best choice for her. Thus, they argued that in order to protect young women "from the consequences of an incorrect decision,"[44] states must be free to insist upon parental consultation.

The Court invalidated the consent requirement because it gave parents the ultimate control over their daughter's decision. However, in so doing, the Court made clear that this did not mean it was suggesting that all minors are able to give effective consent to an abortion, thus signaling that the Court might uphold a less intrusive law. In this way, the *Danforth* Court implicitly distinguished between parental- and spousal-consent requirements, making it clear elsewhere in the decision that states may not seek to advance any interest that a husband might have in limiting a woman's right of choice, since she is the one who "physically bears the child and who is the more directly and immediately affected by the pregnancy."[45]

Establishing the Constitutional Framework: *Bellotti v. Baird*

Like the law the Court invalidated in *Danforth*, the Massachusetts law before the Court in the *Bellotti* case required young women to seek parental consent before having an abortion. However, this law contained one important difference—if a minor's parents refused to give her permission for the abortion, she could seek judicial authorization for the procedure. Thus, at first glance, this law appeared to have avoided the constitutionally fatal parental veto.

In evaluating the constitutionality of the Massachusetts law, the Court, relying upon *Danforth* and *Gault*, again began from a rights perspective, reiterating
that minority status does not place a young woman outside the reach of the Constitution. Pulling in the direction of autonomous decision-making, the Court
recognized that the abortion decision is quite different from most other decisions
a young woman might make during her teen years because of its temporal nature
and enduring impact.

With respect to temporality, the Court recognized that time is of the essence:

> The pregnant minor's options are much different from those facing minors
> in other situations, such as decision whether to marry. A minor not permit-
> ted to marry before the age of majority is required simply to postpone her
> decision. She and her intended spouse may preserve the opportunity for
> later marriage should they continue to desire it. A pregnant adolescent,
> however, cannot preserve for long the possibility of aborting, which effec-
> tively expires in a matter of weeks from the onset of pregnancy.[46]

As with marriage, the time frame for making most decisions does not "expire in a
matter of weeks." For example, take body piercing—if the parents of a 16-year-old
do not grant her permission to pierce her nose (or other body part), she simply
needs to wait two years until she can self-consent to the procedure. Although
she may be disappointed, the nose-piercing option remains open to her until she
reaches her 18th (or for that matter, her 35th or 60th) birthday.

Not only does the piercing option remain open, but also, nothing is lost
or irrevocably altered on account of the postponement. In contrast, not only
is the abortion decision a fleeting one, but denial of consent also has indelible
consequences:

> The potentially severe detriment facing a pregnant woman . . . is not
> mitigated by her minority. Indeed, considering her probable education,
> employment skills, financial resources, and emotional maturity, unwanted
> motherhood may be exceptionally burdensome for a minor. . . . There are
> few situations in which denying a minor the right to make an important
> decision will have consequences so grave and indelible.[47]

Returning to the comparison with marriage, which, unlike body piercing, is a
major life-event, although postponement of marriage may be inconvenient and
difficult emotionally, the consequences of waiting are not "grave and indelible"
as they are in the case of abortion. If denied permission to marry, a young woman
simply continues in the same unmarried status that she occupied before the denial.

In stark contrast to the denial of an abortion, the denial of consent operates to preserve the status quo; it does not result in a dramatic reworking of a minor's present and future reality. Moreover, because the marriage option remains open, any impact of a denial is contained in time and does not "indelibly" spread out over a minor's future life-course.

As discussed so far, the Court in *Bellotti* was clearly reasoning about the abortion rights of minors within an individual-rights framework. As in *Gault* and *Tinker,* the Court was focused upon the minor as a person unto herself and not simply as someone who is enfolded into a family unit. The "grave and indelible" consequences of "unwanted motherhood" were considered by the Court from the vantage point of the pregnant teen, in an implicit acknowledgment that she has a claim to her own life, separate and apart from the life that her parents might claim for her.

But this is just the start of the Court's analysis. Stating that "children have a very special place in life which law should reflect,"[48] the Court then drew upon historic understandings of youth in order to contain the decision's individualistic impulses. It thus concluded that because of the "peculiar vulnerability of children; their inability to make critical decisions in an informed, mature manner; and the importance of the parental role in childrearing," the constitutional rights of minors "cannot be equated with those of adults."[49]

Although aware that there are few situations in which denying a minor the right to make an important decision will have consequences so grave and indelible,"[50] having shifted analytical perspectives, the Court voiced the concern that a young woman might not be capable of making the abortion decision on her own. She might fail to appreciate that abortion is not necessarily the "best choice" for her and might fail to realize that she might be better off marrying the father, making an adoption plan, or raising the baby with the help of her family. Accordingly, the Court asserted that to prevent her from making a bad choice, a minor's autonomy could be limited in favor of the "guiding role of parents in the upbringing of their children."[51]

In focusing on parental guidance, the Court invoked an understanding of the parent-child relationship that emerged with industrialization. It also drew upon the legal approach to youth that is identified with the reforms of the Progressive Era, when laws sought to remove children from the world of adults in order to shield them from grown-up responsibilities, including the making of life-shaping decisions. Reinforcing cultural understandings of the vulnerable child, the laws, much as the *Bellotti* Court did here, distinguished between the protected realm of childhood and the autonomous realm of adulthood.

The *Bellotti* Court did not simply focus on the "guiding role" of parents to justify limiting the autonomy of minors. Identifying it as an even more important consideration, the Court invoked the "natural" authority of parents over their children to justify limiting the rights of young women. In turning to parental authority as a counterweight to full constitutional recognition, the Court drew upon traditional understandings of the parent-child relationship that hearken back to the colonial era:

> Deeply rooted in our Nation's history and tradition, is the belief that the parental role implies a substantial measure of authority over one's children. Indeed, "constitutional interpretation has consistently recognized that the parents' claim to authority in their own household to direct the rearing of their children is basic in the structure of our society."[52]

The Court here does not claim that the invocation of parental authority is for the purpose of helping minors to make better choices. Reflecting an understanding of family relations that is identified with the colonial era, the focus is instead on the preservation of family hierarchies, which, in turn, is directly linked to preserving the "structure of our society." The Court thus reclaimed a model of family relations that "reinforces strong parental authority, and assumes children's choices to be nonexistent, or to be rightly displaced by the choices of their parents, except in the most unique circumstances."[53] By limiting the constitutional personhood of minors, the Court resisted allowing the "impulse of modernity towards autonomous individuality"[54] to dismantle family hierarchies.

The *Bellotti* Court thus comes full circle in its understanding of the legal status of youth. At the start of the decision, teens considering abortions were presented as rights-bearing individuals who had been "freed from . . . the limitations and protections that follow from their inclusion within the holistic social hierarchy of the traditional family."[55] By decision's end, those teens had been re-enfolded into the family, both so that they could benefit from parental guidance and so that "natural" parental authority would not be undercut.

It is here in this push and pull of sorting out the legal meaning of childhood and the nature of the parent-child relationship that the Court crafted the judicial-bypass compromise. Recognizing both the "guiding role" of parents and their "claim to authority" over their children, the Court concluded that states can require a teen to obtain the consent of her parents before having an abortion. However, in recognition of the minor's constitutional right to decisional privacy, if the state chooses to make such a requirement, it must provide "an alternative procedure [the judicial bypass] whereby authorization for the abortion can be obtained."[56] Of defining importance, the law must be constructed in such a manner that the "provision requiring parental consent does not in fact amount to the 'absolute, and possibly arbitrary, veto' that was found impermissible in *Danforth*."[57]

The Court then evaluated the Massachusetts consent law against these requirements. Initially, as noted earlier, it appeared that Massachusetts had solved the parental-veto problem by giving minors the right to seek judicial approval for an abortion in the event parental consent was denied. However, the Court recognized that many parents hold "strong views on the subject of abortion,"[58] and that once consulted, rather than providing their daughter with "mature advice and emotional support,"[59] these parents might prevent her from going to court or from having the abortion, thus effectively having the final say.

For these minors, the court option would be meaningless. They would be no better off than minors in Missouri whose parents had denied them permission for an abortion. For this reason, the Court invalidated the Massachusetts law on due process grounds for "imposing an undue burden upon the exercise by minors of the right to seek an abortion."[60] To resolve the constitutionally fatal veto problem, the Court held that "every minor must have the opportunity—if she so desires—to go *directly* to a court without first consulting or notifying her parents." [61] In short, a minor must be allowed to bypass her parents and have direct, unmediated access to court.

In additional to the parental "bypass" mandate, the Court also set out several other constitutionally necessary requirements. First, the court hearing and any appeals that follow must be completed with "anonymity and . . . expedition" so that the abortion opportunity is preserved. Second, at the hearing, a minor must be given the opportunity to demonstrate that she is mature enough to make her own abortion decision. If she demonstrates maturity, she must be permitted to make her own decision. If a judge concludes that she is not mature enough to give consent, she must be permitted to show that an abortion is in her best interest.

In constructing this bypass model, the Court failed to take note of two self-contained ironies. First, although the bypass process solved the parental veto problem, it did so by transferring the ultimate authority over a young woman's decision from her parents to the presiding judge.[62] If a state cannot vest this authority in a parent, it is even less clear how it can vest it in a member of the judiciary. Moreover, the two-tiered hearing approach means that a judge who determines that a minor is not mature enough to make her own abortion decision could also decide that an abortion is not in her best interest, thus potentially compelling her to carry the pregnancy to term. The decision also contains other serious flaws. As we will see in chapter 3, in deciding that limits can be placed on the abortion rights of minors, the Court failed to seriously consider either the medical decision-making rights of teens or the emerging body of social-science literature on their decisional capacity.

3

(Mis)constructing Adolescent Reality: *Bellotti v. Baird* Reconsidered

I n chapter 2, we saw how in the landmark case of *Bellotti v. Baird*, the Court sought to reconcile competing understandings of young women—as being both rights-bearing individuals and vulnerable children—by creating the judicial-bypass alternative to required parental involvement. In this chapter, we revisit the *Bellotti* decision from a more critical stance. This requires consideration of two distinct, but overlapping, topics—the medical-consent rights of teens and their decision-making abilities. With a more complete understanding of these essential topics, we reexamine the judicial-bypass compromise, which, upon closer consideration, appears to be built upon a partial and incomplete understanding of adolescent reality, thus raising important doubts about the integrity of the *Bellotti* decision.

THE MEDICAL DECISION-MAKING RIGHTS OF TEENS

Drawing upon prior Supreme Court decisions to support its vision of young women as too immature and too subordinate to parental authority to make their own reproductive decisions, the *Bellotti* Court inexplicably overlooked the fact that in the realm of medical decision-making, minors possess significant self-consent rights, particularly when it comes to "sensitive"-health care matters, such as pregnancy. Although this omission is puzzling in its own right, it is even more baffling when one recognizes that *Roe* characterized abortion as a medical decision. As we discuss in this chapter, had the Court, when considering the consent rights of minors, continued to regard abortion as a medical decision, it would have been forced to think about the issue very differently. To set the stage for this discussion, we briefly return to the *Roe* decision.

Roe and the "Reasonable" Physician

Emphasizing the physical and psychological detriments of forcing a woman to carry to term, the *Roe* Court stated that the decision to terminate a pregnancy was "inherently, and primarily, a medical decision."[1] Accordingly, although unequivocally assigning ultimate decisional authority to the pregnant woman, the Court assumed that a woman's physician would play a central role in the decision-making process.[2] In explaining the potential harms of compelled maternity, the Court emphasized the negative impact this would have on a woman's physical and mental well-being:

> The detriment that the State would impose upon the pregnant woman by denying this choice altogether is apparent. Specific and direct harm *medically diagnosable* even in early pregnancy may be involved. Maternity, or additionally offspring may force upon the woman a distressful life and future. *Psychological harm* may be imminent. *Physical and mental health* may be taxed by child care. There is also the distress, for all concerned, associated with the unwanted child, and there is the problem of bringing a child into a family already unable, *psychologically* and otherwise, to care for it. In other cases, the additional difficulties and continuing stigma of unwanted motherhood may be involved.[3]

The Court's "medicalization" of abortion is somewhat unsettling, particularly since, at moments, the Court appears to be more concerned with the rights of physicians to practice medicine free from undue state interference than it is with the rights of women to avoid unwanted maternity. For instance, in summarizing the result, the Court praised the fact that the decision "vindicates the right of the physician to administer medical treatment according to his professional judgment"[4] while neglecting to mention that most significantly, the decision vindicates the rights of women to make self-defining decisions about the meaning and place of motherhood in their lives. This focus both moves women off center-stage and minimizes the non-medical dimensions of the abortion decision.

There is, however, a positive aspect to the *Roe* Court's use of a medical paradigm for thinking about abortion. Given that abortions are routinely performed in medical settings, the Court is normalizing the practice. Stating that abuses of discretion should be subject to the "usual remedies"[5] for physician malfeasance rather than the historical criminal sanctions, the decision moves abortion out of the shadows and into the mainstream of medical practice. As envisioned by the Court, abortion now falls within the realm of ordinary patient care: it is recharacterized as a procedure that a doctor might be called upon to perform in the usual course of caring for his or her patients.

Had the Court continued to reason about abortion within this medical paradigm, it would have been compelled to confront the fact that minors have considerable medical consent rights. In turn, this would have forced the Court to critically examine the assumptions it relied upon to justify the judicial-bypass construct. Starting with an overview of the critical concepts of consent and confidentiality, we now consider the medical decision-making rights of teens.

Consent and Confidentiality: General Principles

Grounded in the "ancient notion that one's body should not be touched without one's approval,"[6] a physician is required to obtain the consent of his or her patient before providing medical treatment, except in emergency circumstances. This consent rule, which is intended to protect a patient's right to bodily integrity, was well established by the early part of the nineteenth century.[7]

Over time, an additional layer was added to this basic requirement, and today, in order for consent to be effective, it must also be "informed." Reflecting the importance of patient autonomy, this rule goes well beyond protecting bodily integrity to also protect the integrity of the decision-making process. As explained in *Canterbury v. Spence*, a leading informed-consent decision,

> True consent to what happens to one's self is the informed exercise of a choice, and that entails an opportunity to evaluate knowledgeably the options available, and the risks attendant upon each. The average patient has little or no understanding of the medical arts, and ordinarily has only his physician to whom he can look for enlightenment with which to reach an intelligent decision.[8]

For consent to qualify as informed, it must be knowing, competent, and voluntary. For a decision to be "knowing," the patient must given enough information about the diagnosis, the risks and benefits of the treatment, and the alternatives to the proposed treatment, so that she or he is aware of the pluses and minuses of the full range of options. For a decision to be "competent," the patient must have the ability to understand and weigh these various options, and for a decision to be "voluntary," the patient must be acting according to his or her own free will—the decision cannot be coerced.[9]

Confidentiality generally follows consent. Accordingly, the duty to maintain confidentiality is owed the party who authorizes the medical care. Subject to limited exceptions, such as when a patient threatens harm to himself or herself or to an identified individual, medical information may not be disclosed to third parties without the consenting party's permission. In short, the patient holds the key to disclosure.

The duty to protect patient confidentiality is "generally acknowledged to be a cornerstone of the physician-patient relationship and 'essential to a patient's trust in a health care provider and a patient's willingness to supply information candidly for his or her benefit.' "[10] The obligation stems from multiple sources, including the various ethical codes of the health-care professions; state and federal medical-privacy laws; the constitutional right of privacy; and state and federal statutes that create and fund various health programs, such as Title X of the Public Health Service Act, which provides comprehensive family planning services.[11]

Consent and Confidentiality in the Provision of Health Care to Minors

What if the patient is a minor—how do the basic principles of consent and confidentiality play out in this context? With respect to consent, the long-standing rule is that authorization for care must be provided by a parent. This rule is predicated on a set of mutually reinforcing assumptions about the decision-making ability of young people, the countervailing wisdom of parents, and the integrity of the autonomous family.

Regardless of age or maturity, minors are presumed to lack the capacity to make informed medical decisions. Counterbalancing this assumption, parents are presumed to possess the wisdom and maturity their children lack and, significantly for our purposes, are presumed to "have an identity of interest with their minor children" such that they will be guided by their children's best interest when exercising their decisional authority.[12] Rooted in the dominant vision of the family as an integrated and harmonious whole, this consent rule assumes that children do not have their own identity and do not exist in the world as separate people. However, as we will see, the multiple exceptions to this rule challenge the assumptions upon which it is predicated.

Turning to confidentiality, the basic rule discussed previously—that confidentiality follows consent—applies here as well. Therefore, if a parent is the consenting party, the confidential relationship typically arises between the doctor and the parent. A doctor can disclose information about the medical care received by the minor directly to the parent, and the parent may authorize disclosure to third parties. However, where the minor is the consenting party, the confidential relationship, following the general rule, should arise between the doctor and the minor. As health-law expert Angela Holder explains,

> It would seem that if the physician does not feel the need to obtain consent of the parents to treat the child, he is by that decision assuring the child that the normal physician-patient relationship that would obtain if he were an adult has begun to apply . . . By accepting the child as a responsible patient who has the right to consent to treatment, the physician has implicitly accorded that child the normal rights of a patient within the patient-physician relationship.[13]

Providers of health care services to adolescents are in general accord about the importance of confidentiality in insuring meaningful access to health-care services, particularly when it comes to sensitive matters, such as reproductive health care,[14] and a number of studies have concluded that without an assurance of confidentiality, teens may postpone or forgo seeking needed care.[15] Confidentiality also promotes the full disclosure of information, which is essential to the provision of good medical care, since a teen assured of confidentiality will not be hampered by the fear that sensitive information will be shared with his or her parents.[16] Another benefit of a confidential relationship is that it allows physicians to help adolescents "incrementally assume greater responsibility for their health and decisions by providing a context in which the adolescent may candidly discuss concerns, worries, and health-risk behaviors."[17]

However, as is often the case where minors are concerned, the law regarding confidentiality is somewhat murky. Although the basic principle—that the duty of confidentiality runs to the consenting party—generally holds true, the laws vary from state to state.[18] For example, in some states, disclosure is permitted under limited circumstances, such as where the minor's medical condition poses a serious risk to his or her health or life.[19] Complicating the picture further, the rules governing confidentiality may vary based upon the identity of the health care provider. For example, a minor in a state with a law that does not expressly link consent and confidentiality may run the risk of parental disclosure if she seeks reproductive health care from her family doctor. However, she will be able to obtain confidential care if she goes to a clinic that receives Title X federal family-planning monies, since funding recipients must provide confidential care to all clients, including minors.[20]

When Parental Consent Is Not Required

As previously discussed, the basic rule is that when the patient is a minor, consent must be provided by a parent. However, the many exceptions to this rule unsettle the dominant vision of parents as hegemonic decision-makers for their children. The exceptions also raise important questions about the validity of the assumptions that underlie the preferred status of parents, at least when it comes to sensitive medical decisions. We begin by looking at exceptions that shift decisional authority from a parent to a third party, and we then consider exceptions that shift authority from a parent to child.

Shifting Decision-Making Authority from a Parent to a Third Party

In situations involving either emergency care or what is commonly referred to as "medical neglect," decision-making authority shifts from the parent to a third party. Although there is no transfer of authority to the minor, these situations are instructive because they challenge the notion that parents have unbounded control over the medical care of their children.

Medical Emergencies

It is well established that a physician may treat a minor without parental consent in the case of a medical emergency, and most states now have statutes that specifically authorize such care. The trend has been in favor of expanding the concept of emergency to include not only life-threatening conditions, but also "those situations where a delay in treatment would increase risk to the patient's health, or treatment is necessary to alleviate physical pain or discomfort."[21] Thus, in many states, a physician can provide care without parental consent when "prompt" treatment is indicated.

The emergency rule is sometimes explained by reference to the doctrine of implied consent, which assumes that under the circumstances, parents, if contacted, would consent to the needed care. However, the essential policy-rationale behind this rule is that doctors must be permitted to provide necessary medical care to minors without fear of liability for the failure to obtain proper authorization for the treatment.[22]

Although the emergency exception does not give minors independent authority to consent to their care, the rule is nonetheless important as we consider the status of minors as medical decision-makers. By privileging the health needs of minors and physician autonomy over the decision-making authority of parents, the emergency exception implicitly recognizes that parental authority is not absolute and sometimes must yield to other more immediate interests. By its very presence, this exception quietly recognizes that children do not exist simply in a family context and that parents may not always be present to prevent injury or tend to urgent needs. Without implying neglect, the exception embodies awareness that in the ordinary course of life, parents and children are not joined at the hip.

Medical Neglect

Parents may be more directly deprived of control over their children's medical treatment in situations involving medical neglect. Here intervention is considered necessary based upon the failure of a parent to provide appropriate medical care for a child, frequently because of religious or spiritual beliefs. In these situations, intervention is usually based upon a child-protection law that is intended to safeguard children from parental abuse and neglect. Most of these laws now specifically identify medical neglect as a category of parental harm that warrants state intervention; where failure to provide adequate medical care is not specifically enumerated, the definition of neglect is usually broad enough that it can be construed to include such failure.[23]

Historically, courts were likely to intervene only if a parent's refusal to consent to medical care posed a direct threat to the life of the child,[24] but as with the emergency-care rule, the recent trend has been in favor of a more expansive definition of the concept.[25] In deciding if intervention is warranted, courts generally balance a number of competing considerations, such as the risk of harm to the child if treatment is withheld, the benefits of treatment, the certainty of results, the express wishes of the child, the religious beliefs of the parent(s), the rights of parental privacy, and the best interests of the child. If a finding of medical neglect is made, the court usually appoints a guardian to act as a substitute decision-maker regarding the treatment in question, without otherwise limiting the rights of the parents.

As in cases of medical emergencies, this limitation on the rights of parents does not shift authority to minors, nor does it challenge the presumption about the decisional incapacity of minors. However, by recognizing the possibility of parental neglect, it directly challenges the presumption that parents always make good medical decisions for their children. By capturing the very real possibility of divergent interests and allowing for parental displacement, this exception forces us to recognize that not all families function as integrated and harmonious units in which a child's essential needs are met by his or her parents.

Shifting Decision-Making Authority from Parent to Minor

The previously discussed exceptions to the parental-consent rule make clear that parental authority over the medical care of children is not absolute. The reality of family life, including the inability of parents to always be physically present and the possibility of potentially harmful inaction (or action), means that decisional authority over a particular aspect of care may need to be shifted to a third party. However, far more important for our purposes are the exceptions that actually transfer authority from a parent to a minor, based upon the minor's status as either emancipated or mature or upon the kind of treatment being sought. These doctrines reveal the narrowness and partiality of the lens through which the *Bellotti* Court viewed the legal world of adolescence, thus enabling it to paint a one-dimensional picture of what turns out to be a far more complex and nuanced reality.

Status-Based Rights: The Emancipated and the Mature Minor

Stated generally, a teen who is legally emancipated can consent to his or her own medical care. Emancipation can occur in a number of different ways. The doctrine was originally developed primarily as a vehicle by which parents could relinquish control over their child, and under the current common law of emancipation, a teen who is "not living at home and is self-supporting, is responsible for himself economically and otherwise, and whose parents (voluntarily or involuntarily) have surrendered their parental duties and rights"[26] may be adjudicated an emancipated minor. This determination generally operates to extinguish the reciprocal rights and responsibilities of the parent-child relationship and vests the child with adult-like rights, including the right to consent to medical treatment.

Although clearly recognizing that minors may be fully independent of their parents, the traditional doctrine of emancipation was not motivated by a vision of minors as persons with claims to self-determination. In part responding to the need for a more teen-centered concept, and in part seeking to bring coherence to the common-law approach, a number of states have enacted emancipation statutes.[27] These statutes can be either general or limited in scope.

Under a general emancipation statute, a minor asks a court to relieve him or her of the full range of age-based limitations. In deciding whether to grant the petition, most states consider the "best interest" of the child, often in combination with other factors, such as whether the minor is capable of conducting his or her own affairs and whether the minor is living separate and apart from his or her parents. If the petition is granted, the minor is generally afforded the full rights and responsibilities of adulthood, including the right of medical self-determination. However, some statutes give judges the right to attach conditions to the grant of emancipation, thus resulting in partial rather than complete emancipation, which could mean that a minor would not acquire medical decision-making rights.

In contrast, a limited emancipation statute grants identified categories of minors relief from specific limitations without the necessity of a court proceeding. Utilizing this approach, many states have enacted what are commonly referred to as "medical emancipation" laws that authorize certain categories of minors, most commonly those who are married, are in the armed services, or are the parent of a child, to self-consent to their own medical care. Here, emancipation does not require actual proof of independence, since the minor's life circumstances are presumed incompatible with parental control. Another statutory approach used in some states is to permit all minors who are above a specific age (most commonly between 14 and 16) to consent to their own health care. In some of these states, self-consent rights are complete, and in other states, they are limited to treatment for specific conditions, such as drug abuse, pregnancy and contraception, and sexually transmitted infections.

Some of these age-based emancipation laws expressly equate minors with adults. For example, in Delaware, minors age 12 and older who are pregnant, who are at risk of becoming pregnant, or who are "afflicted with contagious, infectious, or communicable diseases" may consent to their own related health care, including surgery, and in giving consent, a minor "shall be deemed to have the same legal capacity to act and the same legal obligations with regard to giving consent as if the minor were of full legal age."[28] Significantly, this statute was in effect at the time *Bellotti* was decided and could have served as a model approach. However, by reasoning about the abortion rights of minors outside of the medical paradigm that it set out in *Roe,* the Court avoided having to consider the possibility of treating minors as autonomous decision-makers.

The other important status-based exception to the parental-consent requirement is the mature-minor rule. Developed mainly through judicial decisions, this doctrine allows minors who are mature enough to understand the risks and benefits of proposed medical treatment to give consent. Unlike the law of emancipation, which is premised on objective manifestations of independence, the mature-minor rule directly recognizes that teens may have the cognitive maturity to make informed decisions about their own medical care. Put succinctly, "The legal principle now applied is that if a young person (aged 14 or 15 years or older) understands the nature of proposed treatment and its risks, if the physician believes that the patient can give the same degree of informed consent as an adult patient, and if the treatment does not involve very serious risks, the young person may validly consent to receiving it."[29] Some states now have mature-minor statutes. For example, in Arkansas, "any unemancipated minor of sufficient intelligence to understand and appreciate the consequences of the proposed surgical or medical treatment or procedures" is "authorized and empowered to consent, either orally or otherwise, to any surgical or medical treatment or procedure not prohibited by law which may be suggested, recommended, prescribed, or directed by a licensed physician."[30]

As noted, these status-based exceptions clearly challenge the *Bellotti* Court's depiction of adolescent reality as a world in which teens lack any kind of decisional autonomy. The law of emancipation recognizes that minors may be sufficiently independent of their parents, based either on age or on the objective conditions of their lives, to warrant a transfer of decision-making authority.[31] Here, the presumed identity of interests between parent and child disappears, and it is no longer assumed that parental decision-making will promote the best interests of the minor. Although grounded in notions of independence rather than maturity, emancipation honors the ability of minors to make appropriate life choices. In shifting decisional authority from parents to minors, the doctrine undercuts core assumptions underlying the parental-consent rule—including the assumption that minors are incapable of meaningful self-definition and parents are always the preferred decision-makers.

As with emancipation, the mature-minor rule, by transferring decisional authority from parents to minors, directly challenges historic understandings of capacity and decisional authority. Embodying a dynamic vision of youth, this rule recognizes that minority is not an indistinguishable phase stretching from infancy to young adulthood and that the allocation of authority between parents and children must be calibrated to account for the increasing capacities of children as they move through adolescence.

Treatment-Based Exceptions

Over the past several decades, in response to increasingly visible manifestations of teen sexual activity and drug and alcohol use, states have enacted a variety of "minor treatment" statutes that give minors the authority to consent to treatment for specific types of medical care. Some statutes set a threshold age-of-consent, such as 12 or 14, below which a minor cannot self-consent to care, although the age minimum may only apply to some kinds of care, such as mental health or drug-treatment services. These statutes recognize that if minors are required to involve their parents to obtain care related to potentially sensitive matters, they might delay or avoid seeking needed services. Thus, as a policy matter, these laws privilege the health needs of minors over parental claims of decisional authority.[32]

Accordingly, in most states a minor can consent to pregnancy-related health care (except for abortion); family-planning services, including contraception; the detection and treatment of sexually transmitted diseases;[33] and treatment for drug and alcohol dependency. Many states also allow minors to self-consent to mental health services. In some states, the determination regarding the need for treatment belongs to the minor. Under Pennsylvania law, for example, "Any person 14 years of age or over who believes that he is in need of treatment and substantially understands the nature of voluntary treatment may submit himself to examination and treatment under this act, provided that the decision to do so is made voluntarily."[34] In other states, the responsibility for determining the need for treatment falls more to the clinician.[35]

Minor-treatment statutes are similar to the status-based exceptions in that they transfer decisional authority from parents to minors; however, they are based on public health considerations rather than on teen maturity or independence. Framed neutrally as essential health-related measures, these laws seem to have generated little controversy. Yet, in recognizing the necessity of giving minors control over sensitive medical decisions, this exception more than any of the others (except possibly medical neglect) directly recognizes that the interests of parents and children may diverge and that parental involvement can interfere with the provision of critical medical care. By their very existence, these laws acknowledge the reality of family conflict and unsettle deeply held notions of parents as always being the most appropriate decision-makers for their children.

Interestingly, these medical-treatment laws are generally concerned with activities that are historically associated more with adulthood than childhood. Thus, they seem to implicitly recognize that intergenerational conflicts may be triggered as children reach adolescence and begin to assert their autonomy by engaging in activities that signal their approaching adulthood and separation from their family of birth. By entrusting minors with the authority to manage these sensitive and significant aspects of their lives, these laws, although not directly premised on considerations of maturity or independence, nonetheless acknowledge the ability of minors to respond to the changing realities of their lives at moments in time when their parents may not be able to do so.

When considered as a whole, these exceptions to the parental-consent rule make it clear that parental authority over the health care of minor children is far from complete. Parents may be divested of authority based upon the exigencies of a situation or based upon their own disregard for the medical needs of their child. They may also be divested of authority because of the life circumstances of their child, who, based either upon their status or upon the kind of care that is required, may be empowered to make critical decisions, often with life-altering consequences, for themselves.

THE DECISION-MAKING CAPACITY OF TEENS

Although teens may have considerable self-consent rights when it comes to the making of medical decisions, the U.S. Supreme Court failed to take this reality into account in deciding that when it comes to abortion, the consent rights of young women can be limited in favor of requiring the involvement of a third-party adult. Compounding this omission, the Court also failed to consider more generally that a young woman facing an unplanned pregnancy might have the decisional capacity to determine for herself whether she is ready for motherhood. To frame this discussion, we turn to the frequently cited dissenting opinion of Supreme Court Justice William O. Douglas in the case of *Wisconsin v. Yoder* (*Yoder*).[36]

In *Yoder*, Amish parents successfully challenged the state's compulsory-school-attendance law, arguing that the state's requirement that children remain in school until the age of 16 interfered with the family's right of religious freedom. Concluding that the parents had the right to remove their children from the public school system when the children turned 14, the Court stated,

> Formal high school education beyond the eighth grade is contrary to Amish beliefs, not only because it places Amish children in an environment hostile to Amish beliefs . . . but also because it takes them away from their community, physically and emotionally, during the crucial and formative adolescent period of life.[37]

In dissent, Justice Douglas criticized the majority for failing to consider the interests of the children in these families. In a break with tradition, he argued it was inappropriate to simply assume a harmony of interest between parent and child, since the students might have their own views about what educational course they wished to pursue, which the Court should have taken into account. Viewing the students as individuals with their own separate identities, Douglas also questioned the historic presumption that minors lack the ability to make informed decisions about their own lives. As he explained,

> The parents are seeking to vindicate not only their own free exercise claims, but also those of their high-school-age children. . . . [If the parents are] allowed a religious exemption, the inevitable effect is to impose the parents' notions of religious duty upon their children. . . .
>
> It is the future of the student, not the future of the parents, that is imperiled by today's decision. . . .
>
> It is the student's judgment, not his parents', that is *essential* if we are to give full meaning to what we have said about the Bill of Rights and of the right of students to be masters of their own destiny.[38]

In support of his position that the "essential" voice belongs to the student rather than to his or her parents, Douglas referenced the work of noted experts in the field of child and adolescent development, including the renowned psychologist Jean Piaget, and stated,

> There is substantial agreement among child psychologists and sociologists that the moral and intellectual maturity of the 14-year-old approaches that of the adult. The maturity of Amish youth, who identify with and assume adult roles from early childhood . . . is certainly not less than that of children in the general population.[39]

Although much of the research on adolescent decision-making has taken place since the Court's decision in *Bellotti*, an important body of literature, as evidenced by the Douglas dissent written six years earlier, was in existence at the time the Court rendered its decision. Of this work, the most significant was that of developmental psychologist Jean Piaget, whose stage theory of development, although not immune from criticism, continues to influence the field today.[40]

According to Piaget, cognitive development (cognition refers to "the act or process of knowing including both awareness and judgment"[41]) occurs in predictable stages, starting at birth. Most significantly for present purposes, he determined that somewhere between the ages of 11 and 15, children progress from the concrete-reasoning phase in their development and acquire the ability to engage in abstract reasoning. At this point, they have reached the highest development level—the "formal operations" stage—and possess a reasoning ability that is comparable to that of an adult.[42]

Three primary characteristics differentiate the formal-operations stage from the prior developmental stage: "concrete versus abstract thinking, present versus future orientation, and consideration of only some options versus all options."[43] Thus, upon reaching the formal-operations stage, an adolescent is able to "imagine the past, present, and future conditions of a problem and create hypotheses about what might logically occur under different conditions. They can engage in pure thought independent of actions they see or perform. They can hypothesize and draw deductions, understand theories, and combine them to solve problems."[44]

Since the Court's decision in *Bellotti*, many studies have compared the decision-making abilities of adolescents and adults, and as Piagetian theory would predict, most have found few, if any, meaningful differences in cognitive abilities, at least with respect to adolescents from about age 14 and up. In reviewing much of this research, the Adolescent Health Project of the Congressional Office of Technology Assessment concluded in a major report,

> Although the core studies reviewed vary in geographic location, somewhat in sociodemographic characteristics of participants, in whether or not

they are in a "real" health care decision setting, and in the subject matter domain of the decisions, they generally are uniform in their findings. These studies find few differences in health care decision making as a function of age for adolescents as young as 13 or 14 years of age.[45]

Nonetheless, in subsequent decisions involving the abortion rights of minors, the Court has clung to *Bellotti*'s core assumption about the decisional incapacity of teens. It has not stopped to reconsider this assumption in light of the growing body of research on adolescent decisional capacity—it has simply carried the assumption forward as a fixed and immutable truth.

BELLOTTI REVISITED

Having looked at the medical-consent rights of teens and begun our discussion of their decision-making abilities, we return to the *Bellotti* decision to consider some questions that these new understandings raise. For instance, how can we make sense of the Court's failure to consider the medical-decision-making rights of teens, particularly given *Roe*'s characterization of abortion as a medical procedure? In a similar vein, how can we make sense of the fact that the Court developed (and has since adhered to) the bypass approach in the absence of a meaningful discussion about the decisional abilities of teens? As we revisit *Bellotti*, these questions compel us to ask whether the judicial bypass compromise, rather than reflecting a concern for minors and the integrity of families, might instead be better understood as signaling a shift in the Court's thinking about abortion.

The *Bellotti I* Decision: Abortion Is Different Because It Is Different

The *Bellotti* decision we have been discussing is actually the second of two decisions that the Court rendered in this case. It is by far the more important of the two because it was in the second case that the Court reached the merits of the controversy and decided on the constitutionality of the Massachusetts parental-consent law. However, the first decision, by implicitly singling out abortion for differential treatment, set the stage for the Court's eventual development of the bypass compromise.[46]

When the *Bellotti* case came before the Court for the first time in 1976, the plaintiffs argued that the Massachusetts parental-consent law was unconstitutional because it distinguished between the consent required for abortion and that required for other medical procedures.[47] The Court acknowledged that the issue of differential treatment had "come to the fore" because while the case was pending, Massachusetts had enacted a new law greatly expanding the medical-consent rights of minors. Previously, the primary exception to the parental consent requirement had been limited to medical emergencies, but now teens were vested with considerable self-consent rights based either upon their status or upon the type of treatment being sought. Accordingly, under the new law, pregnant minors (or those believing themselves to be pregnant) had full decisional authority over their own health care, including the right to decide to carry the pregnancy to term, and once the teen became a parent, her decisional authority extended to the making of medical decisions for the child.[48]

Although the Court acknowledged it was now facing a statutory scheme that distinguished between abortion and other medical procedures, it chose not to invalidate the law for discriminating against or burdening the right to abortion. Instead, it decided to remand (send back) the case to the Massachusetts Supreme Judicial Court (SJC) so that the SJC could interpret the statute in accordance with Massachusetts law.[49] However, the Court was not dealing with subtle distinctions that needed careful interpretation. No matter how the statute was read, it was clear that in allowing motherhood, but not its rejection, to be an autonomous choice, Massachusetts was discriminating between minors intending to abort and those intending to carry to term.

Implicit in the Court's decision to remand the case rather than strike down the law is an acceptance of abortion as a stand-alone procedure that can be singled out for more burdensome consent requirements than other types of sensitive medical care. That this is the silent, but powerful, message of *Bellotti I* is made clear by the Court's explanation of why it could not act without the insight of the state court: "As we hold today not all distinctions between abortion and other procedures is forbidden. The constitutionality of such distinction will depend on its degree and the justification for it."[50] As revealed in this quote, the appropriate inquiry is not whether abortion can be singled out for differential treatment, but whether the extent of and justification for the distinction is warranted. It is here—in the Court's acceptance of the singularity of abortion—that we see the first real hint that there may, in fact, be more to the first *Bellotti* decision than initially meets the eye.

Bellotti II Decision: Vesting Abortion with Symbolic Meaning

When the *Bellotti* case came back before the Supreme Court, the Court once again ignored the illogic of the Massachusetts statutory scheme, even though the SJC's interpretation of the parental-consent law indicated beyond doubt that minors in Massachusetts who were seeking to terminate a pregnancy did not have the same consent rights as minors seeking to make other sensitive medical decisions, including those related to pregnancy.[51] Blithely obscuring this reality, the

Court held that in enacting its parental-consent law, Massachusetts was simply seeking "to reconcile the constitutional right of a woman, in consultation with her physician, to choose to terminate her pregnancy . . . with the *special interest* of the State in encouraging an unmarried pregnant minor to seek the advice of her parents in making the important decision whether or not to bear a child."[52] The Court ignored the fact that this state interest was actualized through a consent requirement only when the decision was *not* to bear a child. Narrowly focused on the decisional vulnerability and incapacity of young women and on the authority of parents over their children, the Court did not stop to consider whether teens intending to abort, like teens intending to carry to term, should be allowed to make their own reproductive choices. Instead, it sought to reconcile the competing interests of minor, parent, and the state by constructing the judicial-bypass alternative to the parental-consent requirement,

As discussed in chapter 2, this appears to be a reasonable compromise that respects the reproductive rights of teens while also preserving the ability of states to protect a historically vulnerable population through a parental-involvement requirement. Given the transitional nature of the teenage years, young women are regarded both as autonomous rights-bearing individuals with unmediated claims to legal selfhood and as subordinate members of a parent-centered family unit without claims to a fully autonomous self. However, once the missing pieces of the picture are brought to the foreground, the reasonableness of the compromise is cast into doubt. The Court's selective construction of adolescent life—notably, its disregard for the medical decision-making rights of teens and the existing research on adolescent decision-making capacity—suggests that other considerations may have compelled this result.

Although it did not seem to trouble the Court, the logic of a statutory scheme that treats young women differently based on their intended pregnancy outcome is difficult to grasp. Certainly, if a young woman is capable of deciding to become a mother, with all of the responsibility this decision entails, she is similarly capable of deciding not to become a mother. In fact, as recognized by the *Bellotti* Court, the decision to become a mother is one of particularly profound consequence since "the fact of having a child brings with it adult legal responsibility, for parenthood, like attainment of the age of majority, is one of the traditional criteria for the termination of the legal disabilities of minority."[53] Thus, one could reasonably conclude that a state would have an interest in ensuring that the decision to bring a child into the world is fully informed.

The illogic of linking decisional capacity to the pregnancy outcome is highlighted by the fact that the same young woman might well make both decisions during her teenage years. Certainly, when facing an unplanned pregnancy, most women, whether adult or teen, consider, at least briefly, the implications of each choice for her life, perhaps moving back and forth between options before set-tling on a final decision. Thus, assume for the moment that a young woman's initial decision, upon learning she is pregnant, is to carry her pregnancy to term. Not only is she free to make this decision on her own, but through this decision, she also acquires complete control over her own medical care both during preg-nancy and following the birth of her child. Additionally, upon the birth of the child, she (possibly together with the father) has full authority over the child's medical care. Thus, while pregnant, she can, for example, authorize an amnio, fetal heart surgery, or any surgery that she might need herself; upon the birth of the child, she can consent to open heart surgery for the baby or to the administra-tion of medication that poses certain risks to the baby's health.

Now assume that part way through the pregnancy, the young woman changes her mind and decides instead to terminate the pregnancy. With this change of mind, her decisional capacity suddenly vanishes. She must secure third-party adult permission to abort, and she is divested of her medical-decision-making rights. Or, assume that she does not change her mind and in fact carries to term and becomes a mother with full medical-decision-making rights for both herself and her child. If she were to then become pregnant again, and this time decide to abort, she would suddenly be recast as vulnerable and in need of adult guid-ance to make this decision.[54] Although still able to make the kinds of decisions just described both for herself and for her child, when it comes to abortion, she is unable to make the decision without adult involvement. Of course, should she again change her mind, her decisionmaking ability would be fully restored.

Clearly, decisional capacity is not temporal and contingent, shifting each time a young woman reassesses her pregnancy options. How is it that young women are entrusted to make the kinds of medical decisions described previ-ously both for themselves and for their children, yet when it comes to abortion, adult involvement is necessary because of the "inability to make decisions in an informed, mature manner" that takes into account "both immediate and range consequences"?[55] Yet, this is the real life consequence of a statutory scheme that entrusts teens with the decision to bear a child but not to abort.

It is also hard to make sense out of the contingent nature of the parental role. If parents have an important role to play in helping their daughter make the abortion decision, they certainly could also provide valuable support with respect to the decision to become a mother. This is especially true in light of the multiple medical decisions that pregnancy often entails, in contrast to the singular nature of the abortion decision, and considering that carrying to term is generally riskier for a teenager than having an abortion.[56] Presenting parents as an essential counterweight to teen immaturity, the Court failed to address that the statutory scheme before it made selective use of parents—vesting them with central importance when a young woman seeks to terminate her pregnancy, but casting them aside when the decision is to become a mother. It is not an answer that if the young woman carries to term, her parents will, with the passage of time, eventually learn of her pregnancy whether she wishes them to or not. By the time a pregnancy is showing enough to reveal her situation, it may well be too late for an abortion, thus leaving them without a say in her decision. Moreover, a majority of states permit a minor to place her child for adoption without her parents' knowledge or consent, thus denying them a role in their daughter's decision to relinquish the baby.[57]

So considered, the Court's judicial-bypass compromise hardly seems to strike a reasonable balance between the reproductive rights of young women and the state's interest in ensuring informed decision-making through adult engagement, since there is no reasoned way to differentiate between young women based on their intended pregnancy outcome; it is hard to imagine a scenario in which a young woman would be too immature to choose to terminate a pregnancy, but mature enough to embrace motherhood. Is it thus possible that the only salient difference is the abortion itself? Is it possible that the *Bellotti* decision, rather than really being about protecting minors and parental authority, can best be understood as signaling a shift in the Court's thinking about abortion?

That this may be the truest reading of the case is suggested by the text itself. Having in *Roe* clearly characterized abortion as a medical decision, the *Bellotti* Court introduces a new understanding of abortion. In discussing the desirability of parental involvement, the Court explains that a state may reasonably determine that "as a general proposition . . . such consultation is *particularly* desirable with respect to the abortion decision—one that for some people raises profound *moral and religious concerns.*"[58] The Court thus sanctions the interest of the state in ensuring that young women understand the "moral and religious" dimensions of abortion, even if this limits the right of choice. These concerns therefore create an acceptable legal border between the decision to bear a child and the decision to abort. Read this way, the decision can be understood as indicating a shift in the Court's approach to abortion. No longer a medical decision, abortion has been invested with multiple symbolic meanings that the Court has deemed a young woman incapable of deciphering on her own.

Looking outside of the text, the Court's decision two years earlier in *Maher v. Roe*[59]—a Medicaid funding case—also supports the view that this is the truest reading of the case, since *Maher* offered the first glimpse of a shift in the Court's attitude toward abortion. In *Maher*, the Court held that it was not unconstitutional for states to deny Medicaid funds for abortion while paying for childbirth because the state has a valid interest in encouraging women to have babies. Accordingly, the state may structure the incentives so as to make childbirth a more attractive option to an impoverished pregnant woman. The Court's decision was thus informed by a creeping pronatalism, which was given greater expression in *Bellotti* and subsequent parental-involvement cases before ultimately blossoming into full view in *Casey*.[60]

Since *Bellotti*, in a number of cases involving constitutional challenges to parental-involvement laws, the Court has elaborated on the theme that the abortion decision is laden with symbolic meaning and potentially grave consequences. Three years after *Bellotti*, in *H.L. v. Matheson (Matheson)*,[61] the Court characterized abortion as an act that is fraught with "potentially traumatic and permanent consequences."[62] Suddenly open about its support for the differential treatment of abortion and childbirth, the Court asserted that the state's interests in "full-term pregnancies are sufficiently different to justify the line drawn by the statutes . . . If the pregnant girl elects to carry her child to term, the *medical* decisions . . . entail few—perhaps none—of the potentially grave emotional and psychological consequences of the decision to abort."[63]

Though the Court lacked any reliable support for its claim about the gravity of the consequences of the abortion decision for teens, motherhood is understood as a natural, perhaps inevitable, outcome of pregnancy. Carrying to term is presented as a choice without consequence—only abortion threatens to imperil a young woman's future. Strikingly absent from consideration is the concern about the potentially devastating impact of undesired maternity on a woman's life—a concern that was emphasized by the *Roe* and the *Bellotti* Courts, with the latter noting that the impact may be particularly profound when the pregnant woman is a teenager.

Although recognizing that parental-involvement laws may "inhibit some minors from seeking abortions," the *Matheson* Court concluded that laws encouraging "childbirth except in the most urgent circumstances" are "rationally related to the legitimate governmental objective of protecting potential life."[64] Revealed here for the first time is the pronatalist (an approach that favors child bearing) impulse of parental-involvement laws. The Court recognizes and accepts that the laws are intended to discourage young women from choosing abortion.[65]

Giving weight to the interests of the unborn, several subsequent cases make clear that a primary benefit of these laws is that they give parents the opportunity to discuss the "religious or moral implications" of abortion with their daughter.[66] As the Court explains in the case of *Ohio v. Akron Center for Reproductive Health*,[67]

We believe . . . that the legislature acted in a rational way. . . . A free and an enlightened society may decide that each of its members should attain a clearer, more tolerant understanding of the profound philosophical choices confronted by a woman who is considering whether to seek an abortion. *Her decision will embrace her own destiny and personal dignity, and the origins of the other human life that lie within the embryo. The State is entitled to assume that, for most of its people, the beginnings of that understanding will be within the family,* society's most intimate association.[68]

Similarly in *Casey*,[69] in discussing the Pennsylvania parental-involvement requirement, the Court concluded that the law's benefit is that it gives young women the chance to "discuss the consequences of her decision in the context of the *values and moral or religious principles* of their family."[70]

Largely missing from these latter decisions is an attempt to justify these laws as necessary in order to safeguard young women from their own decisional immaturity. Instead, the emphasis is on giving parents a chance to influence their daughter's decision by enfolding her into the family value system. Thus, it is not a young woman's vulnerability, but her autonomy and the possibility of her forsaking her family's moral code that the Court appears to be most concerned with: the abortion decision may represent a repudiation of her parent's beliefs regarding the origins of human life.

The cumulative message of these cases is clear. Left to her own devices, a young woman may fail to fully consider the "origins of the human life that lie within the embryo" and the consequences of her decision for that life. It is this potential life, rather than what it means to become a mother, that appears to be the Court's primary concern. A teen's own "destiny and personal dignity" does not ensure decisional autonomy since her right to self-determination must be balanced against the interests of potential life—an interest that the state may seek to protect through the intermediary of a young woman's parents.

This shift in focus allows us to understand why, in considering the constitutionality of parental-involvement laws, the Court felt justified in ignoring teens' medical-decision-making rights and decisional capacity. By imbuing the abortion decision with "profound moral and religious" meaning, the Court was able to sidestep the illogic of a statutory scheme that selectively burdens the abortion decision. Draped in symbolic meaning, abortion is no longer comparable to other decisions that a teen may be called upon to make, such as whether she is ready to embrace motherhood. As a result, the Court was able to reason about parental-involvement laws within a self-contained framework that ignores the true status and of capacities of teens.

This reexamination of *Bellotti* sets the stage for the next several chapters in which we consider the actual experience of young women who chose to negotiate the bypass process rather than involve their parents in their abortion decisions. In order to deepen our understanding of the decision-making capabilities of young women confronting an unplanned pregnancy, their experiences are situated in a broader research context. In turn, this body of work leads us back to *Bellotti*, as these stories serve to further elucidate the concerns raised in this chapter regarding the integrity of the *Bellotti* decision.

4

In Their Own Words

As we have seen, when faced with a challenge to the Massachusetts parental-consent law, the *Bellotti* Court sifted through competing understandings of the legal meaning of childhood in order to resolve the question of whether young women were included within *Roe's* promise of reproductive autonomy. Ultimately, the Court concluded that as long as a law also contains an alternative procedure that allows minors to seek authorization for an abortion without informing their parents, states may enact parental-involvement laws. Accommodating the countervailing pulls of autonomy and dependence, this approach initially appears to strike a reasonable balance between competing understandings of youth. However, as discussed in chapter 3, in its failure to account for teenagers' decisional rights and capabilities this compromise is built upon a partial understanding of adolescent reality. Nonetheless, the majority of states now have either a parental-notification or a parental-consent law in place.

As someone with considerable experience representing young women in judicial-bypass hearings in Massachusetts, I have found myself growing increasingly frustrated by the fact that the voices of young women were missing in the public debates over parental-involvement laws. As adults argued about whether young women should be allowed to make their own abortion decisions, I was continuously brought back to the complexity of the lives of the young women I had represented. The richness and texture of their experiences simply did not mesh with the Court's flat portrayal of adolescent reality. Moreover, the common portrayal of young women who abort without parental involvement—depicted as rebellious teens who lack an appreciation of the significance of the abortion decision and their relationship with their parents—did not reflect the experiences of the young women I'd known either.

As my frustration with this gap between the portrayal of these young women and the actuality of their lives grew, I realized that the public discourse would be enriched if the voices of young women were included in the public dialogue about parental-involvement laws. To accomplish this, I conducted a study to learn more about the actual experiences of teens in Massachusetts who had obtained judicial authorization for an abortion, a study that included in-depth interviews with 26 young women.[1]

At our meetings in libraries and food courts, these young women shared their experiences with me. Rooted in the complexity of their lives, these interviews reveal that these young women did not treat either the decision to abort or the decision to not involve their parents lightly. The stories they tell reflect the richness and intricacies of their lives and the depths of their feelings about becoming pregnant, the decision to abort, and their families. They spoke openly about abuse, loss, love, and their often-poignant hopes for the future—a future that often included visions of motherhood.

These young women now take center stage. The presentation of these stories focuses on the depth and meaning of individual experience and the thematic connections between the young women. To deepen our understanding of what the women have to say, their narratives are situated in a broader research context. In turn, their collective voices contribute to this body of work by further illuminating the abilities and challenges of teens who confront an unplanned pregnancy in a state with a parental-involvement law. This dynamic interplay provides a rich counter-narrative to the Court's pinched representation of adolescent life and hopefully will enlarge the boundaries of the public discourse about parental-involvement laws.

To set the stage for the presentation of their experiences, this chapter begins with a brief overview of the Massachusetts parental-consent law and the court process. A snapshot of each young woman is then provided so that they may be heard within the context of their own lives. In the following two chapters, we take a close look at what they said about what it was like to confront an unplanned pregnancy, make the abortion decision without parental knowledge or support, and appear before a judge.

THE MASSACHUSETTS PARENTAL-CONSENT LAW

In 1974, Massachusetts enacted one of the nation's first parental-involvement laws. This law required a young woman who was under the age of 18 to obtain the consent of both parents before having an abortion; if consent was denied, she could seek the consent of a superior court judge for "good cause" shown. Her parents were entitled to notice of the hearing and an opportunity to be heard on the matter.[2]

The law was promptly challenged by a young woman who was afraid to seek the consent of her father because he had previously threatened to throw her out of the house and kill her boyfriend if he ever learned that she was pregnant.[3] This challenge was ultimately heard by the United States Supreme Court, resulting in the previously discussed *Bellotti v. Baird* decision.[4] After the Court invalidated the law because it vested parents with indirect veto power over their daughters' decision, the Massachusetts legislature revised its law to give minors the right to go directly to court without having to first seek parental authorization, thus resolving the parental-veto problem.

The law was then challenged in state court on state constitutional grounds. Taking its cue from *Bellotti*, the Massachusetts Supreme Judicial Court (SJC) concluded that because of the "immaturity, inexperience, and lack of judgment"[5] of young women, the law was necessary to ensure that the abortion decision was "truly free and informed."[6] However, the court decided that it was unduly burdensome to require a minor to obtain the consent of both parents and thus ruled that henceforth the statute would be "enforced as if it stated a requirement only of one-parent consent."[7] Consequently, as it now stands, all minors (except for those who are married, widowed, or divorced) must obtain the consent of either one parent or the court before having an abortion in Massachusetts.

I NEED TO WHAT? THE JUDICIAL-BYPASS PROCESS

Most teens in Massachusetts who are affected by the state's parental-consent law first learn about the law's requirements when they call an abortion provider to schedule an appointment for an abortion.[8] Although this is often unsettling news, young women in Massachusetts, unlike their counterparts in many of the other states with parental-involvement laws, are supported by a well-coordinated counseling and legal-referral process, which begins with a conversation with a trained hotline counselor at the Planned Parenthood League of Massachusetts (PPLM). The counselor reviews a young woman's options with her, including exploring whether she can discuss her situation with her parents. If, after discussion, the conclusion is that she cannot confide in them, the counselor finds an available attorney from a panel of lawyers who have been trained to provide representation in bypass hearings.

The young woman is then responsible for contacting the attorney herself in order to establish an attorney-client relationship, coordinate the logistics of the hearing process (including, for example, determining how she will get out of school), and begin preparing for the hearing. If problems arise—for example, if the attorney does not hear from the young woman in a timely manner, or the young woman expresses some ambivalence about her decision—a hotline counselor remains available to provide additional assistance and support.

Despite this careful coordination, minors often face significant hurdles along the way.[9] For example, although the advent of cell phones has certainly made communication easier, it is not always easy for a teen to find a time and place when she can make and receive confidential phone calls. Given that most hearings are held during school hours, a major hurdle for many teens is figuring out how to get out of school without triggering a phone call home. Young women also often face significant transportation difficulties. Some take public transportation at a time when they should be at school, thus risking the possibility that they will be seen by someone they know. If public transportation is not available, a young woman may need to make arrangements to borrow the family car without arousing suspicion. If her parents change their minds, she may not have a way to get to court. I once represented a teen who had arranged to have a friend drive her to court, only to find out when she arrived at school that her friend had been grounded the night before. Desperate, she borrowed a car from another friend and drove herself to the hearing, even though she did not have a driver's license.

To minimize these burdens, most attorneys arrange to meet with their client at the courthouse on the day of the hearing rather than meet with her in advance. This also reduces the risk that a minor's parents will begin to suspect that something unusual is going on. Before appearing before the judge, the attorney will make sure the client has considered all of her options, can discuss the reasons for the decisions she has made, and understands the abortion procedure.

The bypass hearings are held in the judge's private chambers.[10] Most judges are respectful of the young women before them and limit their inquiry to questions designed to determine maturity or best interest. However, some judges do ask inappropriate questions, such as whether the young woman realizes that she can die from an abortion, that are designed to make a minor feel ashamed or rethink her decision. Although, as discussed in chapter 6, this experience is usually an extremely stressful one, in Massachusetts, unlike in many other states, the overwhelming majority of teens are authorized to consent to an abortion.

FROM ALL WALKS OF LIFE: TELLING THEIR STORIES

The young women I interviewed were from all walks of life. Some came from stable, loving families; others had been removed from their homes due to abuse or neglect. Several were already mothers. Most of them were 16 or 17, although a few were as young as 14. Eleven of the young women I interviewed were white, and eleven others were black. Two of them were Asian, and two were Latina.[11]

Most of the young women I interviewed were enrolled in school, and they generally described themselves as good students. However, at the time of the interviews, five were not in school. Two had dropped out because of motherhood; two had dropped out because of difficulties in their lives (depression, for example); and one had been expelled for disruptive behavior. All of the young women, including those who were not presently in school, had plans for the future. Of those who were in school, most intended to go to college, and some had already identified careers requiring advanced degrees, such as pediatric surgery and adolescent psychology,. Those who were not in school planned to complete their education or prepare for a specific career goal, although as a group, their goals were more modest than the professional aspirations of many of the "in-school" minors.

We now turn to brief snapshots of the lives of each of the young women who shared their abortion stories with me.[12]

Amy Michaels (age 17)

At the time of the interview, Amy was living with her father in a Boston suburb. Her parents had separated several years earlier. Following the separation, Amy had first lived with her mother and younger brother, but after a huge fight with her mother, she had moved in with her father. Since moving in with him, Amy had not had much contact with her mother. Both of Amy's parents are professionals.

Amy's father has a long history of serious depression, and she has considerable anger toward her mother, whom she sees as having very little compassion for her father's condition. Her father also suffers from a number of health problems, which Amy connects to his being seriously overweight.

A serious high school athlete, Amy told me of definite plans to attend college.

Angel Cavanaugh (age 17)

Angel is from a large family of seven children. Her parents have been divorced for many years. After the divorce, Angel and her siblings went to live with her father, but he kicked her out after a fight, and as of our interview, she had not had any contact with him since that time.

Angel's father works as an electrician, but does not contribute to her support. Angel's mother suffers from a serious mental illness and is on disability.

In effect, when I met her, Angel appeared to be raising herself. She had a part-time job and was using her earnings to buy her own food and clothing. She was very proud of being an honor roll student, and she planned to go to college to study computer science.

Anna Lynne Albano (age 17)

When I interviewed Anna, she was living with both parents, and her two older brothers were in college.

Anna's parents came to this country after the war in Cambodia, and she feels that they never fully recovered from the experience of leaving their homeland. She told me that her father had recently been laid off from his position as an assistant vice president of a bank and that her mother worked in a retail store. They were living in an urban community with a large immigrant population.

At the time of the interview, Anna had dropped out of high school because of depression. She had also been quite depressed during her sophomore year and at times felt suicidal. She had been in counseling and had done a lot of reading about depression in order to get a handle on what she was experiencing. She was hoping to return to school and then attend college, although she was worried about making the transition back.

Beth Smith (age 17)

At the time of the interview, Beth was living on her own due to a very complicated family situation. When she was nine, her parents separated, and she went to live with her grandparents. After her grandmother died, she was bounced from relative to relative, and she then returned to her mother's home after a seven-year absence. After a significant fight, Beth left and moved out on her own. Living with her father had never been an option because he suffers from a serious mental illness. He was also addicted to drugs and alcohol and had been in and out of jail during most of Beth's childhood.

Beth was in the process of applying to colleges. She was a strong student and hoped to become an adolescent psychologist so that she could help kids with chaotic lives. She was in the marching band at school.

Bianca Jones (age 17)

Bianca was living with both parents in a middle-class suburb of Boston, in a household also including her two younger siblings, an uncle, and her cousin. Her father is an accountant and her mother works in a bank.

Bianca described herself as a very private person with an avid passion for reading.

She is a straight-A student, and at the time of the interview, had just been accepted to two well-known universities. She is trilingual, and she told me of plans to major in international relationships with a minor in Spanish.

Corey Adams (age 17)

When I met Corey, she was living with both parents in an upper-middle-class suburb of Boston. Her brother, who was in college, was also living at home. Her father owns a small appliance store, and her mother owns a card and gift shop.

Corey, a serious athlete, had played on the basketball team through most of high school. At the time of the interview, she was employed part-time as a secretary. Corey was in the process of applying to colleges and was hoping to become an architect.

Dion Smith (age 16)

Dion was living with her mother and younger brother in a fairly poor Boston neighborhood when we met for our interview. Her father had essentially been out of the picture for most of her childhood, although she had had occasional contact with him. At the time of the interview, he had been in a correctional facility in another part of the state for two to three years.

Although she was struggling with her science and math courses, Dion was hoping to go to college in order to pursue a career in the medical field.

Jane Smith (age 17)

Jane grew up in a family where drugs and violence were ever-present. She and her siblings had been bounced from home to home, and Jane had also spent two years locked up in a juvenile detention facility. At the time of the interview, Jane was living in a housing project with an older brother who both used drugs and was sometimes violent with her.

Jane had recently been expelled from school due to behavioral problems, including drug and alcohol use. In terms of the future, Jane's main hope was to get her own place in order to escape from what she described as the madness of her environment.

Jasmine Cruz (age 16)

At the time of the interview, Jasmine was living in a pre–independent-living group home. When Jasmine was quite young, her mother had lost custody of her to the Department of Social Services (DSS) because of neglect. When Jasmine was 11, custody was returned to her mother; however, her mother essentially left her to raise herself, and several times, she was placed in juvenile facilities. Consequently, when Jasmine was 15 years old, her mother again lost custody to DSS. Jasmine's father was completely out of the picture.

At the time of the interview, Jasmine was not in school. She was, however, starting to work on her GED, which was her primary goal for the future.

Jill Casey (age 17)

Jill, at the time I met with her, lived with both of her parents and two siblings in an upper-middle–class suburb of Boston. Her father works in sales, and her mother is a sculptor.

Jill has been a very strong student, and her favorite subject is behavioral science. She told me about being very involved in extra-curricular activities, including singing in the choir and playing several school sports, such as track and field hockey. With the help of her mother, Jill had just finished applying to 10 colleges, and she was hoping to get into a small elite college in New England.

Kathleen Johnson (age 17)

Kathleen was living with her mother and stepfather in a Boston suburb when we met. She has had minimal contact with her father, who does not live in the United States. Her mother works as a nursing assistant in an old-age home, and she was not certain what either her stepfather or her father does for work.

A member of a rhythm and blues band, Kathleen is passionate about music. She was planning to go to college to study musical performance and business management.

Keisha Wood (age 17)

Keisha was removed from the custody of her biological parents when she was about 10 years old, since which time she had been in the custody of the state's Department of Social Services. She was in their custody when I met her. Since being removed from her parents' care, she had not had any contact with them. At the time of the interview, Keisha had a two-year-old baby and was living in a DSS-run residential facility for teen mothers in Boston. Before this, she had lived with two foster families and was very close to one of her foster mothers.

Keisha is a highly motivated student. She loves to read and write, and her favorite subject at the time of our interview was English. She was planning to become a social worker so that she could provide teen moms with the kinds of support she felt were sorely lacking in the state system.

Keiza Smith (age 16)

I met Keiza when she was living with her mother in a small city west of Boston. Her father had recently walked out on the family, leaving her mother in shock. Keiza did not know what kind of work her father does. Her mother is a nurse's aid.

Although still a high school student, Keiza was already working full-time as a receptionist when I interviewed her and was also involved in sports. Her primary goal when we spoke was to get through high school. She was unsure about whether she would attend college.

Kim Johnson (age 17)

At the time of the interview, Kim was living in a shelter that housed both battered women and teen mothers. She had left her mother's home a few weeks earlier to find an apartment for herself and her infant son, but through the involvement of her social worker, she had ended up in the shelter. Her father was not in her life.

Kim left school in the 10th grade after giving birth to her son. Her primary goal for the future when we met was to return to school and earn her high school degree.

Mary Jane (age 17)

At the time of the interview, Mary was living with her mother and infant son in a low-income urban neighborhood. Her mother was not employed, and although Mary Jane does have a relationship with her father, she did not know his occupation.

Mary Jane had just earned her GED and was planning to attend a community college in the fall. She has a number of hobbies, including reading, listening to music, and dancing, although she was very clear that along with school, spending time with her son is her top priority.

Mary Smith (age 17)

Mary was living with both of her parents and a younger sister in a upper-middle-class suburb. Her father is a psychiatrist, and her mother is a school nurse.

Mary is a very serious student and athlete. She was on her high school basketball, field hockey, track and field, and gymnastic teams. She was also working two part-time jobs when we talked. Mary had just been accepted at college, where she was intending to pursue a career in marketing, her favorite high school subject.

Mary Souza (age 16)

At the time of the interview, Mary's parents had been divorced for several years. When they divorced, she decided to live with her father and younger brother because her mother was moving to a new community, and she wanted to remain near her friends. Mary's father is a real-estate broker, and her mother has her own business.

Mary's relationship with her father, by the time we met, had deteriorated to the point that she no longer felt safe living with him, and she was planning to move to her mother's home at the end of the semester, although that would mean changing schools mid-year. After finishing high school, Mary was hoping to go to college and become an accountant.

Melissa Silver (age 17)

At the time of the interview, Melissa had been living in a Teen Living Program with her infant son for a few months. Prior to this, she had lived with her mother, but she had been removed by DSS due to abuse. Although her parents never married, they had lived together when Melissa was younger, and she had maintained a relationship with her father. Melissa's father had remarried, and his wife disliked Melissa. She also had a stepfather when we met, although he was no longer living with her mother. Melissa's younger brother was also in DSS custody due to abuse.

Melissa dropped out of high school in her sophomore year, but she told me she was hoping to earn her GED.

Miranda Roberts (age 17)

Miranda was residing in a middle-class neighborhood in Boston with both parents and a younger brother at the time of our interview. Her father is a professor, and her mother works in a law office. They both came to this country from Africa, and Miranda told me that she felt like they were trying to raise her as if they were still living in a traditional culture.

Miranda was attending a very prestigious private school. She was on the student council and the senior prom committee and was also serving as a peer mediator. Miranda was in the process of applying to a number of elite colleges in the Boston area. Her goal was to open her own business after graduating from college.

Molly Moe (age 17)

At the time of the interview, Molly had been living for about seven years with her mother and two adult roommates whom she had known since early childhood in a middle-class community near Boston. About a year earlier, her mother's boyfriend had moved in. Molly was quite close to all of the adults in the household. Her parents divorced when she was five, and she has maintained a relationship with her father, who was living about an hour away from Molly with his new wife and Molly's half-sister and two stepbrothers. Her mother is an assistant manager in a bank, and her father works for the telephone company.

Molly is a good student, with a love for art and history. A member of the cheerleading squad, she was exploring going to an art school and thinking about a career as an art therapist.

Monique White (age 14)

Monique was living with her mother and two younger siblings in a low-income neighborhood in Boston. Her mother was quite ill and was not working. When I met her, Monique had minimal contact with her father, who had pretty much abandoned the family. She knew nothing about his line of work.

Monique was a serious student, attending high school through a special program in a suburban community. She was on the girls' softball team and was very definite about going to college, with hopes for becoming a hematologist.

Sandra Kiwi (age 14)

At the time of the interview, Sandra was living in a group home run by the Department of Social Services. After being abandoned by her mother when she was one year old, Sandra was taken in by her grandmother. When she was nine, her grandmother sent her to live with her father. However, his wife physically abused her, so Sandra returned to her grandmother's home. When she was 14, her grandmother kicked her out.

Sandra was struggling in school. In terms of the future, Sandra's mother had recently tracked her down, and they had spent Christmas together. Her goal was to get her life together and go live with her mother in Michigan.

Sandra Llonas (age 16)

I interviewed Sandra when she was living with her mother, her stepfather, and a younger sibling in a Boston neighborhood. Her father was living nearby, and she was in regular touch with him. She was also very connected with a large network of relatives living in the same community. Sandra's mother is a housekeeping supervisor in a Boston hotel, and her father manages a small garage.

Sandra described specific plans for the future. She told me that she intended to complete college and then go on to medical school in order to become a pediatric surgeon.

Stephanie Paul (age 17)

As of our interview, Stephanie was living in a predominantly working-class community near Boston with her mother and six siblings. Her mother was working as a chambermaid in a local hotel. Her father still lives in Jamaica and rarely comes to see his family. Other than occasionally sending money, he has had very little involvement with them. Stephanie had been serious abused by her mother, especially when she was younger.

Stephanie loves children and hopes to become a teacher someday so that she can combine her love for children with her interest in drama and dance.

Taylor Jordan (age 15)

Taylor was living with both of her parents and a younger brother in an upper-middle-class suburb of Boston when we met. Her father is a retired bus driver, and her mother is a teacher.

Taylor is very goal-oriented and spends most of her time focused on her schoolwork. Although only a sophomore when we met, she already had her sights set on attending Yale, where she was planning to major in sociology. She hopes to then go to law school.

Theresa Clark (age 14)

I spoke with Theresa while she was living with both of her parents and two younger siblings in a rural community outside of Boston. Her father is a plumber and her mother works part-time in a local bookstore, although her mother had previously been a homemaker for much of Theresa's life.

When I met her, Theresa's family had recently gone from a seemingly picture-perfect "All-American" family, which included a homemaker mother, a father who provided spiritual counseling at their local church, and three children in a private Christian school, to a family in the throes of chaos. Her mother had slid into serious alcohol addiction, and her father had become severely depressed, leading to a series of hospitalizations. The children had been left to fend for themselves, and Theresa had taken over the raising of her siblings.

Theresa is an avid reader and an athlete, and she enjoys singing. She was enrolled in a technical high school and was studying to become an electrician, while also holding a part-time job, when I interviewed her. Her hope was to work for the electric company as a technician.

5

Facing an Unplanned Pregnancy: The Abortion Decision

Noneof the young women I spoke with had intended to become pregnant. Although some of them responded to the news with a sense of disbelief or denial, all recognized the importance of making a relatively prompt decision. The clarity that they brought to the decision-making process does not suggest an unthinking or mechanical response to their pregnancies. Rather, as demonstrated in this chapter, they all had clearly articulated reasons for deciding that having a child was not a viable option for them, reflecting both an understanding of their present circumstances and a dynamic grasp of future possibilities.

Although they did not involve their parents, these young women did not negotiate the decision-making process on their own. All of them turned to one or more adults as they sorted out what they wanted to do, with most also involving their boyfriend and one or more friends. Although these young women felt the decision was theirs alone to make, the involvement of others provided them with important support as they negotiated this stressful life event.

RESPONDING TO THE NEWS OF PREGNANCY

Like the majority of teens who become pregnant in this country, the young women I spoke with had not intended this result.[1] When asked to describe their reaction to learning they were pregnant, they used words such as "confused," "scared," "upset," and "nervous." Many mentioned crying at the news. For example, Jill described reacting with "uncontrolled sobbing,"[2] and Bianca responded, "I cried. I cried a lot."[3] Several mentioned an initial response of disbelief and denial; a few described how they repeated the pregnancy test to be sure the result was accurate. Miranda's response to her home pregnancy test encompasses many of these themes: "I looked at it . . . and I saw one line. At that point I started crying. I was like 'there's no way.' It wasn't complete yet, but it was like the first line is the one that tells you you're pregnant. I was like 'no way' and I started crying. And then I kept going back to check to see if it was sure. I just wanted to die. It was just awful."[4]

Only one of the young women, Stephanie, responded with an initial sense of happiness to the news she was pregnant. Describing her reaction, she explained, "Well, first, I was happy. I was like 'Oh my god, I have a little baby growing inside of me.'" Her happiness, however, was short-lived and immediately turned to sadness when she considered how her family would respond to the news: "I was happy, and then . . . I was thinking how my family would react . . . and that's when I was like, 'Nope, I can't have the baby.'"[5]

But along with the initial sense disbelief or denial came an understanding of the need for a prompt decision. For some, this awareness was woven into their initial response to the pregnancy. For example, when asked about how she felt upon learning she was pregnant, Molly replied as follows: "Very confused. I didn't exactly know what I wanted to do at the time. . . . I definitely considered all my options."[6] Beth responded,

> I don't want to say "devastation." I mean, life is wonderful—it should never be devastating—but it was really confusing. . . . You know, I've worked since first grade. I knew I was going to college. . . . I did the math in months, and if I had a child, it would be like August, which is right when I would be getting into school, starting my freshman year of college. So many things are just so important . . . it's just not the right time.[7]

Four of the young women struggled with the idea of terminating their pregnancies. Molly and Keiza described having conflicting pulls, and each seemed able to imagine herself as a mother. For Molly, this pull was attributable to the fact that at age 13, she had been involved in an exploitative sexual relationship, become pregnant, and had an abortion. At that time, motherhood was unimaginable. Now, however, at age 17, she was in a caring relationship and was aware of how much more mature she was, thus making motherhood a more realistic option. Keiza was also in a long-term relationship with a man she hoped to marry and have children with one day. Her present reality thus contained within it a picture of her future self, leading her to wonder whether she should actualize that vision now rather than wait until she was older.[8]

For Anna Lynne and Mary J., their difficulties with the decision reflected an ambivalence about abortion. Anna Lynne's doubts about abortion were triggered after the close friend of an older sibling repeatedly told her that by aborting, she would be killing God's creation. Mary J., already the mother of a young son, had always considered herself to be antiabortion. However, when faced with another pregnancy, she was forced to confront her views: "I just feel like I wasn't really for abortions until now . . . I never believed that anyone should have abortions. I felt like if you did, it's your fault. But you know, when certain circumstances . . . you have no choice but to, and that's how I felt."[9]

For the other young women, the decision was quite clear. Characterized by a lack of ambivalence, they were certain that at this moment in their lives, motherhood was simply not a viable option. The clarity that they brought to the decision-making process does not, however, suggest an unthinking or mechanical response to their pregnancy. Rather, their clear understandings of why having a child was not in their best interest at the time show the young women's mature grasp of their present and future circumstances and options.

That none of these young women reacted with a sense of passivity or a relinquishment of control may reflect the fact that teens who choose abortion as the response to an unintended pregnancy tend to have future aspirations and believe that "their future [is] worth investing in."[10] As Kristen Luker writes, the decision to abort often reflects a sense of optimism about the future: "The more successful a young woman is—and more importantly, expects to be—the more likely she is to choose abortion. . . . Even among young women from disadvantaged backgrounds, those who are doing well in school, who are getting better grades, and who aspire to higher education for themselves are more likely to seek an abortion than their more discouraged peers."[11]

According to one study, this optimistic sense of the future animates the abortion decision, whereas teens who become mothers may be likely to have "a strong tendency toward inaction, passivity and an inclination to let 'whatever happens, happen.'"[12] This clearly was not the case for the young women with whom I spoke. All of them took control of the situation and moved quickly into decision-making mode. Acting with a sense of clarity and conviction about what they needed to do in order to preserve both their present situation and their future dreams, they were able to mobilize their social-support systems and take the steps needed to effectuate their decision in a timely way.

As this discussion suggests, the "conventional" wisdom is that between motherhood and abortion, abortion is the more rational response to an unplanned teen pregnancy. It signals a young woman's belief in herself and her future, whereas the choice of motherhood signals an abdication of hope. Although the focus here is on those teens who choose abortion, it is nonetheless important to be aware that this dichotomized view may reflect a pervasive (but often hidden) middle-class bias, and it has been suggested that the " 'problem' of teen pregnancy can be reinterpreted as a different set of choices that are at variance with the White middle-class norm in terms of timing."[13]

Although opting to defer parenthood may be a rational response to an unplanned pregnancy for middle-class teens who typically "have opportunities stretching well beyond age 18 or 19 to become better educated [and] better skilled,"[14] this is not necessarily the case for low-income teens who are likely to "have less to gain from postponing childbearing."[15] In fact, youthful childbearing may be a rational investment in the future of one's offspring, as it increases the possibility that a teen mother will be able to call upon a network of kin support and will live long enough to "see and help her child grow up."[16] Moreover, rather than signaling a sense of hopelessness, having a baby may give a young woman a sense of hope and investment in her future.[17]

REASONS FOR CHOOSING ABORTION OVER MOTHERHOOD

All of the young women I spoke with had more than one reason for choosing abortion over motherhood. Committed to holding onto their place in the world, most of them (except, of course, those who already had a child) saw becoming a mother in high school as unimaginable, and motherhood would have forced them to reinvent themselves in entirely new and unfamiliar ways. In making their decisions, these young women weighed multiple factors and incorporated a future-time perspective as well as a concern for others into the decisional matrix, which, as we discuss in this chapter, has important implications for the debate about adolescent decisional capacity. In descending order of frequency, we now turn to the reasons these young women gave for choosing to terminate their pregnancies.

Safeguarding the Future

More than half of the young women identified future plans as a reason for choosing abortion over motherhood, future plans that, for most, meant continuing their education. Those who were presently in high school planned to go on to college, and many also identified career goals, such as becoming an architect or psychologist, that they knew would require advanced degrees. Those who were not presently in school had plans to return to high school or obtain a GED.

Most expressed a sense of optimism and certainty about their ability to achieve their future goals. As Jill put it, she needed to stick to her plans of going to college and then finding something she was interested in that she would stay with for the rest of her life. Future plans also included marriage and children.[18] Others also spoke in definitive terms, using language that showed no uncertainty about their aspirations. Capturing this confidence, Amy, in describing why she was not ready to become a mother, stated, "I can't even think of it . . . I am going to college. I am definitely going to college."[19] Likewise, Molly, one of the few young women who struggled with the abortion decision, explained, "before, I wasn't even sure if I wanted to go to college. I didn't know the meaning of it . . . how important it was in life. And definitely at this time, now I realize I'm a senior, and this is pretty much what's determining my whole life." [20]

Sandra Kiwi was one of the only minors to mention a future plan that was not related to continuing her education. At the time of the interview, Sandra was living in a DSS shelter, having recently been kicked out of her grandmother's house, where she had spent most of her childhood because of maternal abandonment. As she recounted, "When I turned one, she went somewhere and left me with the baby-sitter, and the baby-sitter decided to leave."[21] Her grandmother took her in. When she was nine, her grandmother sent her to live with her father, but because her stepmother was abusive, Sandra returned to her grandmother's home, only to be kicked out at age 14. While in the shelter, Sandra made contact with her mother for the first time since infancy, and her dream was to go live with her in Michigan. She feared, however, that her mother would reject her if she had a baby. In deciding to abort, Sandra was thus seeking to protect this future plan from disruption; although not educational in nature, the abortion was directly related to Sandra's goal of leaving the shelter and moving ahead in her life.

Although the young women made clear that their future plans were related to their own life objectives and dreams, many also linked achievement of these goals with the ability to be a good parent who could provide a stable life for a child. In drawing this connection, they expressed an awareness of the interconnection between their own well-being and the capacity to create a good life for a child in the future.

Present Realities

More than half of the young women focused on the realities of their present life as a reason for terminating their pregnancy. Some emphasized the impact a baby would have on their life, and others focused on the fact that their present circumstances were not conducive to raising a child. They all worried that they would not be able to juggle everything, which, for most, included both work and school, if they also had to care for a baby.

Highlighting their claim to their teen years, some spoke of the resentment they would feel toward a child who entered their life before they felt ready to be a parent. As Bianca explained, "I wouldn't be able to take care of a baby, with school . . . and financially [and] emotionally it would be a drag. I didn't want the baby to be an inconvenience for me. I wanted the baby to be more like, in a loving environment, where I could care for the baby."[22] In a similar vein, Miranda stated, "It would be awful to bring a child into a situation where a mom doesn't like him cause it ruined her life, you know . . . I don't want [him] to be reminded of that every time he does something bad. I've seen it happen."[23] Exemplifying the dual perspective that permeated the decision-making process of many of these young women, we hear in these two quotes echoes of concern for the child. It is not simply that these two young women did not want to live under the yoke of resentment; both also express concern for the child, with Bianca not wanting a child to experience being "an inconvenience" and Miranda worrying about not liking her child.

Although this reason for choosing an abortion was firmly anchored in the present, these young women were also expressing a concern that extended beyond the immediate—that by impacting the present, having a baby would also alter their life course. Rooted in the immediate, with branches extending out into the future, this reason appears to embrace the meaning and value of their teen years—of the need to respect the integrity of their claim to education and to growing up unencumbered by the responsibilities of parenthood.

Closely related, many of these teens felt that the present circumstances of their lives were not conducive to having a baby. In reflecting on their lives, several spoke poignantly of the need to have things in order before they would consider themselves ready for parenthood. For Sandra Kiwi, this meant not living in a shelter: "I'm 14 and I'm trying to get my life together, go live with my mother in Michigan, and . . . it's just what I need to do . . . before I think of taking care of someone else."[24] For Anna Lynne, a young woman who, at the time of the interview, had dropped out of high school because of serious and recurring bouts of depression (which at times included suicidal tendencies), it meant being able to return to school: "I'm not in school, and I want to get my life back on track with school and then maybe with work and stuff."[25]

In mentioning their present circumstances as a reason for aborting, most also seemed aware of the situational nature of this consideration. As exemplified by the above quotes, contained within the statements of present limitations was a sense of future expectation—of a time when different circumstances, such as a stable living arrangement, a good job, or family assistance, might support a different decision. Thus, although they are rooted in the present, a sense of the future again weaves through the thinking of these young women.

Turning to the teen mothers, all four of them focused on how difficult it would be to have another child in light of their present life circumstances. They spoke about not being able to support another child, either emotionally or financially. This concern was well articulated by Kim, who explained, "My first son is . . . he's hard enough to take care of. He's not old enough and I'm not stable [enough] to be taking care of two kids, and I just can't do it right now. I'm not ready."[26]

Two of the mothers also spoke about how their difficulties were compounded by the fact that they were living in a shelter. For Keisha this was a significant consideration, and she spoke movingly about what it would be like to have another child while living in a shelter: "It wouldn't have been easy for me to have two, and live at Warren House. . . . I know DSS would have definitely looked down on me even more, or said I was irresponsible. You know . . . I feel that's why they treat us—especially teen moms—I think that's why they treat us so bad. . . . But they don't realize that we're teenagers and we're human and things are going to happen. And we're no different from someone that does have a family to stay at and does have a family to support [her]."[27]

These young mothers also seemed to recognize the contextual nature of their decision. As captured in Kim's statement that her son was not old enough and that she just couldn't "do it right now" or in Mary Jane's statement that abortion was the best decision because "right now, my son's not even two," these teens implicitly recognized the potentially changing nature of their lives—that their children would get older and that at some point they might choose to have another child. Thus, although aware of the demands of the present, they also carried with them an awareness that the future might support a different reproductive choice.

Too Young for Motherhood

Being too young for motherhood was also an important consideration, with slightly less than half of the young women mentioning it as a reason for abortion. Not surprisingly, this was more of a consideration for the younger teens. Most of the young women expressed this as a self-evident truth, requiring little or no elaboration. It was simply "I'm too young" or "I'm only 15." Articulated as a self-contained reason, requiring no explication, motherhood seemed an almost unthinkable concept—one that defied their sense of place in the world.

In mentioning being too young as a reason for choosing to abort, a number of the young women mentioned that they hoped to have children in the future. Several also indicated that they might have looked at the situation differently had they been older at the time of pregnancy. As Taylor explained, "I don't think I would be able to take care of it as well as I would have if I was something like 24 or 30."[28] Amy (one of the two 17-year-olds to mention youthfulness as a reason for aborting) expressed the centrality of age in reflecting upon her abortion experience: "I wish I could have done something [else], but I had no options. When I was waiting . . . I was talking to the ladies and they were all older. It makes me sad because I was like, why are you doing this if you're older? I don't think I could do that."[29]

In considering their age and reflecting on how with the passage of time they might make a different decision from the one they were presently making, these young women again seemed to have an awareness of life's transitions. Contained within their present sense of self was an ability to project a more developed future self—one that might welcome becoming a mother.

Child-Related Considerations

More than two-thirds of the minors mentioned concern for the child they were carrying as a reason for deciding to abort. About half of these young women spoke from a self-oriented perspective, focusing mainly on their inability to care for a child because of, for example, the difficulty of balancing school with motherhood or of raising two young children. (See the previous "Present Realities" section). The other young women who gave a child-related reason for choosing abortion spoke directly about concerns they had for the well-being of the potential child, thus incorporating a child-oriented perspective into their decision-making process. Although cutting across all age groups, those speaking from a child-oriented perspective were more likely to be 17, although this group also included two 16-year-olds and one 14-year-old.

The young women spoke with great poignancy about not wanting to bring a child into this world who would suffer or have to go without. Many spoke out of their own experiences of loss and deprivation, wanting to shield any child they might have from the pain they had endured growing up. Others focused more on protecting a child from the sadness of being unwanted.

Jane spoke sadly about not wanting her child to suffer. As discussed in the previous chapter, Jane had grown up in a family where domestic abuse, drugs, and alcohol were a constant presence. She had been bounced from one home to another and had been held in a juvenile detention facility for two years. Now expelled from school and living in the projects with an older sibling (who used drugs and on occasion became violent with her), she recognized that if she had a child in her present circumstances, the child might be doomed to suffer a similar fate. As she explained, when asked why she had decided to terminate her pregnancy, "Because I know right now I'm not capable of bringing a child to the earth because I don't got a job. I don't have my own crib, know what I'm saying? I have nothing to lean back on. Why am I going to bring a child on to this earth if I have nothing to offer it? I don't want my son or daughter to suffer, to go through shit."[30]

Similarly, in deciding to abort, Beth was also seeking to protect a child from having a life as bleak as the one she had suffered. At age 17, she was living on her own with several roommates. Directly before this, she had attempted to live with her mother, after having spent much of her childhood living with various relatives, only to be kicked out after an ugly fight. Although she described her relationship with her father as a close one, living with him was not an option. He suffered from serious mental illness as well as drug and alcohol addiction and had spent much of Beth's childhood and adolescence in jail.[31]

When asked about her abortion decision, Beth explained that after a brief moment of uncertainty about what she should do, the decision was not a difficult one to make: "I always, always promised myself that I would never bring a child into the world if I couldn't give it a life 10 times better . . . than my own. And I couldn't." She continued, "If I had a child now, it wouldn't be good for them. They wouldn't have any kind of life. I wouldn't be able to give them anything. You know, I want to become an adolescent psychologist. I want to make money. . . . I want to have nice things. And I want to give nice things. And I can't do that right now."[32]

Like Beth and Jane, Jasmine also sought to protect her child from the trauma she had experienced growing up. At the time of the interview, Jasmine was in the custody of DSS. She had also been in DSS custody when she was younger, but since the age of 11, when custody had been returned to her mother, she had mostly lived on her own, until custody was again taken away from her mother. When asked about why she had decided to terminate her pregnancy, Jasmine angrily responded, "I honestly don't think it would have a nice life because my mother would have gotten custody of it, and look how the hell I turned out when my mother raised me. I'm not having her raise another kid."[33]

Although Beth's vision of the future was clearly brighter than Jane's or Jasmine's, since she had a sense of certainty about her ability to provide for a child in the future—to give it that better life they all hoped for—all three teens knew that at the present time they could not give a child the kind of life they would want it to have. In terminating their pregnancies, they were seeking to protect a child from another cycle of deprivation.

Not all of the young women who spoke from a child-centered perspective had suffered such difficult childhoods. For example, Bianca, a very high-achieving teen who lived with both parents in a stable, middle-class home, also spoke about wanting to protect her child from suffering. For her, however, this did not reflect a desire to protect her child from suffering the kinds of deprivations she had experienced growing up, but a desire to spare the child the pain of being born to a mother who was not yet ready to care for it. As she explained, "I just don't think that I should bring a kid into my world. I just don't want to bring my kid into misery."[34] Like Bianca, Mary Smith is a high-achieving teen. A National Honor Society member and, until sidelined by an injury, an accomplished athlete, Mary had been accepted into college at the time of the interview. She described herself as being close to her parents, especially to her mother. Her concerns echoed those of Bianca, as she explained, "It wasn't fair for me to raise a child that I couldn't take care of. I want to be able to give it a good life."[35]

In these interview passages, we again see two interconnected threads—the desire to safeguard a child from pain and the desire to provide a better life for a child than would be possible at the moment. Whether speaking from the depth of their own traumas or simply from their own lack of readiness for parenthood, the minors who spoke from a child-oriented perspective grasped the profound connection between where they were in their own lives and what they would be able to offer, or not offer, a child. They also grasped the temporal nature of this concern and expressed the hope that one day they would able to care for a child in the way they thought best.

Anticipated Adverse Parental Response

In identifying reasons for aborting, five of the young women stated that they feared an adverse parental response to their pregnancy. They anticipated that their parents would take some kind of concrete, punitive action against them upon learning they were pregnant and sexually active. Feared reactions included being thrown out of the house, harm to a boyfriend, emotional or physical cruelty, and the initiation of punitive delinquency proceedings. As developed further in the next chapter, these fears were generally well rooted in the realities of the teens' lives, since most of these young women had previously experienced harsh parental treatment.[36]

Though Bianca did not fear the kind of adverse reaction just identified, Bianca's situation is worth noting, since she factored the anticipated reaction of her parents, most notably her mother, into her abortion decision. For Bianca, a very high-achieving teen, the concern was disappointment, since she felt that her mother had no understanding of who she was and made no effort to do so. Expressing concern that her mother "always thinks the worst of me," she also expressed hope that "deep down inside she [her mother] knows I'm a good person." Because Bianca struggled with how her mother saw her, fear of disappointing her parents was an important consideration. As she explained, "I didn't want to disappoint them. They know me in some ways. They know certain things about me, like I don't do drugs. I don't do alcohol. I'm not the type to go around and just party all weekend . . . I just like staying home. To them it would be like, why her?"[37] She feared that by continuing the pregnancy she would validate her mother's tendency to think the worst of her and would risk losing her mother's "deep down" sense that she was, in fact, a good person.[38]

MAKING INFORMED CHOICES

The thoughtfulness with which these young women approached the abortion decision challenges the *Bellotti* Court's assumption that young women lack the capacity to make "fully informed choices that take account of both immediate and long-range consequences."[39] In listening to what they say about why they chose abortion over motherhood, one senses their resolve and the intentionality of this choice. As developed in this section, these young women are not unique; a considerable body of research indicates that at least by mid-adolescence, teens are capable of making informed choices.

Before proceeding, however, a brief cautionary note is in order. Although the research on adolescent decision-making is important—indeed, it is hoped that these interviews will contribute to this growing body of knowledge—the focus on capacity in the abortion context is somewhat problematic, given that teens have considerable decisional autonomy when it comes to other sensitive health decisions, including those related to pregnancy and childbirth.

This duality raises serious doubts about the Court's reliance on capacity as an acceptable rationale for state laws that limit autonomy of young women who choose abortion over childbirth. By focusing on capacity, the Court successfully deflects attention away from its real concern—namely the interest of states in ensuring that young women understand the "profound moral and religious"[40] dimension of the abortion decision. As discussed in chapter 3, the Court ultimately relies upon this interest to explain the need for parental-involvement laws. Accordingly, in reading the following discussion, it is important to keep this broader consideration in mind.

Reasoning in a Multidimensional Framework: The Development of Cognitive Capacity

As noted in a previous chapter, according to developmental psychologist Jean Piaget, somewhere between the ages of 11 and 15, adolescents reach the formal-operations stage of cognitive development.[41]

Upon reaching this stage, adolescents can "imagine the past, present, and future conditions of a problem and create hypotheses about what might logically occur under different conditions. They can engage in pure thought independent of actions they see or perform. They can hypothesize and draw deductions, understand theories, and combine them to solve problems."[42] With abstract reasoning also comes the ability to put decisions into "perspective," which allows one to "frame a decision within a 'bigger picture.' "[43] The ability to put a decision into perspective includes the ability to shift the focus away from one's self in order to assess how "one's actions or decisions affect others."[44]

Although the *Bellotti II* Court was presented with the testimony of two expert witnesses who concurred that most young women are able to understand and give informed consent to the abortion decision,[45] the Court insisted, without reference to either this evidence or other supporting data, that young women are too immature to make the abortion decision on their own. Subsequently, in the 1987 case of *Hartigan v. Zbaraz*,[46] the American Psychological Association (APA) submitted an *amicus curiae* (friend of the court) brief to the Court in which it presented the results of relevant social-science research in order to assist the "Court's resolution of the serious constitutional questions presented."[47] However, once again, the Court chose to ignore this research that challenged its foundational assumption—that young women lack the ability to decide for themselves that they are not ready for motherhood.[48]

As Piagetian theory would predict, this research has generally found few, if any, meaningful differences in cognitive abilities between adults and adolescents, at least with respect to those age 14 and up:

> Overall, the findings of informed consent researchers have been quite consistent. Minors, and especially adolescents, are more similar to adults than the law assumes, in both the choice they make and in the logical process they follow. This is not to say that the results of all of these investigations have been entirely consistent; but, by and large, minors aged 14 years and higher make decisions regarding . . . consent to medical procedures in generally the same manner as adults do.[49]

The few comparative studies that have specifically focused on the abortion decision have likewise concluded that at least by mid-adolescence, young women are able to reason about their pregnancies in complex ways that reflect consideration of multiple factors. In comparing the abortion decision-making of minors and adults, Lewis concluded that although there were some differences in the factors they considered, "minors equaled the adults in their 'competence' to imagine the various ramifications of their pregnancy decision."[50] Likewise, in studying the response of young women and adults to an unplanned pregnancy, Ambuel and Rappaport concluded that age is not predictive of decision-making ability and that with respect to the abortion decision, "minors age 14 to 17 appear to be similar to legal adults in . . . cognitive competency."[51] They also determined that with respect to volition (the ability to make a voluntary decision that is not unduly influenced by others), there was no "evidence of age differences in volition competence from age 14 through age 21."[52]

Significantly, Ambuel and Rappaport found that "psychosocial variables," such as social support, decision conflict, and educational goals, were more far more important in predicting both cognitive and volitional competence than chronological age among those considering abortion. However, the researchers found that when it came to young women who did not consider abortion, age was predictive of competence with respect to those age 15 and under, who as a group were clearly less competent "than the adult . . . group in both volitional and cognitive competence."[53]

Building on this body of research, we now return to the interviews to see what they can tell us about the decisional capacity of these young women. More specifically, we focus in on three critical elements of the abstract reasoning process: the consideration of multiple factors, the incorporation of a future-time orientation, and the ability to consider the impact of one's decisions on others.

Consideration of Multiple Factors

The young women I interviewed all had at least two reasons for choosing abortion, with most giving three or four reasons for their decision. Moreover, they clearly grasped the dynamic links between thematically distinct considerations. For example, a young woman who said she was not ready to have a baby might also mention how having a baby would prevent her from doing what she felt she needed to do in order to become ready for parenthood. Similarly, a young woman who was worried about the disruption of her future plans might further explain that the disruption would mean that she would not have the ability to provide for her child.

Exemplifying the linked consideration of multiple factors, when asked about her reaction to her pregnancy and her reasons for aborting, Beth explained that she'd always known she would go to college and that if she had continued the pregnancy, she would have given birth just as she was getting ready to begin her first year. She acknowledged that it was not the right time for her and that she had also promised herself she would not have a child until she was able to give that a child a life better than her own. At this time, not yet having a college education or a career, she felt like she did not have enough to give to child.

In Beth's explanation one can see both the major thematic reasons that teens in this study gave for aborting as well as the interplay among them. In choosing to abort, Beth was seeking to safeguard her own educational and professional aspirations; she was focused on the well-being of the child, which she linked to her ability to meet her own goals; and she recognized that her current circumstances were not conducive to caring for a child in the way that she would have like to, which again looped back to fulfilling her future aspirations.

Embedded in the interconnected reasons for pregnancy termination, one can also detect an awareness of the contextual nature of the abortion decision. Anchored in the present, these young women recognized the need to have more in place, be it education, greater emotional stability, or financial security, before bringing a child into the world. Almost without exception, they had an awareness of the present as a moment in time and a sense of themselves as dynamic and evolving individuals who might make a different decision in the future. As developed in greater detail in the following section, these young women were clearly able to project a sense of themselves into the future.

Incorporation of a Future-Time Perspective

According to *Bellotti*, one reason minors cannot be permitted to make the abortion decision on their own is that they "lack the ability to make fully informed choices that take account of both immediate and *long range* consequences."[54] From the Court's perspective, teens lack a "future time perspective," which is the "ability to project events to more distant points in the future."[55] Although not citing any literature to support its pronouncement, the Court was certainly correct in one regard—that the ability to take long-term consequences into account is one of the important indicia of decisional maturity. According to researchers Blum and Resnick,

> One aspect of the transition from concrete to abstract reasoning is the understanding of time as an abstraction and the development of a personal sense of future. One is not born with a notion of time; rather it develops from early childhood. . . . It is late in childhood and throughout adolescence that one begins to understand time as an abstract concept which we artificially structure through seconds, minutes, hours and days. Not only is time understood as an abstract concept, but the teenager begins to perceive herself as a being who will live in the future as well as in the present and past.[56]

Where the Court went wrong, however, was in its pronouncement that minors facing an unplanned pregnancy are incapable of considering the future implications of their decision. As the findings of this and other studies make clear, teens are able to think well beyond the present when thinking about whether to terminate a pregnancy. [57]

As discussed previously, an important reason for choosing abortion for these particular minors was the safeguarding of the future plans. The interviews reveal that the young women were clearly able to anticipate the impact that having a baby would have on their ability to realize their goals. As a representative of someone who did incorporate a future-time perspective, Jill explained that, "I'm not saying that it [the pregnancy] is a little problem that gets in your way, that you get rid of . . . because it's not. But you know, to do what I want to do in life . . . and that's not what I want to do. . . . It's not in my plans. My plan is to go to college . . . find something I'm so interested in and just do it for the rest of my life, and get married and have a family."[58] Evident in this quote is Jill's awareness of the future as an abstract concept and "of herself as someone who will live in the future as well as in the present and past,"[59] thus enabling her to consider the long-term consequences of her decision.

Given the approaching end of their high school years, one might well assume that the 17-year-old would have been most likely to identify future plans as a reason for aborting. This assumption would also be consistent with the developmental literature that generally links the acquisition of future-oriented thinking to the increasing maturity of the latter teen years. However, I found this not to be the case with the minors I interviewed. Of the 26 young women whom I met, only four were age 15 or younger; however, all four identified future plans as a reason for terminating their pregnancy. In contrast, only about 60 percent of the 17-year-old (10 out of 16) mentioned this as a reason. This suggests that the link between future-oriented thinking and chronological age is less direct than is usually assumed and that contextual variables may be an important determinant of a future-oriented perspective. We begin by considering the life circumstances of the older teens who did not mention future plans as a reason for aborting, followed by a look at the circumstances of the younger teens who did.[60]

Already having a child may be one of the contextual factors that influences whether a teen identifies future plans as a reason for aborting. Four of the 17-year-olds I spoke with were mothers of very young children (accounting for all of the mothers in the group), and only one, Mary J., mentioned a specific future plan. Having recently obtained her GED, Mary J. was planning to start at a local community college in the fall, and although she had briefly considered having a second child, she felt it would make returning to school too difficult: "Right now, my daughter's not even two; she'll be two in July. And I'm not even doing this with her father. I'm doing this on my own, and I want to go to school in September. I mean, being pregnant, going to school, having another kid, it's too . . . it's a lot.

I am living with my mother. I have a kid already, and I wanted to go to school, and I knew I would be struggling much more than I was."[61]

The other mothers focused mainly on the difficulties of caring for two children as a reason for terminating their pregnancy. Kim, who was living in a shelter at the time of the interview, explained that her first son was still young and hard to care for and that she knew she wasn't stable enough or ready to be caring for a second child as well.[62] Keisha, who was living in a group home for teens, also considered the impact having another child would have on her ability to remain in school and keep her job: "I could probably have done it because of the type of person that I am. I'm strong, you know. I know I probably could have done it, but it just would have been 10 times harder. And I couldn't imagine waking up in the middle of the night again . . . and trying to juggle work and school."[63]

The fact that these young mothers did not focus on future plans as a reason for aborting does not mean that they did not have plans for their future. When asked directly about future plans, they mentioned educational or career goals. However, in the context of the abortion decision, it appears that the more immediate and pressing consideration was to not damage the present by adding the burden of a second child. Protecting future plans thus appears to have been a more remote reality. Nonetheless, these young mothers, as illustrated by Kim's mention of her inability to have another child "right now," recognized that the present would change and that they might be ready to have a second child some time in the future. Their responses thus reflected an awareness that the passage of time might reconfigure their options.

Trauma may also be a contextual variable that influences whether future plans figure into the abortion decision. Stephanie and Jane, two other 17-year-old not to mention future plans as a reason for aborting, had extremely difficult home lives. As with the teen mothers, it may be that the difficult nature of their present lives pushed any consideration of the future into the background.

As previously mentioned, Stephanie initially responded to the news of her pregnancy with happiness. However, having been physically abused by her mother and being quite isolated from her siblings, her thoughts immediately turned to how her family would respond to the news. In deciding what to do, her overriding concern was to not anger her mother or further marginalize her position within the family.[64] These concerns dominated her thinking and may well have overshadowed any ability to project beyond her present vulnerability into the future. Having lived in various homes as a child and now living in the projects with drug-using and sometimes-violent older sibling, Jane in her future dream expressed her longing for security and stability: "As long as I'm somebody. As long as I got a crib, car, and I'm healthy, [and] straight."[65] Overwhelmed by the desperate circumstances of her life, in deciding to terminate her pregnancy, Jane focused on what she lacked in her life and on her desire to protect a child from the kind of suffering she had experienced during her childhood. Given the precariousness of her life, Jane's hold on her future was, at best, tenuous—sadly, for her, there was little in the way of future certainty to disrupt.

Kathleen was the other 17-year-old who didn't mention future plans as a reason for aborting. Although she was neither a mother nor living in an untenable situation, she also may have been so overwhelmed by present concerns that she could not see her way through to the future. In choosing to abort, Kathleen believed she was committing murder. Although certain that abortion was her only option and though firmly believing that it would have been worse to give birth to an unwanted child, she had no doubt that her decision was morally "wrong," and the decision was thus cloaked in a profound sense of wrongdoing. This emotional overlay dominated Kathleen's thinking and may have overshadowed any thoughts about her future.

With respect to the 14-year-olds, the life circumstances of Monique, Theresa, and Taylor may have resulted in the kind of future orientation that is typically associated with older teens.[66] Although only 14, Monique had been entrusted with a great deal of responsibility by her mother—a single parent who suffered from a debilitating illness. As the oldest of three children, Monique recognized her mother's dependence on her, and she assumed responsibility for making sure her siblings pitched in to keep the household running. As indicated by the following remark, Monique was the intermediary between her mother and her younger siblings—functioning in effect as a shadow parent. As she explained, "Well, I mostly . . . I clean, I cook. We all, like we all, chip in. Like my little brother and sister, I always make them help . . . whatever my mom needs done, really, I help her."[67] Although her younger siblings "chipped in," Monique clearly felt that it was her duty to ensure their participation.

Also only 14, Theresa similarly saw herself as responsible for her younger siblings. She felt obligated to see that they remained safe and did not get into trouble as she had done at their age. As their protector, she saw herself as fulfilling a parental role, even though her siblings were only slightly younger than she. Her sense of responsibility had been triggered by recent family traumas, most notably, her mother's development of an alcohol addiction and her father's depression and hospitalizations. As a result of these events, Theresa had begun hanging out with the "wrong" crowd and was both using drugs and getting in trouble with the law. Notwithstanding her own chaos, Theresa felt responsible for her younger siblings during this difficult time.

At the time of the interview, Theresa was working hard to get her life together, and although her family situation had stabilized, she continued to feel responsible for her younger siblings. She explained,

> By the time I was their age, I had already had sex. And I had already been smoking weed for almost a year and drinking for almost a year. So it just kind of scares me, the thought that I was like that when I was younger. So I look after them both . . . I'm like wicked protective. Anything happens to them, I'm right there. Anyone says anything to them, I call them up . . . I [am] almost the way that a parent is supposed to act, where I'm looking out for them, telling them what's right and wrong, and what not to do. And the thing is they listen to me.[68]

Theresa saw herself as a parent with direct authority over her siblings. Seeking to shield them from what had happened to her at their age, and perhaps commenting on her parents' shortcomings in relation to her upbringing, she saw herself acting in "the way that a parent is supposed to act."[69]

What stands out is the sense of responsibility that both Monique and Theresa felt and their awareness that others in their family depended on them. This early assumption of adult-like responsibilities gave them a well-developed sense of their own capabilities and place in the world, which, in turn, may have contributed to their focus on the future. In short, their life experiences may have vested them with a maturity beyond what one typically associates with their chronological age.

Another consideration emerges from the interview with Taylor. Taylor, age 15, lived in a relatively stable family in an upper-middle-class community and attended a high school where the vast majority of graduates go on to a four-year college. For her, having a professional ambition had been a motivating force since she had been quite young. As she explained, "My whole life, I've always wanted a good education. I've always wanted to become a lawyer."[70] These plans were an integral part of Taylor's vision of who she was in the world. With such a clear sense of her future, it is not surprising that even at a young age, these plans assumed a prominent place in her decision-making process.

These interviews thus suggest that strict reliance on age as a predictor of a future-time perspective, at least in the decision-making context of abortion, is overly simplistic and that incorporation of the future as a decisional variable reflects a complex interplay of factors. When a young woman is overwhelmed by her present circumstances, this reality, rather than the more remote future, may be her primary focus. When, for example, she is focused on the demands of keeping herself sheltered and safe, or of raising a young child, these concerns may dominate the decision-making process and push out consideration of the future. Conversely, certain experiences, such as the assumption of important responsibilities or a well-developed and supported set of goals, may, independently of chronological age, contribute to a greater sense of control or mastery over contemporary circumstances, thus freeing up energy to consider the future.

Challenging a simplistic link between age and a future orientation, it thus appears from the interviews that the ability to consider the future requires reasonable control over the present, so that the future appears visible and within reach. When the urgency of present-day concerns requires attention, the future may be too remote of a consideration to play a role in the decision-making process. Accordingly, the failure to focus on the future may reflect a consuming engagement with the present rather than a lack of cognitive ability.[71]

Although not all of the young women mentioned future plans as a reason for aborting, the interviews reveal another dimension of a future-time perspective. In statements such as "right now, I couldn't support a child"; "now, my son is only two"; "when I am older, I plan to have a family"; or "when I am older, my boyfriend and I will have our own place and better jobs," these young women were expressing an awareness of the present as time-limited and were recognizing the changing and dynamic quality of their lives. Grasping the transitory nature of time, these young women had a clear sense of themselves as evolving persons who would command different resources as they moved into adulthood. They anticipated the possibility of an older self who, facing changed circumstances, might make a different decision from the one they were presently making, thus indicating both an awareness of time as an abstract concept and an ability to locate themselves in the future.

Concern for the Prospective Child

Many of the young women incorporated a concern for the child they might bear into the decision-making process. Some worried they would not be able to give a child what it would need; others, particularly the older teens in the group, focused on wanting to protect a child from suffering. Of those who focused on protection, some spoke out about the chaotic circumstances of their own childhoods and a desire not to visit this kind of suffering on the next generation; others reflected on what it would be like for a child to be born to a mother who was not ready to assume the responsibilities of parenthood. In either case, these young women were able to imagine the impact of their decision on another individual and to loop this information back into the decisional matrix as one of the variables to be considered. As mentioned, this ability to move beyond the self and incorporate another perspective or interest into the decision-making process again suggests the complex and abstract nature of the decisional process these young women engaged in when faced with an unintended pregnancy.

TALKING TO OTHERS ABOUT THE ABORTION DECISION

Although the young women I spoke with did not involve their parents in the decision-making process, all but one (who only spoke with one other person) discussed their decision with at least two people, with a significant number speaking with three or more people. Although adults were an important source of support, a greater number of peers were taken into their confidence. Virtually all of the young women who had become pregnant in the context of an ongoing relationship turned to their boyfriend for support, and more than half of them involved one or more friends. [72] They also tended to turn to their peers before turning to an adult.

In talking to their peers, the young women found consistent support for their view that abortion was the best option for them at this moment in their lives, but with the possible exception of Keiza, whose boyfriend wanted to wait until they were married to have a baby, none reported feeling any pressure from their peers to choose abortion. Perhaps not surprisingly, if the issue came up during the course of their conversations, their peer confidants generally agreed with the young woman's perception that it was best for her to proceed without the involvement of her parents.

In addition to confiding in their peers, all of the young women I interviewed spoke with at least one adult in the course of the decision-making process, with many turning to several adults for support and guidance. A number of them also mentioned that the fear of disclosure prevented them from confiding in adults who otherwise could have served as additional sources of support.[73] For example, Molly mentioned that there were several adults at school she would have liked to have spoken with, but she was worried that they would have to report her to the Department of Social Services, which, in turn, would have led to her mother finding out about her situation.

In terms of adult contacts, about 60 percent of the young women turned to a professional, such as a nurse, a guidance counselor, or a teacher, and about 30 percent turned to a trusted relative, most often an older sister or an aunt. The adult confidants were generally also quite supportive of the young women's desire to have an abortion, and as with their peers, none of the young women reported feeling pressured into having an abortion by the adults they spoke with. In the course of their conversations with adults, the issue of whether the young woman was planning to talk with her parents almost always came up, and although many of the involved professionals offered to help her figure out how to speak with her parents, ultimately, all respected her decision not to involve them.

Other studies have likewise found that most teens who terminate a pregnancy without parental involvement turn to other trusted sources of support during the course of the decision-making process.[74] Moreover, researchers have found that, particularly at the lower end of the age spectrum, at least one confidant is likely to be an adult.[75] As to which adults teens tend to seek out, existing research suggests that similar to the young women I interviewed, professionals, such as nurses, doctors, school counselors, and social workers, are generally preferred over relatives.[76]

There is, however, some indication that patterns of adult involvement may be different for black and white teens, with data from Massachusetts showing that black teens were significantly more likely than white teens to involve an adult in the decision-making process. Moreover, although these teens also turned to professionals more frequently than relatives, it is striking that when compared to white teens, they were almost three and a half times more likely than white teens to turn to relatives, but only about two times more likely to turn to a professional.[77] Further suggesting the importance of family ties, a study of black urban teens in Baltimore found that almost all of the young women who did not involve their mother turned to a parent surrogate, defined as an adult who had helped to raise them or to whom they felt responsible, rather than to a professional. Thus, even if not formally related, it appears that persons who functioned as relatives were far more important to these young women than were adult professionals.[78]

Although not enough is known about adult involvement in the decision-making process of young women who terminate a pregnancy without parental involvement to draw any definitive conclusions about this apparent difference, one intriguing possibility is that it reflects the particular importance of family ties to black youth, which, in light of the uncertainty of the external world, may serve as a "'safe haven' or anchor."[79] Consequently, "black adolescents may negotiate the difficult transition to adulthood without the same level of distancing from family which has been described so often with reference to white youth."[80]

Social Support and Decisional Competence

The young women I spoke with were clear that motherhood (or having a second child) was not a present option for them, but communication with trusted individuals during the decision-making process was still important to them. These interactions allowed them to review their decision, explore alternatives, and learn about the requirements of the state's parental-consent law. These confidantes also provided them with critical emotional support.

Although autonomous decision-making is often regarded as a benchmark of maturity, and there is a correlation between age and the likelihood that a teen will confide in an adult, with younger teens more likely to involve an adult, this linkage is overly simplistic as it fails to take the importance of help-seeking behavior into account. As explained by Steinberg and Cauffman in looking at maturity of judgment in adolescence, "Healthy decision making is not equivalent to decision making that disregards the advice or expertise of others. Indeed, one of the hallmarks of mature judgment is knowing where to turn for advice, knowing how to solicit it, and knowing whether and to what extent to follow it."[81] Similarly, Lewis writes that across adolescence, teens become increasingly likely to "consider information and opinion from diverse sources."[82]

Thus, rather than suggesting immaturity or decisional incompetence, the support-seeking behavior of minors who make the abortion decision without parental involvement may be a purposeful compensatory strategy. It may mean that younger teens are aware that they are not experienced decision-makers and would benefit from drawing upon the experience of others.[83] The seeking of advice may be a purposeful, adaptive strategy that enables them to fill in the gaps in their own knowledge base with the experience-based wisdom of others.

In addition to playing a role in the decision-making process, help-seeking behavior may serve as a buffer against stress and contribute to better outcomes. Teens who call upon existing support networks when they encounter difficult situations, which is viewed as a "problem-focused coping strategy," may be more successful in negotiating the transition to adulthood, since these networks have been shown to buffer the effects of stress.[84]

Although valuing the involvement of others and considering what they had to say, the young women who tell their stories here nonetheless saw the abortion decision as one that they needed to make, with several resisting pressure from others who wanted them to have the baby. That these young women saw this as a decision that was theirs to make fits with studies showing that during adolescence, teens become increasingly self-reliant in their decision making and less subject to both parental and peer influence.[85] To borrow a phrase from Lewis, these young women seemed to "own" their abortion decision, something Lewis concluded was increasingly likely to occur during the course of adolescence, as conformity to parents and peers declines.[86]

In their study of how teens made the abortion decision, Ambuel and Rappaport reached an intriguing conclusion that may help to weave together these two aspects of the decisional process—support-seeking behavior and self-ownership of the ultimate decision. Of the psychosocial variables that they looked at, including, for example, educational goals, decision conflict, and abortion knowledge, "social support" was the most consistent predictor of decision-making competence. Seeking to understand this connection, Ambuel and Rappaport theorized that social support enhanced competence "by providing a forum to obtain information, receive emotional support and practice decision making"[87]

Thinking about help-seeking as a strategy that enhances individual functioning in the face of a difficult situation is a useful framework within which to view the decision-making process of young women I interviewed. Although they clearly sought out and valued the involvement of others, they also exerted control over the decision and saw it as theirs to make based on an assessment of their present and future circumstances and the impact that motherhood would have on their lives.

In listening to the voices of these young women, one cannot help but be struck by the comparative flatness of the *Bellotti* Court's depiction of adolescent life. Although one can certainly hope that young women who are faced with an unplanned pregnancy will confide in their parents, it is wrong to presume that those who do not are casually making uninformed decisions that fail to take the short- and long-term consequences of avoiding motherhood into account. Aware of the impact that motherhood would have on their present and future lives, young women mobilize existing support networks and appear well able to reason about abortion in multidimensional ways that take into account the present and future impact of motherhood. As we see in the next chapter, the decision to not involve parents is also one that reflects the depth and complexity of young women's lives.

6

Parents or the Judge?

Young women who seek to terminate a pregnancy without their parents knowing about it are often characterized as "typical" rebellious teens who do not appreciate the significance of the abortion decision or their relationship with their parents. Under this view, it is hoped that parental-involvement laws will play a valuable channeling function—by presenting young women with the unappealing option of appearing before a judge, the laws will redirect them back to loving parents who can then provide them with wise counsel.

However, the reality is that more than half of all teens considering abortion turn to one or both parents, regardless of whether they are legally required to do so.[1] The fact that legal compulsion does not seem to significantly influence rates of parental disclosure raises doubts about the channeling function of parental-involvement laws. It suggests that teens who believe they can safely confide in a parent will do so, and those who do not feel they can do so will not, even if this means having to go to court to seek judicial authorization, which, as subsequently discussed, is generally a traumatic experience that does not appear to enhance the nature or the quality of a young woman's decisional process.

To deepen the understanding of why some teens choose not to involve their parents, I explored this issue with the young women I interviewed. As developed in this chapter, they took this decision very seriously. They had multiple reasons for nondisclosure that were based firmly in the realities of their lives and that reflected the individualized nature of their relationships with their parents. Their decisions were rooted in a history of harsh parental treatment, the lack of meaningful connections with one or both parents, and, perhaps a bit surprisingly, in a desire to preserve existing relationships.

The seriousness with which they made this decision is underscored by the near universal dread they had of going to court. As discussed in the final section of this chapter, court felt like a high-stakes test that the young women had to "pass" in order to effectuate their decision not to become a mother. Although, it is possible, of course, that some of these young women erred in their assessment of how their parents would react to the news of their pregnancy and intended abortion, this possibility does not detract from the seriousness and sincerity of their decision not to confide in their parents.

To contextualize the nondisclosure decision, I asked the young women to describe their relationship with their parents. Of particular interest was whether they had a history of open communication about sex, since one concern about parental-involvement laws is that they may pressure teens into disclosing they are sexually active in an environment where sex has been off-limits as an acceptable topic of conversations. These young women appear to have had far less communication about sex than what is typical between teens and parents. This suggests that disclosure may be less likely in situations where there is not a prior history of engagement that a young woman can draw upon in order to gauge how her parents are likely to respond to the news of her pregnancy.

"BUT WE DON'T TALK ABOUT SEX": CONTEXTUALIZING THE NONDISCLOSURE DECISION

Relationships with Parents

Half of the young women I spoke with said that they a good relationship with one or both parents.[2] Of those who had a good relationship with one parent (usually the mother), almost all reported that their relationship with the other parent was either bad or nonexistent. In describing what it meant to have a good relationship with a parent, the young women mentioned things such as being able to talk openly about problems they were having in school or with friends, having a comfortable sense of being able to chat about the events of the day, or just enjoying spending time together. However, most spontaneously described the limits of their connection—making it clear that the relationship did not encompass discussions about the deeper, more intimate aspects of their lives, that this was where the limits were drawn. Thus, despite the closeness, almost all of these relationships were what can best be described as "bounded," encompassing only certain domains of the lives of these young women.

As Molly explained, despite her good relationship with her mother, "It's not very often that we have conversations about intimacy and stuff like that. . . . My mom gets really uncomfortable. Like she doesn't know how to approach the situation. . . . I never ask. I'm embarrassed myself, you know."[3] Similarly, Anna Lynne, who also has a good relationship with her mother, explained, "She just wants to hear about like, school and stuff, and what I like to do and everything, but when it has to do with like guys . . . She's just like 'Oh, your friend?' It's just like she doesn't want to hear about me having a boyfriend . . . or me going out."[4] As Taylor put it, "My mom and I are close, but we don't really talk about things that would, like, get her angry, or like things that would cause an argument. We sort of, like, avoid that, and so we don't really talk about, like, sexual things."[5]

A possible explanation for this demarcation of domains is, as discussed later, that at the time these young women became pregnant, almost none of the parents had initiated meaningful or positive conversations with their daughters about sexuality or even about their changing bodies. This failure may well have signaled to these young women that these matters lie outside the borders of the parent-child relationship. It is also possible that the sense of demarcation reflects the developmental process of separation and individuation.

The other young women did not feel that they had a good relationship with either parent.[6] Of these, eight characterized their relationship with at least one parent as "okay," and like the majority of the young women who felt they had a good relationship with one parent, they generally described their relationship with the other parent as bad or nonexistent. Where a young woman described a relationship as "okay," she usually meant that there was not a sense of closeness, sharing, or connection, but, unlike the more troubled relationships, there was not overt hostility, frequent fighting, violence, or complete detachment either.

The remaining five young women in this group had a bad or nonexistent relationship with both parents, and three had been removed from the custody of one or both parents due to abuse and neglect. When a relationship was characterized as bad, it almost always meant more than simply not feeling close or connected. Rather, the relationship was characterized by frequent fighting, abuse, a complete and total breakdown in communication, or a combination of these problems.

For example, Mary Souza, who, when we met, had been living with her father for the past four years since the divorce of her parents, described her relationship with her father as follows:

I live with my dad, and we get into a lot of fights. . . . It's gotten to a point where we just argue and I don't feel comfortable around him. . . . We just clash . . . and I don't feel, like, really wanted. When I walk in the door, I just go to my room. . . . Little tiny things that blow up into big arguments. We talk back and forth with each other and it gets so overblown that we end up yelling, he starts, like, spitting or whatever, and then it just gets blown up into a bigger argument.[7]

Feeling frightened much of the time, Mary was planning to leave her father's home and move in with her mother, with whom she had a good relationship.

Although Stephanie said that her mother very sweet and was one of the best moms in the world, her description of the relationship belies this sense of sweetness:

I cannot say she doesn't care about me, but sometimes I feel like she doesn't because if I do something, I get beat up sometimes. I get beat up most in my house—more than my brothers and sisters. So, sometimes, that is why I feel like, you know, I am the one that she loves the least. . . . And people I talk to, they always say that [the] kid that gets beat up and gets blamed all the time will probably be the one she's gonna love more in the future. Well, I don't think so. Then it's probably gonna be too late for her. I'm still going to think that she . . . doesn't care and stuff.[8]

Although less explosive, Corey's relationship with her mother had deteriorated over the past few years, so that now they could not even go out to a restaurant together, which they had previously enjoyed doing. As she explained, "My mom and I fight . . . a lot now. I mean we have always argued and fought, but I used to always go out to eat with my mom, but now we always fight, no matter what. Like wherever we go, even if I'm in the car with her for ten minutes, we fight."[9]

In most instances, where a young woman said she did not have a relationship with a parent, she was referring to a father who simply was not part of her family's life.[10] As Sandra Llonas explained when asked about her father, who lived apart from her and her mother, "My dad? Well he's practically never been around. Like when I was younger, I used to see him like two or three times a year. And then a couple of years ago, I went to go live with him, and I lived with him for a year and a half; but he was always working, because he had a full-time job and then he had a part-time job. So I would never seen him."[11] Stephanie's father maintained a business in his home country and would come to see his family once or twice a year. She explained why he did not really seem like a parent to her: "My dad, to tell the truth he was only here physically and financially. He wasn't here like a real dad to . . . show me what's good in life . . . and help me do the right thing. He was only here physically."[12]

When asked about their relationship, Monique conveyed her resentment toward her absent father, who had only been to see her twice since she was a young child:

> He's been to my house on two occasions. He doesn't make an effort to come see me. So I take it as, I'm the child—why should I make an effort to go see him? . . . I remember before he told me not to talk to boys on the phone. . . . And I was just like, "Who do you think you are?" I don't know, I guess I make him feel smaller, less manly. It just surprised me, like "How are you going to tell me what I can do? I mean, you never even bought me a gift. You don't even know my birthday."[13]

After Sandra Kiwi left her father's home at the age of nine, due to abuse by her stepmother, she had attempted to stay in touch with him through letters, but she sadly explained, "I guess he don't want to talk to me. I sent him letters, but they keep on coming back."[14]

These young women cannot be pigeonholed regarding their relationships with their parents. As the interviews make clear, it is too simplistic to assume that all minors who do not involve their parents come from abusive or dysfunctional families. Although this abuse and dysfunction was certainly present for some of them, others enjoyed a good relationship with at least one parent and clearly valued the connection. As developed further in this chapter, this complexity is reflected in the reasons given by these young women for not telling their parents; as their narratives show, both the lack and the presence of meaningful connections were factored into the decision not to disclose.

Talking about Sex

Overall, the young women I spoke with did not feel comfortable talking with either parent about sex. None of the parents had initiated meaningful or informative conversations with their daughters about what it means to become sexually active. (See, however, mention of Beth below.) They had not sat down and talked to them about the potential risks of sexual activity, how to make wise choices, or contraceptive options. However, a few of the parents, perhaps upon suspecting that their daughter was having sex, had provided snippets of advice, such as "use a condom." In turn, perhaps not surprisingly, none of the young women had told either parent that she was sexually active.

For about half of the young women, this silence was consistent with long-standing patterns of communication. As they reported it, their parents had never talked to them about sex, including the basic facts of life, or if they had, the message they had conveyed was quite negative. Perhaps seeking to protect their daughters, some parents presented a sole message about sex—that it was bad and fraught with lurking dangers.

For example, the attitude that Miranda's parents sought to instill in her was that sex was for bad teens: "My parents and me have never talked about me having sex. Sex is always the bad thing; bad teens have sex. Teens who have sex get in trouble." Miranda mentioned that when she would randomly try to bring up the topic of sex, her mother would consistently respond, "Don't have sex. It's bad for you; something bad is going to happen. You don't want to be one of those bad teens or get pregnant."[15] A similar message was conveyed to Taylor, who understood her mother to be saying that even when people were married, sex was something bad—something to be avoided whenever possible.[16]

For Angel, who had lived with her father until he kicked her out of the house after a fight, and whose mother suffered from a serious and debilitating mental illness, the only communication she had had with a parent regarding sex consisted of her being called a whore by her father because she had friends who were boys. This was also the only kind of communication about sex between Mary Souza and her father, with whom she lived. As Mary explained, her father's basic attitude was that teens who had sex were tramps, resulting in his calling her a whore when he learned she was sexually active.[17]

The other young women described having had some earlier communication about sexual matters with at least one parent, almost always a mother. For some, this communication consisted of being given basic information about the facts of life; for others, it also included a caution about using protection if she had sex. Most felt that their mothers were uncomfortable talking to them about sex. The sense many conveyed in the interview was that their mothers seemed to feel some kind of responsibility to provide them with basic information but were not looking to initiate an ongoing dialogue with their daughters or invite them to come to them with questions as they matured. In a rather poignant example of this tension between discomfort and responsibility to inform, Anna Lynne described how her mother would "happen" to turn on the Discovery Channel when educational shows about sex were on and then casually suggest that Anna Lynne sit and watch television while she finished preparing dinner.

In contrast, three of the young women felt that a parent, and in Beth's case, both parents, had been open and direct with them about sexual matters, although this did not necessarily mean they recognized or accepted their daughter's sexuality. Jill and Theresa were both able to talk openly with their mothers about sex; however, mirroring their mother's discomfort, neither felt able to raise the issue of her own sexual activity with them.

Jill's mother began talking to her about sex when she was in elementary school. Jill described these conversations about sex as being relatively informative and relaxed; despite this, her mother had never broached the topic of Jill becoming sexually active, nor had she talked to her about birth control. As Jill understood it, this was because they lived in a very sheltered, middle-class community, where people did not think teenagers had sex. As she related, "I didn't think that teens of the age of 16 [her current age] would ever, you know what I mean? And I think they [her parents] think that too. They just don't think . . . especially where I live. Nice little town, no real issues."[18] Theresa also felt comfortable talking openly with her mother about sex and felt that she could ask her anything she wanted to about sexual practices. However, like Jill, she could not bring up birth control or her own sexual activity because her mother strongly opposed premarital sexual relationships on religious grounds. Thus, although certainly more open about sex than the other parents, neither of these mothers comprehended her own daughter's sexuality. This topic remained off-limits, notwithstanding the general ease of communication about sex.

In contrast, in addition to feeling that her parents were pretty comfortable talking with her about sex (she joked that her parents did not break out into cold sweats), Beth indicated that her parents actually acknowledged the possibility that their daughter might become sexually active during her teen years. Beth explained that although her father was clear that he preferred that she wait until she was older, he understandingly told her that if she were going to be sexually active, he hoped it would be in the context of a caring relationship: "If I was going to be, [he thought] that it should be with someone special . . . who cares for me as I care for them. That was his big thing."[19] Her mother also echoed this concern. Interestingly, these communications did not occur within the context of a stable parent-child relationship. As described in chapter 4, Beth had spent most of her childhood moving from the care of one relative to another due to her parents' inability to care for their children, inability that, in her father's case, related to a history of chemical dependency, depression, and incarceration. Of the entire group, only Beth's parents seemed able or willing to comprehend and respond to their daughter's sexuality in a direct and immediate way.

Even given what these young women had to say about the lack of open and meaningful communication about sex, it is possible that had their parents been asked, they would have painted a different picture since parents and children often differ in their perception as to whether "real" communication about sex has occurred, with parents more likely to report that it has.[20] One explanation for this discrepancy is that parents may underestimate how much their children want to know; another possibility is that children do not regard the conversations as meaningful because "parents tend to equate 'meaningful' discussions of sex with the teaching of morality."[21]

Although teens and parents have a difficult time communicating about sex, studies consistently show that a majority of parents do speak with their children about sex.[22] According to a 2002 survey of a nationally representative sample of teens between the ages of 15 and 17, 61 percent of young women and 42 percent of young men had discussed with a parent "how to know when you are ready to have sex." The same survey found that 54 percent of young women had discussed condoms, and 63 percent had discussed other forms of birth control with a parent.[23] Given these statistics, even if one assumes some "underreporting" on the part of the young women I spoke with, it is still striking how little communication there was between these teens and their parents regarding sexual matters and how much of the communication, when it took place, was negative. With very few exceptions, even in the relationships that these young women described as being close, sex was simply not an open topic of conversation. As developed next, this silence may have played a role in the teens' nondisclosure decision.

THE DECISION NOT TO INVOLVE PARENTS

As with the abortion decision, the interviews make clear that the minors gave considerable weight to the decision not to involve their parents. Despite common assumptions about teens as devaluing the relationship they have with their parents, these teens were neither flip nor casual about the nondisclosure decision, and their reasons were well-grounded in the realities of their lives. Thus, for example, minors who worried that they would be forced to keep the baby related this concern to their parents' long-standing and strongly held opposition toward abortion, premarital sex, or both. Young women who feared their parents' anger related this to past incidents of violent or other adverse actions, such as being thrown out of the house after an argument.

Further suggesting the careful consideration they gave to the decision not to confide in their parents, almost all of the minors had multiple reasons for nondisclosure, and, as with the abortion decision, the interviews revealed an ability to draw connections between the reasons. For example, a minor who worried that a parent was under too much stress to cope with the revelation of her pregnancy might also have worried that this additional burden would increase the strain on an already fragile relationship, thereby further taxing the family system. Similarly, a minor who feared that a parent would react with extreme anger might also be concerned that the anger would destroy whatever relationship they had.

Another indication of the seriousness and complexity of the young women's decisional process, the interviews revealed that these young women, including those who were living with both parents, distinguished between their parents when thinking about disclosure. They saw each parent as a separate person and their relationship with each as having its own dynamic. They did not simply or indiscriminately lump their parents together with a dismissive "they'll never understand" or "they'll be pissed" attitude that one might anticipate from teens. Rather, reasons given for noninvolvement reflected the individualized nature of these relationships. For example, a minor might have been concerned with protecting her mother from the burden of the news, while focusing on her father's anticipated anger. This delineation between parents and the corresponding differentiation of reasons for not disclosing to them enables us to see how, as further explored here, their reasons were well-grounded in the reality of their lives, rather than simply being expressions of adolescent rebellion or disdain for their parents.

Neglect, Pressure, and Anger: The Reaction of Parents Who Learned of Their Daughters' Intended Abortion

The parents of four of the young women I interviewed actually knew about their daughters' pregnancy and about the intended abortion. The mothers of two of the young women had been informed directly by their daughters, and the parents of the other two learned of their daughters' situation through either a third party or inadvertent means. Before looking at the reasons for nondisclosure, it is instructive to consider how these parents responded upon learning that their daughter was pregnant and wished to have an abortion.

Both Melissa (already the mother of a young child) and Jasmine told their mothers about their pregnancy and intended abortion. Somewhat ironically, both of these young women were in DSS custody due to parental abuse and had extremely troubled relationships with their mothers.

At the time of the interview, Melissa was in a teen living program, having been removed several months earlier from her mother's custody due to severe abuse. Growing up, the only instruction Melissa had received about sex or the facts of life was when her grandmother, with whom she was very close, told her about the "period situation." When Melissa first became sexually active, she had hoped that this would be an opportunity for her mother and her to sit down and talk about things. So one day, she announced to her mother that she was "no longer a virgin," hoping desperately that her mother would "talk to me about it. She don't talk to me."[24] She also hoped her mother would express some concern for her well-being and tell her to "use condoms." However, this disclosure had no impact on her mother. She expressed no interest in or concern for her daughter.

When Melissa became pregnant for a second time, she again hoped that if she confided in her mother, it would be a way to connect with her. She also hoped her mother would support her abortion decision. Apparently not realizing that having lost custody to DSS, she no longer had the authority to consent to the abortion, Melissa's mother said that she would come to the clinic to give permission for the abortion, but she never showed up.[25] Sometime later, she told Melissa she had overslept. Adding to the poignancy of her situation, Melissa, although much closer to her father than to her mother, chose not to tell him about her pregnancy because she knew he would be very upset. Still grieving the recent death of her grandmother, who had been the most stable adult figure in her life, Melissa could not bear the thought of losing the support and respect of her father.

Jasmine was a very angry young woman who had not lived with her mother for most of her life due to abuse and neglect. At the time of the interview and during her pregnancy, Jasmine was living in a halfway house, and her pregnancy had been the result of a rape. It was not clear why Jasmine decided to tell her mother about her pregnancy and abortion plans, since her mother had never been a supportive presence in her life. After learning her daughter was pregnant, Jasmine's mother put tremendous pressure on her to have the baby.[26] To this end, she enlisted relatives to call Jasmine at the halfway house to try to persuade her to keep the baby.

Dion was not sure how her mother had learned she was pregnant, but once she realized her mother knew, Dion told her of her plans to terminate the pregnancy. Her mother responded to this news with complete indifference. Her only response was that she was not going to help Dion pay for the abortion. In light of her mother's lack of interest or concern, Dion decided to seek court authorization for the abortion rather than try and involve her mother further. Following their initial conversation, Dion's mother remained completely indifferent to her situation and never even asked Dion about whether she had gone through with the abortion.

Corey's parents learned of her abortion when they found information regarding postoperative care from the abortion clinic in her room. Her father responded with rage and one morning before school threatened to break down Corey's door in order to force her to speak with them. Once she opened the door, he grabbed her arms and dragged her down the stairs. He then held her down on the couch and would not let her leave the house until she told them what had happened.

With reactions ranging from indifference to abuse, these parents hardly appear to be the wise and caring presence envisioned by the Court. That none of these parents reacted in a supportive or constructive manner underscores the importance of listening to what young women have to say about why they think it best not to disclose their situation to their parents. It also makes it clear that the Court's one-size-fits-all approach to parent-child relationships is at best naïve—and at worst a danger to the well-being of young women facing an unintended pregnancy.

Reasons for Nondisclosure

Clustered thematically, the primary reasons that the young women I interviewed gave for not involving their parents included fear of a serious adverse response or anger; relational considerations, such as lack of relationship or a problematic relationship, anticipated harm to the relationship, and concern for a parent; and a fear of being pressured into having the baby. This is generally consistent with the results of other studies. For instance, in a study of a representative national sample of teens, reasons for nondisclosure clustered around the same themes, with relational concerns and fear of parental anger being the two most important considerations.[27] Similarly, another study concluded that "avoidance of parental notification was only partly due to perceived parental disagreement with the decision. There were many other reasons for not notifying parents: an absent father, multiple concurrent family stresses, family violence, parental substance abuse, and a feeling of having 'betrayed' the family by becoming pregnant."[28] Accordingly, as we consider what these young women had to say about why they did not involve their parents, although it is clear that each experience is unique, when taken as a whole, these experiences provide considerable insight into the dynamics of the nondisclosure decision.

Anticipated Severe Adverse Parental Reaction or Parental Anger

Five of the young women did not tell their parents about their pregnancy and abortion plans due to fear of a serious adverse reaction; an additional five feared that their parents would be very angry or upset with them.[29] With the possible exception of Miranda (see below), the young women who feared a serious adverse reaction had all experienced harsh parental treatment; their fear was thus well-grounded in past patterns of harm. Significantly, no young woman who felt she had a good relationship with a parent gave fear of an adverse parental reaction as a reason for nondisclosure. Similarly, minors who feared parental anger generally pointed to a history of relationship difficulties, which frequently included recurring and often bitter fighting. Fear of an adverse reaction or parental anger was almost always linked to other reasons for nondisclosure, such as lack of a relationship, parental beliefs about abortion, or concern about disappointing a parent. The following discussion illustrates the kinds of adverse reactions that the minors feared.

As described earlier, Stephanie was regularly beaten by her mother and had been singled out among her siblings for this kind of harsh treatment. Already isolated within the family, she feared disclosure would reinforce her mother's sense of her as the worst of her children, thereby resulting in Stephanie's further marginalization and deprivation of family affection. This worried her more than being beaten, both because she hoped the knowledge that "she had something inside" would keep her mother from harming her physically and, sadly, because she was so accustomed to being beaten that the prospect of it no longer frightened her—"I'm no longer afraid if she beat me and stuff 'cause you know when you get used to something, you're just like, well, it happens. . . . I always tell her if she thinks beating me will change me, it won't change me at all."[30]

Mary Souza was afraid her father would "flip out." Although this perhaps seems like the kind of response that a teen might give without much thought to whether a parent really would respond harshly, the history of Mary's relationship with her father makes real the fear behind the words. Mary had lived with her father since her parents' divorce a number of years earlier. Before the divorce, she had not had much of a relationship with her father, but she chose to live with him because her mother moved to a new community, and she wanted to remain in her hometown. Following the divorce, the father-and-daughter relationship rapidly deteriorated. It became punctuated by extremely angry and hostile arguments in which Mary's father would spit at her, and although she did not elaborate, she indicated there had also been other abusive behavior of a more serious nature. She felt increasingly afraid of him and was planning to move in with her mother at the end of the school term, although this meant changing schools mid-year and leaving her lifelong friends.

In addition to fearing for her physical safety, Mary also worried that her father would respond by once again labeling her a whore[31] and taking out a delinquency petition on her in juvenile court. This was no idle fear, since her father had previously filed such a petition upon learning that she had been sexually active with a former boyfriend. He had also filed a second delinquency petition against her following a particularly bad argument.

To complete the picture of Mary's situation, it is worth noting her reason for not involving her mother here. In contrast to her relationship with her father, Mary felt quite close to her mother, describing her as her "best friend," and she was looking forward to moving in with her. However, over the years, her father had told her mother that Mary was a bad girl, and she worried that if her mother learned she was pregnant, her mother might think less of her and not want her to come live with her. She was also worried about the fact that her mother was under a lot of pressure, and she was concerned that the news of her pregnancy would be too much for her mother to cope with. (See later section entitled "Concern for a Parent.")

Severing family ties as a way of dealing with anger had been a longstanding pattern in Angel's family, and she feared that if she told her mother about her pregnancy and intended abortion, she would be thrown out of the house. Angel's parents had divorced many years earlier. Her father had received custody of all five children because her mother suffered from a serious and debilitating mental illness. Angel described how her father hated her mother so much that after the divorce, he lied in court to get restraining orders against her so that she could not see her children. However, four years prior to my meeting with Angel, Angel's father kicked her out of the house following an argument, at which time she began living with her mother and stopped having any contact with her father.

Angel had no idea how her mother would respond to the news of her pregnancy. Sadly, she recounted, "I really [don't] know her that well compared to what most women know about their moms because I didn't see her for like a couple of years after my parents got divorced. And she's mentally ill, so she was always lying in bed and stuff when I was younger." Shifting to the present, Angel continued, "And now it's hard to get along with her because she's a little insane. She's on SSI for being insane, and she takes pills, and it's hard to talk to her because she talks to herself and stuff."[32] Angel also described how her mother constantly yelled at her. Since she was unable to predict her mother's reaction, Angel's fear of being kicked out of her mother's house was very real in light of her family's history of cutting ties based on hatred and anger. This was a risk she was unwilling to take, since, with her father having made it clear that she was not welcome in his home, it would have resulted in her becoming homeless

Miranda worried about a different kind of negative reaction. Miranda was born in the United States to immigrant parents, whom she described as very strict and traditional and unable to adjust to the American way of life. As mentioned earlier, her mother had constantly drilled into her that sex was for bad teens who had not been brought up right.

Previously, Miranda had seen her mother become extremely angry and agitated when she learned that a second cousin who was visiting them had had an abortion. Miranda recounted how her mother had dragged the whole family into the matter and had angrily confronted the friend who had driven her cousin to the clinic. Knowing how her mother felt about both premarital sex and abortion, Miranda anticipated that her mother would react to her pregnancy with extreme anger. Although she did not fear being harmed physically, since there was no history of abuse, she feared that her mother would respond by forcing her to return to her home country to give birth and raise the child among her relatives, so that she could be closely supervised by an extended family network. Of course, there is no way of knowing for certain whether her mother would actually have done this. However, Miranda's fear was very real and well-grounded in the belief structure of her mother, as reflected in her mother's response to her second cousin's abortion.

Although proponents of parental-involvement laws often assert that most teenagers, when asked how their parents would react if they found out she was pregnant, would reflexively respond, "They'd kill me," this discussion makes clear that with respect to the young women I interviewed, the fear of an adverse parental response was generally well-rooted in a history of troubled relationships and past negative treatment. The young women who had a good relationship with one or both parents did not worry about an adverse parental response—in the absence of a history that would support this concern, it was not a consideration in the decision not to disclose. Likewise, the young women who did fear parental anger also looked to their family's history—generally a history of significant difficulties in the relationship, including frequent and serious arguments—in deciding not to discuss their pregnancy and intended abortion with a parent. Again, where the relationships were good, this was not a concern.

Concern for the Relationship

Eleven of the young women feared that disclosure would harm the relationship they had with one or both parents.[33] They worried that their parents would not trust them again, would lose respect for them, or would be profoundly hurt or disappointed. Almost all of the young women who did not tell a parent because of a concern that disclosure would negatively impact their relationship had a "good" or an "okay" relationship with that parent.

Both Jill Casey and Mary Smith expressed concerns about the impact that disclosure would have on the relationships that they enjoyed with their parents. As mentioned earlier, Jill lived in a fairly wealthy suburb, where, according to her, adults simply assumed that their high-achieving children were not sexually active. Thus, although her mother had talked openly with her about the facts of life, they had never discussed the possibility of Jill's own sexuality. Focusing on the importance of her relationship with her parents, Jill explained, "If I had told my parents, eventually they would have let me have the abortion. . . . Yet, our relationship would never have been the same after that. I'm sure of it. The respect, the trust—it would be gone. . . . I didn't want to jeopardize that."[34]

Like Jill, Mary came from a middle-class professional family and was planning to attend college in the fall. Also describing herself as close with both of her parents, she feared that her mother would be horrified to learn she had been sexually active and would lose respect for her: "She would have been disgusted. . . . I feel that she would look at me different; she would just think of me different. She'd act different toward me." Mary explained that the only situation under which she would have told her mother about being pregnant was if the pregnancy had resulted from a rape—because then it wouldn't have been her fault:

> If . . . I had gotten pregnant, say, not by choice,[35] but by rape . . . then I think she would've completely understood. . . . If I had told her it was because of my own mistake . . . I think she has this assumption like I'm too smart to make a mistake because I'm in the National Honor Society and going to college. . . . I think it would've definitely affected her viewpoint . . . She would think I was irresponsible about everything.[36]

A number of the young women mentioned the high expectations that their parents had for them—expectations that they feared would be destroyed with the news of their pregnancy. In not telling, they hoped to preserve their parents' vision of and faith in them. As Sandra Llonas explained when discussing why she did not tell her mother, "I'm the oldest kid on both sides of the family. All the grandkids, all the cousins look up to me, and everyone depends on me—you're the oldest, you're doing so good in school, you're gonna go to college, and you're going to do this and that, without messing up with dudes."[37]

For the most part, the concern that disclosure would disrupt a relationship was not an important consideration where there was no relationship to protect. However, both Corey and Bianca, who at the time of the interview characterized the relationships they had with their mothers as terrible, were concerned that their mothers would be deeply disappointed in them, thus further damaging their already tenuous relationships and perhaps destroying the chance of future reconciliation. This difference may reflect the fact that, in contrast to the others who reported having a bad or nonexistent relationship with a parent, both Corey and Bianca had previously enjoyed times of closeness with their mothers and, during the course of the interview, expressed sadness over the deterioration in the relationship. As Corey, who was constantly fighting with her mother, explained, "There was no need to tell them because it would just hurt them. It would make it worse; it would make them more disappointed in me. And it would make them think like, 'she's making such a bad decision. She's irresponsible' . . . and they would just worry so much. I just think it would just make it worse."[38]

Although there is no way to be certain that all these young women were correct in their belief that disclosure would permanently damage the relationships they had with their parents, the seriousness and sincerity of their concern was striking. This is made evident by the fact that rather than risk disruption of these connections, these minors were willing to submit this intimate decision to the authority of the court, which, as discussed later, was a daunting prospect for all of them. Thus, rather than signaling family dysfunction or a flip "teen" attitude toward parents, nondisclosure may well represent the desire to preserve connection rather than risk its disruption.

Concern for a Parent

Distinct from the concern for the impact that disclosure would have on a relationship with a parent was the concern that eight of the young women expressed about the impact disclosure would have on the well-being of a parent.[39] In this regard, a number of the young women expressed concerns about burdening a parent who was suffering from a serious physical illness or condition. Mary Smith, who did not talk to her mother because she worried it would harm their relationship, detailed, "I never once thought of telling my dad. He has high blood pressure . . . and I think this would have just set him off. It would have made him worry too much. A lot has been going on with him medically, like he had a stroke a few years ago. He's retired now actually. So . . . I didn't want to push because he gets upset easily. . . . I never thought of telling him."[40]

Both Anna Lynne and Monique considered the health of a parent in combination with other factors in deciding not to disclose their situation. Anna Lynne's father had suffered a heart attack several years earlier and was now under considerable stress. In discussing why she did not involve him, she recalled,

> I just didn't think it was the right time because my dad—he was the assistant vice president at a big company—and he just got laid off because of a corporate merger, and since then, he hasn't had a job. . . . They're kind of tight with money right now; they have a lot of financial problems. It's just my mom working, and she doesn't like her job at the department store, and she wants to quit . . . they're pretty stressed right now.[41]

For Monique, it was her mother's chronic, debilitating illness and the fact that her mother was a single parent of three children that prompted her nondisclosure decision. Speaking not just of the abortion, Monique said, "I wouldn't put the burden on my mother . . . she has enough problems. I just keep on."[42]

For other young women it was an acute awareness of parental vulnerabilities. Thus, although Beth, the young woman who was living with roommates after being kicked out of the house by her mother, could talk openly about her emerging sexuality with her father, she felt that she needed to protect him from the news of her pregnancy. "I don't know how he would have handled it. He's a manic-depressive. He's an alcoholic, and . . . right around the spring [the time of her pregnancy], it's his time to try and commit suicide, and . . . I didn't want to add to any of his problems."[43]

Molly, who had told her mother about a prior abortion, sought this time to shield her from further stress:

> My mom has a lot of stress—she's got bills to pay off, she's working two jobs. . . . She goes to work at six in the morning and gets out of there at four, and then she has to go to work at five and do another job for three more hours. I think that if she were to find out about it, she would have been . . . even more emotionally stressed. And to bring her through something like that again would be . . . really hard for her to deal with. So I figured that to save her the emotional . . . stress and stuff, I would keep it from her.[44]

As these quotes make clear, these young women were very attuned to the difficulties in the lives of their parents and felt a sense of responsibility to shield them from further distress. As with the focus on not damaging relationships, they were seeking to prevent inflicting harm through disclosure of information that they believed would be upsetting to their parents. Thus, again, nondisclosure was rooted in a protective impulse—in a desire to prevent harm and safeguard existing familial patterns.

Lack of Relationship

Close to one-third of the young women did not involve one of their parents due to the lack of a relationship him or her. In most instances, this was a father who was living apart from the family and was simply not part of the young woman's life. Several of these fathers were living in other states, a few were in other countries, and one or two were in jail.

Reflecting the profound lack of connection with their absent fathers, many of these young women, when asked why they did not involve their parents, spoke only of their mothers. Their fathers were so removed from their lives that it was as if they had been shorn of their parental status and were thus outside the scope of the inquiry. Only upon being specifically asked about why they did not talk to their father did they consider him. As Monique succinctly put it when explaining why it never even crossed her mind to tell her father about her pregnancy, "I didn't even call him to say Merry Christmas, so I definitely didn't call him."[45] Reflecting the total lack of engagement, and in contrast to the dominant pattern of multiple reasons for noninvolvement, the absence of a relationship was the only given reason for not involving these absent fathers.

The context was different for several of the young women who did not involve a parent because of the lack of a relationship. Here, the consideration was less the total absence of a parental bond and more the sense of distance and lack of a context for disclosure. For both Amy and Corey, the lack of a relationship was a relatively recent occurrence. Both of them had been engaged with their mothers while growing up but had entered into stormy times with them. Unlike the young women who did not even think of mentioning their absent fathers, both Amy and Corey were painfully aware of the shift in their relationship with their mothers and mentioned how they would have told their mothers had the relationships not deteriorated so badly.

Amy commented, "My mom and I have no relationship. . . . Her and my relationship basically dissolved. . . . If I hadn't moved out, I would have thought about talking with her, but not now. I have no relationship with her."[46] Similarly, Corey, who was also worried about parental disapproval, revealed, "I felt like if I had a better relationship with her, I really would have [told her]. And it's too bad that we had such a bad relationship when like the worst thing happened to me. But I couldn't tell her at that point."[47] For Amy and Corey, the absence of a relationship was intertwined with other considerations—for Amy it was a fear that her mother would tell her father, and for Corey it was anticipated anger, disappointment, and the risk of an irreparable breach in the relationship—and thus reflected a shifting dynamic rather than a fixed, categorical lack of connection.

Parental Pressure and Ideology

Five of the young women were concerned that if one or both of their parents knew about the pregnancy and intended abortion, they would be pressured or forced into having the baby.[48] Interestingly, none mentioned being afraid that her parents would pressure her into marrying the father of her child.

For the most part, these young women described their parents as staunchly antiabortion and identified this ideology as the wellspring of anticipated parental opposition to their intended abortion. Several also expressed concern that they would be forced to have the baby as a kind of penance for their "wrongdoing." For Beth, however, the concern was that her mother would push her to have the child based on her mother's desire to care for a child: "She loves children—loves them—and she would want me to have it. Not because she's antiabortion, but because she wants to be a grandmother. Like, if I had it, and gave it to her, she would be fine with that. . . . There's the whole situation with how . . . the child would be raised the same way I was raised, and that's just not good enough."[49]

Autonomy

It is easy to assume that many young women do not tell their parents about their pregnancy and intended abortion because they are seeking to assert their independence from parental control. Depending on one's perspective, this might be viewed as an unreasoned act of defiance or as a normal aspect of adolescent development in which separation from parents is considered an essential step toward healthy adulthood.

However, autonomy did not emerge as an important theme in the interviews. Only two of the young women, Jane and Kim, spoke of "autonomy" as a self-contained reason for nondisclosure. As described earlier, Jane had an extremely troubled relationship with her family, and at the time of the interview, Kim was living in a shelter with her infant daughter. Kim's father was long absent from her life, and she had sporadic contact with her mother. As Kim saw it, her abortion was simply none of her mother's business; for Jane, her decision represented a claim to her own body and an assertion of attempted control over the chaos in her life: "It's my life. . . . It's my body. My brain runs my body. I run my body. I run my mind. . . . I'm going to do what I gotta do . . . because I'm the one that's really going through this shit. That's the way I see myself."[50]

For others, considerations of autonomy were subtler and more contextual. Several of the young women, for example, articulated their claim to autonomy within a broader context of assessing the harm that disclosure would have. This dynamic is captured in the following quote from the interview with Keiza: "It just wasn't their decision. I just made my decision of whether or not to have it, and why if I'm just going to have it [the abortion], should I bring them down . . . if I don't have to."[51] Molly felt that rather than upsetting her mother, she should take responsibility for her own actions: "She would probably blame it on herself, say 'why did I let this go happen,' and stuff like that. You know, it's not her fault. I can't . . . put her through that because of the choice that I made."[52] This was also a consideration for Monique, who was deeply concerned about burdening her mother: "Me, I feel like you just don't involve . . . you got in this situation; why involve your mother? I felt if I got in this situation, I can get out of it."[53]

Thus expressed, autonomy appears as an expression of contextual considerations rather than as an absolute claim to self-expression. The consideration of self was linked to the relationships these young women had with their parents and was weighed against the impact that disclosure would have on them. In short, it was not a separateness that was devoid of consideration for others.

The Role of Fear and Connection in the Nondisclosure Decision

As the previous discussion makes clear, both the fear of and the connection to parents were significant factors in the nondisclosure decisions of the young women I interviewed. These are clearly very different, and one might say contradictory, considerations; yet, each tells us quite a bit about the complex and variable nature of the decision not to involve parents. They also play an important role in the policy debates about parental-involvement laws.

As already established, a considerable number of the young women I spoke with were afraid of how their parents would respond to the news they were pregnant and wanted an abortion. The importance of this thematic consideration is underscored by the fact that almost one-third of the young women who sought judicial authorization for an abortion in Massachusetts over a 12-month period mentioned fear of parental anger or an adverse parental reaction as a reason for nondisclosure, with the percentage rising to almost 40 percent for those young women living just with their father.[54] Although, as we have seen, the Supreme Court has ignored critical dimensions of adolescent reality, in the case of *Hodgson v. Minnesota,* which involved a challenge to a two-parent notification requirement that did not include a bypass option, the Court acknowledged that many teens "live in fear of parental violence."[55] Based on the recognition that the consequences of a notification requirement are "particularly pronounced in the distressingly large number of cases in which family violence is a serious problem" and that disclosure of a daughter's pregnancy "can provoke violence, even where parents are divorced or separated,[56] the Court invalidated the Minnesota law for failing to provide a bypass option.

Nonetheless, supporters of parental-involvement laws often discount the fear that many young women say prevents them from confiding in their parents, asserting that if asked how her parents would respond to the new of her pregnancy, most teens would reflexively respond that her parents would kill her—that this is simply how teens think and talk about their parents. However, underscored by the Court's recognition of the reality of parental violence, the interviews make clear that fear is not an invented or unthinking response of young women in the throes of adolescent rebellion.

First, not all of the young women gave this as a reason. Second, and more important, when fear was mentioned, it was almost always grounded in a history of harsh parental treatment. Moreover, fear of an adverse reaction was almost never a stand-alone reason, but was entwined with other considerations, such as the lack of a relationship or parental beliefs about abortion. Also significant is the fact that none of the young women who characterized their relationship with a parent as good mentioned fear of an adverse reaction as a reason for nondisclosure. Thus, far from being an unconsidered response, which can be disregarded as expressive of "typical" adolescent disdain for parental authority, the fear expressed by these minors was well-anchored in longstanding family patterns and interwoven with other elements of the relationships they had with their parents.

Perhaps less immediately obvious than fear of a harsh parental response, the connection that these young women had with their parents was also an important thematic consideration. As discussed earlier, this consideration manifested itself in two primary ways. Some of the young women chose not to disclose their situation because they did not want to damage the relationship they had with a parent, and others sought to protect their parents from the burden of disclosure. For some, both of these considerations were present. As with fear, the interviews make clear that these were not casual or unthinking factors in the nondisclosure decision.

A deep concern to the young women who did not want to disappoint or upset their parents was that disclosure would permanently alter the relationship that they had with them. It was often the case that a young woman's parents held her in high esteem and had encouraged her to reach for the stars. She thus feared that if her parents learned of her "mistake," they would come to believe that their longstanding confidence in her had been misplaced and she would tumble from grace.

Nonetheless, however sincere their beliefs, this reason for nondisclosure can seem somewhat paradoxical. It is easy to understand why a minor who fears that a parent might harm her or force her to carry to term would not want to disclose her situation, but it is harder to grasp why a minor who values a good relationship with her parents would likewise want to keep her situation from them:

> This reason for requesting a waiver of parental consent may seem irrational to some. After all, if a girl loves her parents and does not want to hurt them, their relationship is probably healthy enough to survive the news of the pregnancy. As adult onlookers, we might be tempted to deny a petition for waiver of parental rights, sympathizing with loving parents, who, we believe, could help their daughter in crisis. This is contrary to the teen's view. Her interest in maintaining a stable and loving relationship with her parents may be paramount in her eyes. The thought of confessing a pregnancy to the parents she loves is possibly the worst fate imaginable.[57]

Accordingly, nondisclosure may be a purposeful strategy to safeguard connection rather than risk its disruption.

In this regard, it is worth noting that of the young women I interviewed, the two who chose to tell their mothers about their pregnancy and intended abortion (Melissa and Jasmine), had no relationship to speak of with them, both having been removed from their mothers' custody due to either abuse or neglect. For them, disclosure carried no risk, since there was no connection to protect. Further elucidating this dynamic, Melissa was also very clear that having recently lost her grandmother, who had been the most important adult in her life, she was not about to risk the connection she had with her father by telling him of her intended abortion.

In a similar fashion, in a study looking at communication about sexual behavior, researchers were surprised to find that "contrary to our predictions, maternal underestimation of sexual activity increased as the quality of the mother-teen improved."[58] Seeking to explain this unanticipated result, researchers suspected that "mothers who have good relationships with their teens are less prone to believe that their teens would engage in 'inappropriate' behaviors, and hence are more likely to deny the possibility of sexual activity. Alternatively, teens who feel positive about their mothers may not want to tell them of their sexual activity so as to not hurt or upset the mother."[59] Thus, although it seems perhaps somewhat counterintuitive, we again see that the importance of the connection may mean that adolescents make deliberate choices to keep certain information outside the borders of their relationship with their parents.

The importance to adolescents of maintaining a relationship with parents has recently received a fair amount of attention in the developmental literature. At least in part, this focus is attributable to feminist psychologists who have been dissatisfied with the exclusion of women from seemingly neutral models of psychological development. Flowing from this concern, efforts have been made to reconstruct understandings of human development that, rather than focusing on the self as "separate and bounded,"[60] look to a more relational-focused approach to identity formation[61]—a framework that many have argued is more appropriate for exploring women's sense of self.

This paradigm shift has contributed to a reconsideration of the nature of the parent-child relationship over the course of the teen years, and a number of studies have concluded that "contrary to the popular stereotype that parent-adolescent relations are conflictual in nature and that adolescents vigorously reject their parents' advise and counsel,"[62] many teenagers value the support and guidance of their parents as they traverse these transformative years. This valuing of communication and guidance extends to the sexual domain, where studies indicate that teens wish that parents would be more "open, supportive and empathetic" in their communications about sex[63] and believe that such communication would make it easier for them to delay sexual activity and avoid pregnancy.[64]

Distinct from concerns about protecting the relationships the teens had with their parents, the importance of family connections was also evident in the expressed desire to protect parents from additional stress. Identifying the difficulties and complexities of their parents' lives, including the burdens of physical and mental illness, job and financial pressures, and marital woes, many of these young women worried that their parents simply could not handle any more difficulties.

As the interviews made clear, nondisclosure under these circumstances was again rooted in a protective impulse and in the desire to safeguard established patterns of family life.

Highly attuned to the burdens under which their parents were struggling, these young women revealed a sense of responsibility and a desire to not increase existing difficulties. In effect, these concerns reflect a role reversal, with the child taking on the protective function normally associated with parenthood. The ability to move beyond the self and incorporate another perspective or interest into the decision-making process again suggests the maturity of these young women. Not bound, as a child might be, by the dominance of self, these teens had an awareness of the ramifications of their actions on others.[65]

Taking Existing Patterns of Communication into Consideration

Excluding from consideration young women who do not confide in their parents based on a fear of anger, a harsh response, or pressure to carry the pregnancy to term, an important question is whether certain family characteristics make it more likely that a young woman who is facing an unplanned pregnancy will disclose her situation to her parents. The interviews I conducted certainly lend support to what others have concluded, which is that it is not the law, but rather the nature and quality of the parent-child relationship, that shapes her course of action.

This suggests a rather obvious proposition—that where there is no history of communication about intimate matters, a teen may be unwilling to test the waters at such a critical moment in her life. In the absence of such a history, not only would a young women be revealing that she is pregnant and wants an abortion, but she would also likely be initiating the first parent-child conversation about her own sexuality. Lacking any way to gauge how her parents would respond to the news of her pregnancy, the risk of disclosure may well be too great.

On the other hand, if parents have recognized and accepted the emerging sexuality of their adolescent daughter and have been able to respond to this reality in "age-appropriate ways," their daughter would be more likely to feel that she can turn to them when faced with an unplanned pregnancy.[66] Supporting the link between established patterns of communication and the increased likelihood of disclosure, one study found that more than half of the teens who had not discussed birth control with their parents did not tell their parents about their abortion, whereas two-thirds of the teens who had discussed birth control with their parents chose to confide in them.[67] It thus appears that if a teen can call upon a history of open and honest exchanges, the risk of disclosure is minimized. This established pattern of communication gives her a way to assess how her parents are likely to respond to the news of her pregnancy. Rather than taking the chance of jumping off a cliff into the unknown, she is provided a safety net by this history.

THE COURT EXPERIENCE

As a consequence of their decision not to confide in their parents, the young women I spoke with were required under Massachusetts law to seek judicial authorization for an abortion. Although all were found mature enough to make their own abortion decision, the process was fraught with tremendous anxiety. Moreover, the stress did not appear to be offset by any appreciable benefit or gain.

Capturing the distress that many of the young women felt upon learning that they had to go to court, Mary Souza explained,

> I think that [when] a girl under 18 . . . finds out she's pregnant . . . [it's] already nerve-wracking. . . . Finding out that you're pregnant—it's just so scary. Alone, you feel so alone . . . and then, you know, you can't tell your parents. So automatically you feel alone. . . . And then you have to go to court . . . it was just so scary. Thank God I had my friends with me. . . . If I ever had to go to court on my own, I probably would have been crying every day.[68]

As their court dates approached, the young women grew increasingly anxious. Jill Casey was so worried that she would not make it on time to court that she made a dry run: "Two days before I was actually going, I drove out there and looked for it. And I found my parking space, the exact one I was going to park in. And I went in, and I found exactly where I was going to sit, and then I went home. And two days later I went. I sat. I parked. I did all the stuff that I had practiced doing."[69]

Overall, their greatest fear was that the judge would deny them consent for the abortion. Over and over they described how, despite assurances from their lawyers or health care providers that virtually all teens in Massachusetts are granted consent, they worried they would be the one teen to be denied permission. Focusing on the fear of being turned down, Monique recalled, "I was nervous. I was actually scared. . . . Because my doctor . . . she's like, '99 percent of the time she [the judge] agrees,' but I'm like 'what about the 1 percent? I could be the 1 percent' . . . and I was nervous."[70] Similarly, Miranda described her anxiety: "The whole time waiting, I was just nervous. I was thinking, what happens if they don't give me the consent? What am I going to do now? . . . That's the only thing on my mind. . . . You know then I [would] have to go through all that I was trying to avoid."[71] Amy echoed the same kinds of fears: "I was . . . aaaah, scared just thinking about . . . if I don't get this, what am I going to do? . . . If this doesn't work, what am I going to do? . . . What if the judge says 'no'? That's the only thing you think about. What are you going to do next?"[72] Melissa described being so frightened that she forgot the answers to some of the questions she was asked: "They asked me, 'How do you know you are pregnant?' and I was going to say 'ultrasound,' but I couldn't think of the word because I was so nervous. I was like 'Oh, my God'; then I said 'test,' because I forgot."[73]

Afraid of being denied consent, they worried about making a mistake that would make them appear stupid or immature. They worried that they would not be able to convey their maturity to a judge who knew nothing of them or their life circumstances or that their reasons for not involving their parents would not be considered satisfactory. Taylor worried about how she would come across to the judge: "They're, like, judging you to see if you are mature or not. And like wondering what you're going to say. Like 'what if I say this, and then maybe they don't think I'm mature enough,' or 'what if do this' and . . . stuff like that."[74]

In worrying that she would be denied consent, Jill's primary fear was that the judge would not approve of her reason for not involving her parents:

> I felt uncomfortable. I was proving something to her. . . . I felt like my rea-
> son for not involving my parents wasn't good enough, like I needed to have
> a better reason, like "oh, my mom and dad would throw me out of the house
> if I told them," and that's the only way that I would be able to get her to say
> "ok." . . . I've never felt my hands so sweaty . . . [from] nervousness, being
> uncomfortable. Intimidated. Scared that she would say no—that was the
> main thing.[75]

This fear of being denied consent for an abortion reflects the minors' sense of powerlessness and lack of control over the outcome and their awareness of the power that the judge had over their futures. What if I say the wrong word? Give the wrong reason? Or convey the wrong impression? Will this lead to my being turned down and forced into motherhood? These kinds of worries played themselves out over and over again as the minors entrusted their futures to the court. The following quote from Beth captures this sense of powerlessness in describing how court made her feel: "Just unsure of myself. I'm very confident of myself and my decisions, and going through all that, I just felt very unsure of myself. Very uncomfortable. Very weak and vulnerable. And I'm not a weak person."[76]

Closely related, a number of the young women angrily questioned how a judge who knew nothing about them or their life circumstances could possibly make a meaningful determination about their maturity or readiness to have a child. The following quote from the interview with Mary Jane illustrates this concern:

> I don't understand why you have to go to court and have another proce-
> dure, another step. . . . I mean, if we are old enough or mature enough . . .
> however you want to see it . . . to have sex and get pregnant . . . I think that
> we should be able to make our own decisions. I don't think that someone
> else should be able to make our decision for us and tell us if they think we're
> old enough, mature enough, you know, to have the right mentality. I don't
> think that someone else should have to judge you on that one—because,
> well, what they see and what you know, living your own life, they don't
> know. I mean, they might listen to you and think one way, [and] you know
> how it is another way.[77]

Another important reaction was that it was uncomfortable to have to divulge such intimate details about their lives to complete strangers. Some expressed feeling exposed or invaded; one young woman expressed this as a loss of boundaries. Others spoke about a sense of shame or wrongdoing. As Beth put it,

> It was just so overwhelming. I mean to have so much going on and then to
> have to go to a huge courthouse to sit and talk to a judge who was going
> to make this decision that really doesn't involve them. . . . I mean it was
> uncomfortable . . . having to share something so intimate and so personal
> with strangers. I don't want to say it's embarrassing to have been pregnant,
> but it didn't fit in my picture of what I was supposed to be, how I'm sup-
> posed to be viewed by people. And then here I was with my big mistake,
> and strangers saying if my decisions were right or wrong.[78]

For Mary Smith, going to court made her feel as if she had done something wrong: "I was like, 'wow, I've never been to court before.' You would think that when you went to court, you were doing something wrong. It kind of made me feel like 'Oh well, I'm doing something wrong here. I have to get the court's per-mission to let me fix it.' "[79] Mary Souza reported similar feelings when describing what it was like having to hook up with a lawyer to go to court:

> That was actually the most nerve-wracking thing. Like, I just found out I'm
> pregnant, and then, you know, you have to go to a courtroom with a lawyer.
> To me, I've never seen anything good go on with authority in courtrooms
> and stuff . . . you're getting locked up, you know. And it's so nerve-wracking.

Like I was so nervous the day I had to go, and then after that, you have to look forward to your appointment. I'm only 16, and usually at this age, you know, you don't see people going to court for good things. I mean, I see kids going there because they're arrested . . . not for something great, you know? So I look at it as something just frightening.[80]

For Taylor, the sense of wrongdoing engendered by the court experience was particularly unsettling because she planned to be a lawyer, and court now felt to her like a very scary and horrible place.

A number of the young women described the experience as being overwhelming—it was simply too much to have to handle so much at such a difficult time in their lives. Critical in this regard was having to negotiate all of the logistical details related to the bypass hearing, including contacting their lawyer, arranging to miss school, preparing for the hearing, and figuring out how to get to court. Of course, compounding their stress was the need to accomplish all of this without arousing suspicion. In this regard, Jill raised an important concern. For her, the focus on having to negotiate the legal requirements meant she did not have time or energy to focus on the emotional aspects of her situation—the burden of arranging to go to court interfered with what she thought was important in this situation:

The big issue is that I'm pregnant. And that's what I'm crying about, and yet all we talk about is what am I going to do to be able to have an abortion. I had to be focusing on what am I going to do . . . you're crying because you didn't want this to happen to you . . . because it's emotional. I mean it's not just nothing, you know; you could have a child. That's huge. But, then you have to add in . . . what if I go and try to do this and they say no. What am I supposed to do?[81]

For most of these young women, there was nothing positive about the court experience to counterbalance the overwhelming sense of fear and anxiety, although a few did mention a sense of pride at being found mature by a judge. Already clear about their decision to abort and their inability to involve their parents, with the exception of Melissa, who appreciated having supportive adult contact, the young women did not feel that going to court helped them with their decision. According to Beth, "The court wasn't really a supportive thing. It was more just this person who didn't know you saying whether or not you're stable enough to get an abortion."[82] Similarly, Angel, in explaining that court did not help her with her decision in any way, stated, "I don't see what was helpful about some person just trying to decide whether I was mature or not . . . All they did was ask questions. . . . I just think that going to court is completely pointless."[83] For Corey, court was a lesson in irony: "I think that it was ridiculous—because they either were going to decide whether I was mature enough to make the decision, but if I wasn't mature enough, then why would I have the kid? Obviously, if I wasn't mature enough to make a decision like that, I wasn't mature enough to have a child. . . . It was just a huge step that I didn't feel needed to have been taken."[84]

In reflecting on their experience, a number of the young women mentioned that they thought it would make better sense for there to be an alternative to court for teens who cannot involve their parents. Focusing on the logistical difficulties, Theresa explained it this way:

> It would be easier if you could just go with someone over 18 because [with] the whole court thing, you have to spend a whole day getting into Boston. My parents, I had to lie to them about the whole day. . . . I think actually there should be someone at the abortion center to decide if you're mature enough to make your own decision. It would have been much easier instead of worrying, 'Am I going to get there on time? Am I going to get consent from the court?' It's just so confusing. I was so full of stress for like the month before. Just trying to get everything in order and trying to get there and get it done before it was too late, and it's just so stressful for you.[85]

For most of these young women, court was like a high-stakes test they had to pass. Terrified of failing and being forced into motherhood, they focused on not making mistakes or giving the wrong impression to the judge. They did not experience court as a supportive or informative process that enhanced their decision-making capacities or helped them view their decision in a new light. They felt unknown and resentful of the power that the judge had over their lives and the accompanying loss of privacy.

As a number of court decisions make clear, the traumatic nature of these young women's experience with the bypass process is far from unique. In the case of *Hodgson v Minnesota*, the evidence at trial clearly established that the court experience "produced fear, tension, anxiety and shame among minors."[86] One witness in the case described the process as "nerve-wracking," and a judge from Massachusetts testified that "going to court was 'absolutely' traumatic for minors."[87] According to Doctor Hodgson, the named plaintiff in the case, some of her patients returned from court "wringing wet with perspiration. They're markedly relieved . . . they dread the court procedure often more than the abortion procedure."[88] Echoing sentiments expressed by the young women I spoke with, a guardian ad litem testified that the teens who appear in court "are often exhausted . . . They talk about feeling that they don't belong in the court system, that they are ashamed, embarrassed, and somehow that they are being punished for the situation they are in."[89]

Although the court experience was clearly a very difficult one for the young women I spoke with, it can be even more difficult in other states, where the process is not well-coordinated, as it is in Massachusetts, and the granting of consent is a far less predictable outcome. (See chapter 4 for more details.) In some states, courts are not prepared to handle bypass hearings, and if a young women calls to inquire about her right to a hearing or the court process, she is likely to be given inaccurate information. Some courts also refuse to hear these cases or have made it known that any petition that is heard will be denied.[90]

In other states, minors face an array of idiosyncratic requirements that are intended to make the process more burdensome, dissuade minors from abortion, or make it more difficult to obtain consent. For example, in Arizona, rather than the "preponderance of the evidence" standard that is typically used in civil cases, a young woman must introduce "clear and convincing" evidence of her maturity.[91] In Alabama, a young woman may have to endure the presence of a "pro-life" guardian ad litem (GAL) whom the judge has appointed to represent the interests of the fetus[92] or receive counseling from a "pro-life" group, known as "Sav-A-Life," in order to be granted consent; she may even be subjected to both requirements.[93]

In either situation, the process may be infused with religious indictments of abortion. In one hearing, which lasted nearly four hours, the GAL, who elected to name the fetus "Ashley," asked the young woman "whether she was familiar with a quote in which God says to the prophet Jeremiah: 'Before I formed you in the womb I knew you,' " and upon learning that the minor believed abortion was a sin, the GAL inquired of her, "You are aware that God instructed you not to kill your own baby, but you want to do it anyway? . . . you want to interfere with God's plan for your baby?"[94] This did not seem to trouble the judge, who, although allowing the petition, saw fit to mention in the order that his decision was certainly "not in the best interest of the unborn child" and that "what we call life is but a brief passage in eternity. There must be a special providence for the unborn who not only are deprived of the opportunity to live but of the opportunity of having a saving faith in spite of the sin whose commission is the natural inheritance of man."[95]

In other states, petitions are routinely denied. Moreover, because the concepts of "maturity" and "best interest" are relatively indeterminate and subjective, it can be hard for a young woman to determine in advance whether she is likely to be given consent. The following examples illustrate the indeterminacy of the bypass process.

In Ohio, the state's high court upheld the denial of consent to a 17-year-old senior in high school who was planning to attend college. She also worked 20 to 25 hours per week; paid for her car, telephone, and medical expenses; was active in team sports; and maintained a B average. But the court found that she was not mature enough to give consent because this was the second abortion she had sought within a 12-month period, after having had sexual intercourse with two different men. Moreover, she apparently had discontinued her use of birth control.[96] The court also concluded that it could not determine that "parental notification would not be in her best interest," despite the fact that on at least two occasions, her father had hit her hard enough to leave bruises on her body.[97]

In Texas, a trial court denied the abortion petition of an almost-18-year-old young woman because she failed to "understand the intrinsic benefits of keeping the child or adoption," despite the fact that she worked with children as a volunteer, had taken a parenting class in high school, and had read books about and done internet research on the alternatives to abortion.[98] In addition, on two separate occasions, she had spoken for more than an hour and a half with counselors who had carefully reviewed all of the options with her and had talked to with several women who had also faced unplanned pregnancies. Fortunately, the decision was reversed on appeal, based on the court's determination that the minor did understand "the alternatives to abortion as they apply to her and . . . has thoughtfully considered their implications," although a dissenting justice argued that the denial should have been upheld because she failed to consult with anyone who was opposed to abortion.[99]

In the last case under consideration, a judge in Alabama denied consent to a 17-year-old minor who was a straight A student and involved in extracurricular activates. She planned to attend college in the fall, which was why she did not want to have the baby, and had been awarded two scholarships. She also had a part-time job and was saving her money to help with college costs. In addition to speaking with her boyfriend about the abortion, she had spoken with nurses both at Planned Parenthood and at two medical clinics, with a woman from a local health department, with a family friend in her late thirties, and with the friend's sister-in-law, who had previously terminated a pregnancy. She understood the abortion procedure as well as the alternatives to abortion. At the hearing she testified that she understood she "would receive counseling immediately before the procedure, and that counseling also would be available at any time after the procedure. . . . [and] that she would do whatever was necessary if she had any complications.[100]

However, the trial judge determined that she was not sufficiently mature to give consent because she had not spoken with a physician about the abortion, since the clinic had denied her request to do so in advance of the procedure:

> Petitioner has been denied the opportunity to engage in pre-op counseling with the physician, evaluate the physician, or interview and question the

physician. Likewise, the physician hasn't evaluated petitioner or furnished information to petitioner[,] so the court finds the petitioner is not mature or well-informed and that abortion at this time . . . is contra to her best interests.[101]

Despite the fact that she had spoken with several adults, including reproductive health care professionals, understood both the alternatives to abortion and the abortion procedure, and was yet to receive further counseling, Alabama's Supreme Court upheld the denial on the grounds that it was neither "plainly erroneous or manifestly unjust."[102]

The young women I spoke with are not alone in questioning the value of a system that places such great authority over their lives in the hands of a complete stranger and that does not appear to enhance the quality of their decision-making. According to one Massachusetts judge, who is personally opposed to abortion, the law is "utterly preposterous. The court is a pure rubber stamp. All the law does is to harass kids. It sets up a barrier to abortion." Similarly, a judge from Rhode Island commented, "The law is a vehicle for making abortion more difficult for minors to obtain. That is all it is."[103]

Given that most young women are clear about their decision by the time they appear before the judge, court looms like an obstacle that must be surmounted rather than a constructive process that contributes positively to either the decisional process or its outcome. If the court option does not serve a channeling function by directing young women who otherwise might not have turned to them to their parents or does not enhance the quality of the decision-making process, it is hard to justify the burden it imposes on young women, particularly in light of the fact that teens who choose not confide in their parents generally do so for reasons that are well-rooted in the multilayered realities of their lives.

7

Child or Adult? The Indeterminate Legal Status of Adolescents

At the heart of this book has been an inquiry into whether young women who are facing an unplanned pregnancy should be treated as legal adults, or whether the realities of youth disqualify them from this status and the autonomy that attaches to it. In addressing this issue, considerable attention has been paid to research, including the interviews with the young women from Massachusetts, which supports the view that young women should be treated as adults because they are capable of making an informed choice about whether they wish to carry their pregnancy to term. This work also responds to the *Bellotti* Court's reliance upon differences between adult and adolescent women as an acceptable justification for state laws that limit the reproductive rights of young women, which, as exemplified by the Court's invalidation of spousal-involvement requirements, would be unconstitutional if imposed upon adult women.

At the same time, the book has raised the question of whether the focus on capacity really addresses the animating concerns of the *Bellotti* Court, in light of the Court's abject failure to address the differential legal treatment of young women based on their intended pregnancy outcome. As discussed in chapter 3, this failure calls into doubt the sincerity of the Court's focus on developmental differences between adults and minors as the justification for limiting the abortion rights of minors, instead suggesting that the decision reflects the Court's increasing willingness to allow states to limit the rights of young women based upon concerns about the moral and religious implications of the abortion decision.

If *Bellotti* is understood as signaling a shift in the Court's thinking about abortion, its acceptance of this differential treatment of pregnant teens who seek to terminate a pregnancy and those who wish to carry to term makes more sense. If the Court, rather than focusing on abortion as a medical procedure, as it did on *Roe*, is now vesting abortion with moral and religious meaning, the animating impulse behind the decision may well have been to make abortions more difficult to obtain rather than to shield minors from the consequences of their immaturity. As we have seen, this "consequentialist" reading of *Bellotti* (meaning that the outcome is a consequence of an unstated agenda) is born out by the Court's opinion in *Planned Parenthood of Southeastern Pennsylvania v. Casey*,[1] in which the Court asserts that "there are philosophical and social arguments of great weight that can be brought to bear in favor of continuing the pregnancy to full term," thus giving states the green light to enact laws that evince a "profound respect for the life of the unborn."[2]

Having arrived at this understanding of *Bellotti*, I felt quite certain that this consequentialist reading was the best way to make sense out of the decision. Confident in my critical view of the Court's approach to the abortion rights of minors, I nonetheless found myself bothered by a nagging doubt, which was triggered by my uneasiness over the growing push to treat juvenile offenders as adults.

With some smugness, I had always thought it ironic that the "conservative" forces who are fueling this transformation are also likely to support parental-involvement laws. As Donald Beschle succinctly writes, "The stereotypical conservative will call for full application of adult penalties to adolescent criminals, but will deny the right of teenagers to make decisions in a wide variety of contexts, presumably on the grounds that one so young cannot be fully capable of making such significant choices."[3] Seen from a consequentialist position, "The conservative values both a low incidence of youth crime and a strict adherence to traditional morality, and chooses a set of positions to bring about both ends."[4] How inconsistent, I thought. This shifting view of adolescent capacity is clearly calculated to achieve desired social outcomes—thwarting youth crime and limiting a woman's right of reproductive choice—and has nothing to do with the actual reality of teens who either have committed a crime or are confronting an unintended pregnancy.

However, this is where the nagging doubt enters. Without fully being able to explain why, something inside of me recoils at the thought of a 15-year-old being treated in the same manner as an adult who has committed a similar wrongful act. Hence, my quandary. Am I no different from the conservative who argues for treating minors who commit crimes as adults but who would deny them this status when it comes to reproductive decision-making? Is it possible that I believe that minors facing an unintended pregnancy should be treated as adults because I support the right of choice, while I reject this status when they commit crimes because I am uneasy with the retributive "just desserts" approach to crime? Beschle addresses this seeming inconsistency as well: "The stereotypical liberal calls for expanded recognition of adolescents' rights in a wide range of civil contests, while defending a juvenile justice system that is based on the premise that an adolescent's choice to commit a crime is rendered less culpable because of the adolescent's age."[5]

The question I was thus forced to confront is whether there is a principled way to reconcile these "liberal" perspectives.[6] Can one seek to shift the boundary of adulthood downward when it comes to reproductive rights while simultaneously decrying the trend toward treating adolescents who commit crimes like adults, without falling into the consequentialist trap? Is there a principled way to reconcile these seemingly conflicting views of adolescence? These questions are the focus of this chapter. To answer them, we begin with a conceptual framework within which to situate this comparative inquiry, and we then look at the historical development of the juvenile court system.

SHIFTING BOUNDARIES

The age of majority is weighted with tremendous symbolic and practical importance. It cleaves the world of legal rights and responsibilities into two dichotomous realms—the dependent realm of childhood and the self-governing realm of adulthood. Upon turning 18, one crosses over from one side of this divide to the other.[7] In the space of a literal moment, one is transformed from a legally incompetent "infant" into a fully competent legal person.

If a single moment in time creates the two legally significant age-based categories of child and adult, an obvious question is, where in this binary classification do adolescents fit? Although "most experts in developmental psychology agree that the period between twelve and seventeen occupies a crucial place in contemporary human development,"[8] this reality is not reflected in the law. There is no formal legal counterpart to the developmental construct of adolescence. There is no fixed intermediate legal stage between the worlds of childhood dependence and adulthood autonomy through which adolescents progress in a predictable and sequential manner to shed the limitations of childhood and incrementally assume the rights of adulthood. Rather, for the most part, adolescents have been incorporated into the legal world of childhood.

Although there is a fixed age-based divide that cuts the life cycle into two wide swaths, it is nonetheless incorrect to conclude that the law makes no allowances for the developmental advances of the teen years. First, as we have seen, in a number of cases involving the rights of teens, the Supreme Court has made clear that teens, although not the legal equivalent of adults, do possess constitutional rights—that rights do not "mature and come into being magically only when one attains the state defined age of majority."[9]

Second, one need only to think of the automobile to realize that the law is cognizant of the changes that come with adolescence, as teens in most states can obtain a driver's license at the age of 16, although they may be subject to limitations that are not imposed on adults. Teens also have the right to make certain medical decisions. Depending upon the state, they can make the decision to leave school or put a baby up for adoption. They can work and are generally given a greater say in custody disputes between their parents. However, as Elizabeth Scott explains, rather than representing the creation of a third legal category, these variations represent the shifting of the boundary between childhood and adulthood for designated purposes.[10] With a shifting of the boundary, adult-like rights can be extended to teens without disruption of the binary classification system.[11] In effect, this means that childhood ends at different ages in different contexts.

A critical question in this regard is, how are these boundary shifts determined? What considerations influence whether, in a particular context, adolescents remain on the child side of the age-divide, or whether the boundary shifts downward in order to provide them with adult-like rights? Do lawmakers ground the shifts in developmental facts? Are they grounded in policy considerations? Or perhaps, as Scott suggests, it is some combination of the two, reflecting "both the public interest and the interest of adolescents."[12] Another possibility is that the shifts are consequentialist in nature, reflecting agendas that have little to do with the reality of adolescent life.

To play out these out these alternatives, imagine for a moment a public debate over the issue the Court faced in the case of *Tinker v. Des Moines*[13]—whether junior high and high school principals could suspend students for wearing black arm bands to protest U.S. involvement in the Vietnam War, or whether the students' actions were a protected form of free speech. To resolve this, one might take a developmental approach and ask whether young teens have the capacity to develop cogent views on complex policy issues, thus entitling their speech (in this case, their symbolic speech) to First Amendment protection. Or one might focus on related policy considerations, such as that this kind of behavior should not be tolerated because the proper function of schools is to "make us a more law-abiding people . . . and that school discipline, like parental discipline, is an integral and important part of training our young people to be good citizens—to be better citizens."[14] From a consequentialist perspective, an individual's position on the issue would be informed by his or her views on the war effort rather than by an understanding of adolescent capacities or of the place of schools in public life. Accordingly, support for the principal's position would flow from approval of the war effort, whereas support of the student's right to wear armbands would signal the opposite view.[15]

This concept of boundary-shifting gives us a framework for thinking about whether there are valid differences between the reproductive rights and the criminal domain that would justify setting the boundary between childhood and adulthood at different places on the age continuum. Before tackling this question, we look at the evolving legal status of the juvenile offender, with a focus on the recent "get tough" approach.

REHABILITATION OR RETRIBUTION? ADOLESCENTS IN THE CRIMINAL JUSTICE SYSTEM

As we have seen, when it comes to abortion, the prevailing legal view is that minors should not be treated as adults with comparable rights of reproductive self-determination. With *Bellotti* as the legal mooring, lawmakers in most states have enacted parental-involvement laws that limit the ability of young women to decide for themselves that they are not yet ready for motherhood. However, when it comes to juvenile offenders, the picture is quite different. Over the course of the past 30 or so years, as the public has become increasingly concerned about youth violence, there has been a "convergence between juvenile and criminal courts [that] eliminates virtually all of the differences in strategies of social control between youth and adults."[16] Central to this convergence, the historic emphasis on rehabilitation has been eclipsed by the spirit of retribution.

The Emergence of the Juvenile Court

With the passage of the Juvenile Court Act in 1899, the state of Illinois established the nation's first juvenile court system, and within 20 years all but three states had created a juvenile court system patterned after the Illinois model. Prior to the development of separate juvenile courts, children charged with wrongdoing had been tried in the adult criminal courts. Under the common law, "rule of sevens," there had been a sliding scale of criminal culpability. Children under the age of seven were presumed incapable of forming a criminal intent and thus were not regarded as criminally responsible for their actions. Children between the ages of 7 and 14 were governed by a rebuttable presumption of incapacity, and at age 14, a minor was deemed to have the same capacity as an adult. Accordingly, children as young as seven were potentially "subjected to arrest, trial, and in theory to punishment like adult offenders."[17]

The juvenile court system was a product of the Progressive Era reform movement, which emerged at the turn of the century to address the social and economic dislocations spawned by industrialization and urbanization. This movement,

> was composed primarily of middle-class men and women who attempted to address the array of social problems that accompanied rapid urban growth and industrialization, including poverty, crime, [and] disease . . . Progressive reformers . . . used the techniques of empirical research and sociological investigation to study the ills that afflicted American society. . . . They did not see poverty and unemployment as the result of individual moral failings . . . but rather as the result of environmental forces over which the poor had little control. . . . These reformers . . . called on the state to intervene in social and economic relations in order to protect the common good . . . They created bureaucracies and commissions to manage social problems and relied on trained experts to develop and administer policies.[18]

As discussed in chapter 2, reformers increasingly emphasized the vulnerability of youth and sought to enact reforms that would create a separate realm for children and thus protect them from the harsh adult realities. Reformers launched initiatives that "were intended to structure child development and to control and mold children while protecting them from exploitation."[19] Appalled by the fact that children "could be given long prison sentences and mixed in jails with hardened criminals,"[20] reformed pushed for the creation of the juvenile court system as a centerpiece of their child-focused innovations.

This new system reflected the belief of the reformers that crime was the product of environmental forces, which for children usually meant their home environment and neglectful parents (or perhaps, more accurately, neglectful mothers), rather than an expression of free will. Progressive reformers believed in the "Rehabilitative Ideal."[21] Accordingly, if a child was brought before a judge, the focus was not to be on determining whether the child had committed a wrongful act, but instead on how to rescue him or her from a life of crime.

Children were to be "treated" and "rehabilitated" rather than found guilty and punished, and this required a flexible and informal approach: the proceedings were characterized as civil rather than criminal in nature, and the formal rules of criminal procedure were discarded. So that they could direct their attention to "the child and the child's character and lifestyle rather than on the crime,"[22] judges were vested with virtually unfettered discretion. This discretion also enabled them to craft a dispositional outcome that was carefully tailored to meet the "real" needs of the child before the court.[23]

The Downside of Informality: *In re Gault* and Procedural Reform

In 1967 the Supreme Court issued a landmark ruling that helped set the stage, although perhaps inadvertently, for a dramatic reconceptualization of the juvenile offender. Fifteen-year-old Gerald Gault was adjudged delinquent and committed to a state industrial school until he turned 21 (the age of majority at the time) for making "lewd" telephone calls to a neighbor. Had Gerald been an adult, the maximum punishment he could have received would have been a 5- to 50-dollar fine and imprisonment in jail for no more than two months. In reviewing the case, the Court was troubled by the dispositional outcome as well as by the informal nature of the proceedings. For example, Gerald was not given adequate notice of the charges against him; neither he nor his parents were informed of his right to a lawyer; and his "admission" was obtained without his being informed of his right to remain silent.

These concerns prompted the Court to take a searching look at the juvenile court system. In tracing the system's historic development, the Court concluded that the juvenile court system had failed to live up to its rehabilitative ideal:

> Juvenile Court history has again demonstrated that unbridled discretion, however benevolently motivated, is frequently a poor substitute for principle and procedure. . . . The absence of substantive standards has not necessarily meant that children receive careful, compassionate, individualized treatment. The absence of procedural rules based upon constitutional principle has not always produced fair, efficient, and effective procedures. Departures from established principles of due process have frequently resulted . . . in arbitrariness.[24]

To address these concerns, the Court held that the "fundamental fairness" requirement of the due process clause applies to juvenile court proceedings and that juvenile are thus entitled to many of the same procedural rights as adults, such as notice of the charges against them, the appointment of counsel, and the privilege against self-incrimination. However, the Court also made clear that it still believed in the rehabilitative mission of the juvenile court system and that it was not seeking to eliminate all of the distinctions between juvenile and adult criminal court proceedings.

Following *Gault*, the Court extended other procedural safeguards to juvenile proceedings, such as that guilt must be established beyond a reasonable doubt[25] and that teens cannot be put at risk of double jeopardy. [26] However, the Court continued to reiterate its continued support for the juvenile court's rehabilitative purpose:

> The juvenile concept held high promise. We are reluctant to say that, despite disappointments of grave dimensions, it still does not hold promise, and we are particularly reluctant to say . . . that the system cannot accomplish its rehabilitative goals.[27]

Accordingly, although seeking to introduce "procedural orderliness into the juvenile court system," the Court made clear that it was not ruling that "all rights constitutionally assured for the adult accused are to be imposed upon the state juvenile proceedings."[28] Significantly, it declined to extend to juveniles the right to a trial by jury, stating that this would "remake the juvenile proceeding into a fully adversary process and [would] put an effective end to what has been the idealistic prospect of an intimate, informal protective proceeding."[29]

In retrospect, this post-*Gault* period can best be understood as a transitional time between the more optimistic vision of the Progressive Era reformers and the contemporary emphasis on the unredeemable nature of the juvenile "superpredator." In this intermediate period, "policymakers grappled with the challenge of constructing a retributive system that recognized the youth and immaturity of juvenile offenders . . . [and recognized] that adolescent criminal conduct was less culpable that that of adults.[30] During this transitional phase, teens were granted some adult-like constitutional rights but were still regarded as belonging in a separate legal category. Although, as we have seen, this dual conceptualization has remained fairly constant in the abortion context, in the juvenile arena, the push has been toward a more complete adult configuration.

From Rehabilitation to Retribution

Starting sometime in the 1980s, the growing public perception that juvenile behavior was out of control and that the rehabilitative approach had failed spawned a "get tough" attitude toward juvenile crime.[31] Reflecting this increased anxiety, a 1993 Gallup poll reported that 73 percent of respondents favored trying violent juveniles as adults.[32] Although perhaps representing the far end of this perspective, the following passage from a 1985 article in *Policy Review* nonetheless captures the changing sentiment:

> Liberals argue that crime results from such things as inadequate education, economic deprivation, and low self-esteem. Consequently they favor early

intervention government programs aimed at preschoolers, government-initiated job opportunities, and treatment-oriented responses for young criminals.

Conservatives, on the other hand, argue that crime results from a lack of moral self-restraint. The absence of such restraint ordinarily follows from the absence of nurturing parental care. Families and government are not interchangeable . . . government must focus on what it was created to do—catch and convict lawbreakers.

The challenge for conservatives now lies in suppressing juvenile crime at the first sign of trouble . . . Government's role is to enforce the law, and it should be vigorous and purposeful in the acceptance of that duty . . .

Every step of today's juvenile justice system reflects its orientation toward treatment and rehabilitation and away from accountability and punishment. . . .

The juvenile justice system must become a tough criminal justice system for young lawbreakers. Three principles must guide its reform. First, the gap between law breaking and accountability must be significantly narrowed . . . Second, violent crimes must be punished with appropriate penalties . . . Third, there must be sanctions for every crime.[33]

Although not expressly stating that distinctions between minors and adults should be eliminated, this perspective on youth crime clearly rejects a dual system of justice premised on the assumption that youthful offenders are less culpable than their adult counterparts due to developmental differences.

Reflecting these changing views, during the last two decades of the twentieth century, most states enacted laws making it easier to prosecute juveniles in the adult criminal court system. Some of these laws exclude certain categories of juveniles from the jurisdictional authority of the juvenile courts based upon age or the severity of the crime or a combination of the two. Others make it easier to transfer minors from the juvenile to the adult criminal court system based on the nature of the offense, without requiring an individualized assessment to determine the appropriateness of the transfer, which in the past had typically required a showing that the minor was not "amenable to rehabilitation."[34]

The other main avenue of change has been to shift the dispositional approach away from rehabilitation towards retribution. Rather than focusing on the needs of the juvenile offender, a retributive approach is based on the assumption that "the criminal should be hurt, and that the injury caused by the criminal offense calls for a like infliction of injury on the criminal as a moral penalty."[35] Put another way, retribution "relies on the more general principle that justice prevails when people get what they deserve,"[36] regardless of whether the punishment serves any useful social function. With this shift, the penalties that juveniles remaining in the juvenile system are subject to have increased and, in some cases, now extend into adulthood, rather than ending at the historic cut-off age of 17 or 18.[37]

These changes suggest that the concern voiced by the Court—that with reform, there was a danger that the positive aspects of the individualized, rehabilitative nature of juvenile court proceedings might be lost—has been realized. Although initially the extension of adult-like rights to juvenile offenders was intended to ensure that they were not subject to unfair and arbitrary proceedings, reforms have gone well beyond that point, such that "juveniles who have barely reached adolescence can be tried as adults, and incarcerated in adult prisons."[38] As was true prior to the reforms of the Progressive Era, once again, juvenile offenders are becoming "indistinguishable from adults."[39]

CHILD OR ADULT? IT ALL DEPENDS, OR CONTEXT MATTERS

Having considered the legal status of juvenile offenders, we return to the question that lies at the heart of this chapter—whether one can support a different approach in the two domains without falling into the "cognitive dissonance" bind.[40] Of critical importance is the argument raised by many developmental experts who have studied the conduct of juvenile offenders: the assertion that juveniles should not be treated as adults because developmental differences make them less responsible for their actions. In light of these differences, subjecting them to the same treatment would violate the "core principle of penal proportionality . . . [which] holds that fair punishment is measured not only by the among of harm caused or threatened by the actor but also by his or her blameworthiness."[41]

Central to this body of work is a convincing argument that the cognitive approach is too narrow a framework within which to evaluate the decisional competency of adolescents who commit criminal acts and that in order to understand the differences between adolescents and adults, psychosocial factors must be taken into account. Assuming this is correct in the criminal context, the question becomes whether this view has any crossover implications for the abortion decision. As developed in the following discussion, it appears that the differences between the two domains support the extension of adult-like rights in the reproductive realm while supporting the preservation of historic distinctions between teens and adults in the juvenile justice realm.

The Critique of the Cognitive Approach

Although recognizing that adolescents "have the cognitive capacities for reasoning and understanding necessary for making rational choices" and that research generally supports the conclusion that there are "few, if any, differences between the cognitive processes of adults and children,"[42] the developmental theorists assert that the focus on cognition is too narrow because it minimizes the noncognitive, psychosocial variables that influence the decision-making process.[43] They suggest that it is in the realm of "judgment" rather than cognition that important differences in the decision-making ability of adults and minors are likely to be found.[44] Developmental theorists have thus called for a "framework of adolescent competence and maturity that includes not only cognitive factors such as understanding, reasoning, and appreciation, but also . . . psychosocial factors that would be irrelevant or excluded under an informed consent framework."[45]

Their work indicates that psychosocial factors are particularly influential when it comes to "decision-making by adolescents in ways that are relevant to competence to stand trial and criminal responsibility. Particularly salient in this context are factors such as (1) conformity and compliance in relation to peers, (2) attitude toward and perception of risk, and (3) temporal perspective."[46] The following passage provides an excellent summary of how these judgment factors are likely to impact the teen actor in the criminal context:

> [T]he evidence suggests that developmental factors characteristic of adolescence contribute to immature judgment in ways that seem likely to affect criminal choices . . . [P]eer conformity is a powerful influence on adolescent behavior, and may lead teens to become involved in criminal activity to avoid social rejection. It is not surprising that, in contrast to adult crime, most juvenile criminal activity takes place in groups. Adolescents also seem to perceive risks differently or less well than adults, and they are more inclined to engage in risky activities. . . . Finally, time perspective changes with maturity. As compared to adults, adolescents tend to focus more on immediate, rather than long-term, consequences.[47]

Based on these considerations, these theorists have challenged the contemporary drive to eliminate the distinctions between juvenile and adult offenders. At the same time, they have avoided calling for a return to the Progressive Era model, which essentially absolved adolescents of any criminal culpability:

> Developmental differences affecting decision-making are likely to be substantial enough to provide categorical excuse from responsibility for only the very young juveniles . . . A categorical presumption of adolescent nonresponsibility, such as that which was endorsed by the traditional juvenile justice system, is hard to defend on grounds of immaturity alone . . .

On the other hand, the perspective on adolescent criminal conduct offered by developmental psychology also challenge the retributive arguments of modern advocates of punitive policies. . . . The evidence disputes the conclusion that most delinquents are indistinguishable from adults in any way that is relevant to culpability.[48]

In rejecting both the categorical exoneration of adolescents based upon their immaturity and the "just desserts" model of adult retribution, the suggested approach is that youthfulness be taken into account as a "mitigating factor." This approach would place "the culpability of a guilty actor somewhere on a continuum of criminal culpability, and, by extension, a continuum of punishment."[49]

Abortion and the Cognitive Approach to Decision-Making

In questioning the appropriateness of the cognitive approach for evaluating the capacities of adolescents in the criminal context, developmental theorists point out that the emphasis on cognition is due to the "early attention to medical decision-making and the standard of informed consent . . . [a]ccording to [which], consent for medical treatment must be made knowingly, competently, and voluntarily."[50] Rooted in the medical realm, this approach does not, therefore, take into account the kinds of noncognitive factors that, as discussed previously, contribute to age-related differences with respect to participation in criminal behavior.

In contrast, the cognitive approach is well-suited for the abortion decision, since, as the *Roe* Court recognized, abortion is "inherently, and primarily, a medical decision,"[51] and although the *Bellotti* Court may have invested abortion with other meanings as a way of justifying the imposition of limitations on young women, the fundamental nature of the decision remains unaltered—it is a medical decision that is realized in a medical setting. Thus, it is very much the kind of decision that research has shown minors are able to make in an adult-like manner.

Reinforcing the appropriateness of the cognitive approach, it is important to recognize that almost all minors involve at least one responsible adult in the decision-making process[52] who can provide information and advice that can be incorporated into the decisional matrix. Moreover, before an abortion is performed, a teen, like any woman, receives counseling about both the abortion procedure and the available alternatives. She thus receives information from a knowledgeable professional in a structured setting, which gives her the opportunity to reflect on her decision, albeit at a rather stressful moment in time.

Clearly, this decisional process bears little, if any, resemblance to the "on the street" setting in which decisions to engage in criminal activity are most likely made, often in accordance with "street codes that reward displays of physical domination and social approval for antisocial behavior."[53] Youth crimes are often "unplanned or hastily planned events, the result of a chance of coming together of motivation and opportunity."[54] As will be further developed in the next section, these contextual differences clearly make it appropriate to use different models of decision-making—one focused on cognitive variables and the other on psychosocial variables—when assessing the capabilities of adolescents in these two domains.

Abortion and Juvenile Crime: The Salient Contextual Variables

As discussed, the cognitive approach is appropriate in the abortion context because it directly relates to the ability to give informed consent. Further supporting the view that this is the appropriate standard, it is also clear that the judgment factors that are so salient in the criminal context, namely peer pressure, risk-taking, and temporal perspective, have little direct bearing on the abortion decision-making process.[55]

Peer Influence

A frequently mentioned consideration when it comes to adolescent decisional capacity is the role of peer influence, and a decision may be seen as less mature if it results from peer pressure rather than from individual choice. However, research indicates that peer pressure generally peaks by about age 14 and that, in general, it is more salient with respect to minor, rather than life-altering, decisions. Adolescence is thus marked by an increased self-reliance in decision-making abilities,[56] which, as established in chapter 5, extends generally to the medical context and more specifically to the abortion decision itself.[57]

However, the picture is quite different when it comes to participation in criminal activity since peer pressure exerts considerable influence that is far more significant for teens than it is for adults. According to expert Franklin E. Zimring,

> The ability to resist peer pressure is yet another social skill . . . not fully developed in many adolescents. A teen may know right from wrong and may even have developed the capacity to control his or her impulses while alone, but resisting temptation while alone is a different task than resisting the pressure to commit an offense when adolescent peers are pushing for misbehavior and waiting to see whether or not the outcome they desire will occur. Most adolescent decisions to break the law take place on a social

stage where the immediate pressure of peers is the real motive for teen crime. . . .

The cold criminological facts are these: the teen years are characterized by what has long been called "group offending." . . . When adults commit [crimes], they are usually acting alone.[58]

In fact, according to Zimring, "no fact of adolescent criminality is more important than what sociologists call its 'group context,' " and teens who participate in crime may be seeking to avoid being labeled a "chicken."[59] For some, "status attainment may depend . . . on manifestations of physical power or domination. . . . The continual demand for respect, coupled with limited avenues by which to attain it, sets up conflicts that often are resolved through fighting and crime, the most readily available paths to high status."[60]

For adolescents, engagement in criminal activity tends to be a very public event. Participation often reflects peer influence, and in turn the participation helps to determine a teen's place in the social order. This could not be more different from the decision-making process in the abortion context. The abortion decision tends to be a highly private one. Teens who do not involve their parents generally turn to a few carefully selected confidants, such as a boyfriend, a best friend, and a few trusted adults, but it is not a public act with social ramifications. In fact, as it emerged in the interviews, the young women were very clear that although they valued the input of those they chose as confidantes, they had a clear sense of ownership over the decision,

Thus, although peer pressure is highly relevant in the criminal context, there is no evidence to support the view that peer pressure interferes with a teen's ability to make the abortion decision, thus limiting her sense of responsibility and control over this choice. The contested stage is her own body and her desire to shape her own destiny—abortion is a self-contained decision rather than one that is played out in a highly visible manner in a teen's social universe.

Risk-Taking

It is generally believed that adolescents are more likely to engage in risky activities than are adults and that this tendency contributes to youthful participation in criminal activity (it may also, of course, contribute to participation in risky sexual behavior). There are many explanations for this developmental difference. One explanation is that adult and adolescents perceive risks differently[61]—that teens are less aware of the risks that inhere in certain courses of action, although considerable evidence indicates that in fact, "adolescents are well aware of the risks they take."[62] Another possibility is that adolescents and adults attach different weights or values to decisional variables; in particular, teens may be more likely to focus on the immediate rather than the long-term consequences of their actions.[63] The greater proclivity of teens to engage in risky behavior may also be attributable to the role of peer influence; they may participate in certain activities in order to obtain the approval of their peers or to avoid social ostracism.[64] There has also been a growing interest in looking at the possible links between adolescent brain development and risk-taking behavior, with some scientists now suggesting that the portion of the brain that regulates impulsivity is one of the last to develop."[65]

When it comes to abortion, there is no indication that risk-taking proclivities have any relevance. In fact, by its very nature, the abortion decision is rooted in "conservative" impulses. In electing not to plunge into the unknown world of motherhood, young women are seeking to protect their current lives as well as to exert control over their futures. They may also be seeking to protect family relationships from the disruption of disclosure and the dislocations that would come in the wake of a decision to have a child. The abortion decision can thus be viewed as a form of risk-avoidance, as an expression of a young woman's desire to safeguard her life, her family, and her future from disruption. Like peer influence, the developmental factor of risk-taking appears to be irrelevant in the abortion context, in contrast to the criminal arena, where it tends to shape youthful involvement in very powerful ways.

Future-Time Perspective

As we saw in chapter 5, children tend to be present-oriented in their thinking, and an important developmental gain that occurs during adolescence is the acquisition of a future-time perspective, the "ability to project events to more distant points in the future":[66]

> One aspect of the transition from concrete to abstract reasoning is the understanding of time as an abstraction and the development of a personal sense of future. One is not born with a notion of time; rather it develops from early childhood. . . . It is late in childhood and throughout adolescence that one begins to understand time as an abstract concept which we artificially structure through seconds, minutes, hours and days. Not only is time understood as an abstract concept, but the teenager begins to perceive herself as a being who will live in the future as well as in the present and past. The child and early adolescent rooted in the present is unable to conceptualize, let alone plan for the future.[67]

Once oriented to the future, an individual is more likely to consider the long-term consequences of a decision.

A person is also more likely to consider the future consequences of his or her actions if he or she has some sense of hope and vision for the future; otherwise, there is little to consider. Often lacking meaningful options, juvenile offenders may be particularly inclined to disregard the future implications of their actions, since their ability to locate themselves in the future is "inhibited by the realities of adolescence in modern urban culture . . . Many delinquents develop a sense of 'futurelessness' and fatalism, engendered by their inability . . . to escape neighborhoods in which violent death is a daily occurrence and incarceration is considered a relative routine life event."[68] Where the future holds little promise, the immediate gains of participation in criminal activity (such as easy money) may overtake consideration of the "the long-term costs . . . of conviction of a serious crime."[69]

As we have seen, the desire to safeguard the future is often a significant factor in the abortion decision. As a group, "girls who are doing well in school before the pregnancy and who have a strong future orientation are more likely to choose abortion to resolve an unintended pregnancy than those who are not good students and lack high educational and vocational goals."[70] Again emphasizing this future orientation, Kristen Lucker writes,

> The more successful a young women is—*and more important, expects to be*—the more likely she is to obtain an abortion. . . . Even among young women from disadvantaged backgrounds, those who are doing well in school, who are getting better grades, and who aspire to higher education for themselves are more likely to seek an abortion that their more discouraged peers.[71]

In contrast, teens who choose motherhood are thought to be less likely to weigh the impact of their decision on the future, since their options tend to be more circumscribed and vulnerable to disruption. In short, for teens without future possibilities "that are both attainable and worth attaining motherhood, may be the best alternative available . . . [and] there is little impetus to defer it to a later age even if one has the cognitive capability to do so."[72]

Thus, once again, we see how a key developmental variable plays out quite differently in the two domains. When it comes to abortion, the decision generally embodies a careful consideration of the future and a desire not to take chances with what it holds. In contrast, teens who engage in criminal actions may lack "future possibilities that are both attainable and worth attaining" and thus have little motivation to consider the ways in which their actions might alter their life course.

Distinguishing Characteristics of the Juvenile Population

In comparing the decision-making of teens facing unplanned pregnancies and those who are engaged in criminal activity, another critical distinguishing factor must be taken into account: juvenile offenders are far more likely than other adolescents to be suffering from mental disorders. Research has documented the "high rates of mental disorder, including substance abuse disorders and multiple co-occurring diagnoses, among children incarcerated in juvenile facilities,"[73] and almost 80 percent of delinquent youth present with at least one mental disorder—a rate that is approximately four times higher than the rate in the non-delinquent population.[74]

These findings have important implications. First, as a general matter, mental illness is a risk factor for participation in criminal activity.[75] Second, mental disorders can interfere with the developmental process, which means that the decision-making abilities of juvenile offenders are likely to be less well-developed than the decision-making abilities of other adolescents of the same age.[76] Illustrating this developmental gap, when compared to non-offender adolescents, those engaged in criminal activity were less likely to have developed an abstract understanding of a right as "an entitlement guaranteed by social agreement."[77] Also relevant is the fact that when juvenile offenders are compared to adult offenders, the presence of mental disorders appears to have a greater impact on the capabilities of teens.[78]

These differences lend further support to the view that a different legal approach is warranted when it comes to the abortion decision and the treatment of juvenile offenders. Not only is the decision-making ability of teens who are engaged in criminal activity more likely to be compromised by the impact of psychosocial factors, but their baseline capacity is also more likely to be diminished by the presence of a mental impairment. Moreover, if a teen seeking to abort was suffering from a mental disorder, it is hard to imagine how one could argue that her decision to not become a mother was the outcome of an impaired decisional process rather than of a realistic appraisal of her life circumstances.

CHILD OR ADULT? A PRINCIPLED APPROACH TO BOUNDARY SHIFTING

Returning to the concern that prompted this chapter—whether there is a principled way to argue for shifting the boundary between childhood and adulthood downward in the abortion context, while arguing that a distinction should be retained between teens and adults in the criminal context—it is clear that important differences between these two domains justify distinct approaches.

A young woman facing an unintended pregnancy does not stand in the same shoes as an adolescent considering participation in criminal activity.

The impulses, the pressures, and the structures within which these choices are made influence the decisional process in very different ways. Generally, the abortion decision is made in a quiet, reflective way. Teens are able to draw upon the support of others, but the decision remains fairly private in nature. It does not have public ramifications and does not define her place in her community. Conservative in nature, the abortion decision embodies a desire to safeguard that which the teen holds dear, including existing relationships and plans for the future. In contrast, participation in criminal activity is not usually the result of a thoughtful decisional process. It tends to be an impulsive act, often undertaken in response to peer pressure. Far less private in nature, the decision may determine a teen's place and status in his or her community. It may also represent the reality that there is little to risk.

In light of these differences, it is actually the demand for parallel treatment that creates the "cognitive dissonance." To disregard these differences in the name of consistency would, in fact, lead to an inconsistency in results, either overvaluing the abilities of teens in the criminal context or undervaluing their abilities relative to the abortion decision. Respect for the transitional nature of the teen years requires a domain-sensitive approach that takes the developmental process into careful consideration, rather than insisting upon than a simplistic line-drawing approach that disregards these realities.

Conclusion

As explored in this book, there are serious flaws with the Court's approach to the abortion rights of minors. At first glance, the judicial-bypass "solution" that the Court offers in *Bellotti* to the autonomy-versus-dependence dilemma appears to be a well-crafted compromise that recognizes that young women have a foot on each side of the great divide that separates the legal worlds of children and adults. However, this approach fails to account for the complexity of teens' lives and their decision-making abilities.

Young women are able to reason in thoughtful and informed ways about why motherhood is not an appropriate option for them at a particular moment in their lives. Whether seeking to protect the integrity of their teen years, safeguarding their plans for the future, or considering the well-being of the prospective child, they are able to grasp the enormity of what it means to bring another life into this world. Likewise, whether seeking to protect themselves from parental abuse, protect the relationship they have with their parents, or protect their parents from additional stress, young women have well-grounded reasons for not involving their parents in the abortion decision, reasons that reflect both the circumstances of their lives and the complex dynamics of their families.

These considerations take on even more weight when the limited abortion rights of minors are compared to the significant self-consent rights that they possess in the medical realm. Most importantly, as a general rule, a pregnant teenager who wishes to carry her pregnancy to term may elect to do so without having to discuss this decision with an adult. Not only is this decision hers alone to make, but also, she is likely to be vested with full authority over her pregnancy-related care and, once a mother, then over the care of her child. If she instead chooses to relinquish her child for adoption, she can do so in most states without the consent of her parents. And broadening our focus to include the criminal justice arena, we have seen how states are increasingly demanding that juvenile offenders be processed and punished like adults, based on the view that they are as accountable for their actions as adults are.

We are then left to face the reality that running underneath the Court's expressed concern for the vulnerability of young women and the supportive role of parents is a strong antiabortion sentiment. One senses, tucked into discussions about the procedural requirements of bypass laws, the Court's fear that a young women might make a decision that is at odds with her parents' moral and religious view of abortion. It is here that the bypass compromise comes to makes more sense, and we can see why the Court stopped short of declaring that *Roe's* promise of decisional privacy is broad enough to include young women in its embrace. Left to her own devices, a young woman might not fully appreciate the "origins of the human life that lies within the embryo," which apparently is a far weightier concern than what it means to become a mother. A teen's own "destiny and personal dignity" thus does not translate into decisional autonomy because her right to self-determination must be balanced against the interests of potential life—an interest that the state may seek to protect through the intermediary of a young woman's parents.

Despite the fact that parental-involvement laws have been subject to considerable criticism, in various arenas, they appear to enjoy a great deal of public support. There is also no indication that the Court is going to move away from its belief in their constitutionality; in fact, a growing concern is that if there are any changes, they are likely to be in the direction of further limitations rather than greater autonomy.

Accordingly, although it remains important to challenge these laws, other approaches must also be considered that, although not as respectful of adolescent reproductive autonomy, would provide young women with more flexibility than is available under the prevailing paradigm. In fact, a number of states have enacted laws to expand the pool of adults that young women who cannot involve their parents may turn to in lieu of having to seek judicial authorization for an abortion.[1] These laws fall into two broad categories: some allow for the involvement of specified family members, and others allow for the involvement of designated professionals (with a few states employing a hybrid approach) as an alternative to seeking judicial authorization.

The adult-relative alternative permits designated family members to receive notice of or grant consent to the abortion in lieu of a bypass hearing. Some laws authorize the involvement of a fairly broad pool of relatives, and others limit it to grandparents. The states that have carved out a formal role for professionals generally give that person (most commonly a doctor or mental health professional) decision-making authority. Thus, she or he is authorized to waive the parental-notice or parental-consent requirement based on a determination that the minor is mature or that notice would not be in her best interest, in lieu of seeking a waiver from the court. In effect, a designated professional substitutes for a judge as the arbiter of maturity or best interest. In some states, the professional cannot be affiliated with a facility that performs abortions or, more narrowly, with the facility where the minor is planning to have her abortion.

Connecticut has taken a different approach. It does not have a parental-involvement requirement (thus obviating the need for judicial-bypass hearings, since there is nothing to bypass.) Instead, the law requires that all minors receive adequate counseling and information from either a counselor or a physician (the physician may be the one who is performing the abortion). The counseling must be done in an objective, noncoercive manner and must explore all pregnancy options and the possibility of parental involvement.

RECOMMENDATIONS

Although the preferred policy-recommendation is to allow young women to decide for themselves whether or not they are ready for motherhood, other recommendations are included along the lines suggested previously. Expanding options for young women who cannot turn to their parents at this stressful time in their lives reduces the burden of the court process while also formalizing the kinds of meaningful adult engagement that most young women already avail themselves of.

In reviewing these recommendations, it is important to keep several considerations in mind. First, remember that young women can decide to become mothers without adult involvement. Second, although states may require adult involvement in the abortion decision, they cannot mandate that the adult be a parent—the constitutionally required bypass option already permits "alternative" adult involvement. Third, if the focus of these laws is truly to enhance the decision-making of minors, utilization of trusted and knowledgeable adults is a more appropriate option than forcing minors into the legal system, a process that is burdensome, frightening, and of no demonstrable benefit. The following recommendations begin with the least burdensome alternative and proceed accordingly.

1. Counseling Requirement: As an alternative to a parental-involvement or judicial-bypass provision, minor abortion laws could contain a counseling requirement, such as the one found in the Connecticut statute. Any such statute should specify that the counseling be nondirective, include a discussion of all pregnancy options, and encourage the possibility of parental involvement. To minimize any potential burden of this requirement, the law should not prohibit professionals who are from the facility performing the abortion from doing the counseling.

2. Expanded Pool of "Alternative Adults": If a law is to contain a parental-involvement requirement, it should expand the pool of "alternative adults" whom minors may involve in lieu of seeking court authorization to include both professionals and adult relatives. Each category should be as inclusive as possible, and no restrictions or preconditions (such as that the minor demonstrate fear of parental abuse or that the professional not be affiliated with the abortion provider) should be imposed on a minor's ability to involve one of these designated adults.

3. Preference for Professionals over Relatives: If a choice must be made between allowing adult relatives or professionals to constitute the pool of alternative adults, research suggest that preference should be given to professionals. However, all relevant factors need to be assessed. For example, a nonrestrictive option that includes a broad pool of adult family members may be preferable to a professional option that excludes otherwise qualified persons because they work for the facility where the abortion is to be performed.

4. Nature of Professional Involvement: With respect to professional involvement, a counseling role is preferable to a decision-making role, since this would provide guidance to the minor while allowing her the ultimate authority over the decision.

5. Retention of Judicial Bypass: Judicial bypass should remain an option for those minors who lack a relationship with or access to an alternative adult.

Although not providing minors who choose abortion with the decisional rights of either minors who choose childbirth or adult women who make either reproductive choice, these alternatives seek to provide young women with options that more closely correspond with their preferred patterns of interaction when seeking to terminate a pregnancy without parental involvement.

Notes

PREFACE

1. Kristen Luker, *Abortion & the Politics of Motherhood*, p. 194 (1984).

CHAPTER 1

1. *Roe v. Wade*, 410 U.S. 113 (1973).

2. *Id.* at 118–119.

3. Kristen Luker, *Abortion: The Politics of Motherhood*, p. 126 (1984).

4. *Planned Parenthood of Southeastern Pennsylvania v. Casey*, 505 U.S. 833 (1992).

5. James C. Mohr, *Abortion in American: The Origins and Evolution of a National Policy, 1800–1900*, p. 20–21 (1978).

6. The common law is "a body of law that is based on custom and general principles and embodied in case law and that serves as precedent or is applied to situations not covered by statute." *Merriam-Webster's Dictionary of Law* (1996), http://dictionary.lp.findlaw.com.

As a general matter, colonial lawmakers drew heavily on English common-law precedents and relied upon them as "the rule of decision in legal controversies." Morton J. Horwitz, *The Transformation of American Law, 1780–1860*, p. 4 (1977).

7. According to the *Roe* Court, the historical evidence is not entirely clear regarding the status of post-quickening abortions, and it is possible that abortion at any stage was never "firmly established as a common-law crime." *Roe*, 410 U.S. at 137.

8. Leslie J. Regan, *When Abortion Was a Crime: Women, Medicine, and Law in the United States, 1867–1973*, p. 8 (1997).

9. Mark S. Scott, Note, *Quickening in the Common Law: The Legal Precedent Roe Attempted and Failed to Use*, 1 Mich. Law & Policy Rev. 199, 212 (1966).

10. *Id.* at 210–212.

11. The doctrine of mediate animation was incorporated by Gratian into the *Decretum*—a core text in the definitive body of Canon Law until the early twentieth century. *Id.*, at 215; *Roe*, 410 U.S. at 134–35; and note 22.

Note that some texts refer to a 40/80-day time frame for animation, and others refer to a 40/90-day time frame.

12. The Church actually abandoned the mediate animation doctrine for a brief period in the late sixteenth century under Pope Sixtus V as well. In his effort to "cleanse" the Church, the pope declared that abortion was murder at any point in pregnancy. Lawrence Lader, *Abortion*, p. 79 (1979).

13. Lawrence H. Tribe, *Abortion: The Clash of Absolutes* (1992).

14. Mohr, supra note 5, at 16.

As will be discussed, most of the women who had abortions at this time were single women seeking to escape the stigma of unwed motherhood.

15. *Id.* at 44.

16. This section is based mainly on the following work: Paul Starr, *The Social Transformation of American Medicine: The Rise of a Sovereign Profession and the Making of a Vast Industry* (1982); *see also* Luker, at note 3.

17. Starr, supra note 16, at 38.

18. *Id.* at 39.

19. One needs to be very careful when speaking of these democratic impulses; although antielitist in nature, the egalitarian ideology of Jacksonian America was applied essentially to white males only—women and blacks, particularly slaves, remained hidden in the shadows.

20. Starr, supra note 16, at 47.

21. *Id.* at 58.

22. According to Starr, although they gave doctors some measure of comfort, these early licensing laws were not terribly effective, since they essentially served to confer "approval authority on the recipient without excluding anyone else from practicing medicine." *Id.* at 44.

23. *Id.* at 90.

24. Mohr, supra note 5, at 148.

25. *Id.* at 157.

26. Luker, supra note 3, at 27, 31.

It should be noted that most historians of the medical profession, Starr included, do not focus on abortion as a key element in the doctors' drive to professionalize. Rather, they focus on scientific breakthroughs in the field of medicine, shifting political ideologies that were less condemning of privilege, and issues of class privilege and prestige. *See also* Charles Rosenberg, *The Therapeutic Revolution: Medicine, Meaning, and Change in Nineteenth-Century America*, Perspectives in Biology and Medicine 20 (1977). This link between the drive for professionalization and the doctors' antiabortion activism has been drawn by scholars such as Mohr and Luker in their pioneering works on the history of abortion.

27. Luker, supra note 3, at 27–35.

28. Horatio Storer, *Why Not?: A Book for Every Woman*, (1868), at 29, 32.

Storer's book is based on the prize-winning essay he submitted to the American Medical Association's contest for the best antiabortion paper.

29. However, according to Luker, doctors were not the only ones with this knowledge; rather, it was a matter of general understanding. Luker, at note 3.

In fact, Storer himself seems to recognize this; later on in *Why Not?* he discredits the reasons a woman might have for terminating a pregnancy, stating that the only understandable reason would be "ignorance of the true character of the act of willful abortion" but that such ignorance would be incredible "in these days of the general diffusion of a certain amount of physiological knowledge." Storer, at 70.

Doctors began trying to convince the public of the meaninglessness of the quickening distinction at about the same time the Catholic Church abandoned the doctrine of mediate animation for that of immediate animation. However, this shift in church doctrine probably did not have a direct bearing on the thinking of doctors, since religious institutions played little role in this first antiabortion movement.

30. This passage is from a lecture given in 1854 by Professor Hugh Hodge at the University of Pennsylvania, as reprinted in *Why Not?* at 82 (emphasis added).

31. AMA Report on Criminal Abortion, 1859. For the text of this report, *see* http://www.abortionessay.com/files/11859ama.html.

32. There is some disagreement among scholars regarding the extent to which beliefs about the sanctity of fetal life motivated doctors to speak up against abortion. According to Mohr, many doctors genuinely believed that the fetus had an absolute right to life and that abortion was therefore the equivalent of murder. Mohr, at note 5.

However, Luker argues points to the fact that doctors did not seek an absolute ban on the practice, but rather sought laws giving them the authority to decide when an abortion was necessary. This, Luker asserts, indicates that physicians believed that a fetus had a "conditional" rather than an "absolute" right to life. Luker, supra note 3, at 28–35.

33. Mohr, supra note 5, at 46.

34. *Id.*

35. Storer, supra note 28, at 76.

36. H. S. Pomeroy, *The Ethics of Marriage*, p. 97 (1888).

37. Storer, supra note 28, at 82.

38. Riva Siegal, *Reasoning from the Body: A Historical Perspective on Abortion Regulation and Questions of Equal Protection*, 44 Stan. L. Rev. 261, 301 (1992). This article provides an excellent analysis of the wider social implications of the doctors' campaign.

39. For the text of this speech, see http://www.abortionessay.com/files/Humphreys.html.

40. *Id.*

41. Mohr, supra note 5, at 168.

42. For further elaboration of these themes, see Siegal, supra note 38, at 302–308.

43. The classic work on this topic is Linda Gordon's book, *Women's Body, Women's Right: A Social History of Birth Control in America* (1977). *See also* Siegal, supra note 38, at 308–314.

44. Siegal, supra note 38, at 309–310.

45. Regan, supra note 8, at 62.

46. Lawrence Lader, *Abortion*, p. 64–69 (1977); *see also* Regan, supra note 8, at 137–38, 193–94, and 206–213.

47. Luker, supra note 3, at 42–44.

48. This second wave of antiabortion activism is discussed in detail in chapter 3 of Regan, supra note 8.

49. *Id.* at 132.

50. Regan, at 138–140.

51. Regan, supra note 8, at 174–77.

For a detailed discussion of how these boards worked and of the obstacles that they placed in the way of women seeking an abortion, see chapter 4 in Lader, supra note 46.

52. Herbert L. Packer and Ralph J. Gampell, *Therapeutic Abortion: A Problem in Law and Medicine*, 11 Stan. L. Rev. 417 (1959).

53. *Id.* at 418.

54. *Id.* at 447.

55. According to Regan, this growing conservatism reflected broader social influences, including McCarthyism and a backlash against the perceived increasing independence of women. Regan, supra note 8, at 162–64.

56. Eva Rubin, *Abortion, Politics, and the Courts*, p. 18 (1987).

57. Regan, supra note 8, at 219–220.

58. *See also* Luker, supra note 3, at 62–65.

59. *Id.* at 79–80.

60. This burst of legal activity is explored in great detail in David J. Garrow's book, *Liberty and Sexuality: The Right to Privacy and the Making of Roe v. Wade* (1994).

61. *Griswold v. Connecticut*, 381 U.S. 479 (1965).

62. *Id.* at 485.

63. *Id.* at 484.

64. *Id.* at 486–87.

65. *People v. Belous*, 458 P.2d 194, 71 Cal.2d 954, 80 Cal. Rptr. 354 (1969).

66. *Eisenstadt v. Baird*, 405 U.S. 438 (1972).

67. *Id.* at 454.

68. The cases involving the abortion rights of minors are addressed in the next chapter.

69. *Roe v. Wade*, 410 U.S. 113, 119 (1973).

70. *Id.* at 154. As discussed in chapter 3, the Court characterized the abortion decision as one that is medical in nature.

71. *Id.*

72. *Id.* at 159.

73. *Id.* at 164.

74. For details on the efforts of antiabortion forces to limit a woman's right of choice, *see also* Lawrence H. Tribe, *Abortion: The Clash of Absolutes*, chapters 7–8 (1992); Luker, supra note 3, chapter 6; Rubin, supra note 56 *Abortion, Politics, and the Courts: Roe v. Wade*

and Its Aftermath, chapters 4–9 (1987); and Faye D. Ginsburg, *Contested Lives: The Abortion Debate in an American Community* (1989).

75. As discussed in the next chapter, the Court also struck down the law's parental-consent provision.

76. *Danforth*, 428 U.S. at 70.

77. This method involves withdrawing amniotic fluid and replacing it with saline or another fluid in order to induce an abortion.

78. *Danforth*, 428 U.S. at 78.

79. *City of Akron v. Akron Center for Reproductive Health, Inc*, 462 U.S. 416 (1983).

80. *Id.* at 445.

81. *Id.* at 714, citing *Whalen v. Roe*, 429 U.S. 589, 604, note 33 and note 37 (1977).

82. *Id.* at 713.

83. *Id.* at 709.

84. *Thornburgh v. American College of Obstetricians and Gynecologists*, 476 U.S. 747 (1986).

85. *Id.* at 763.

86. *Id.* at 801 (internal citations omitted and emphasis added).

87. The Medicaid program was established by Title XIX of the Social Security Act (42 U.S.C. sec. 1396 et seq.). It is a cooperative federal-state undertaking through which the federal government provides funding to states for the provision of medical care to low-income persons.

Congress followed suit in restricting Medicaid funding in 1976. The federal funding-ban is commonly referred to as the Hyde Amendment, after its initial sponsor, Representative Henry Hyde of Illinois. The ban has been renewed by Congress on a yearly basis. In its most restrictive forms, funding has been cut off for all abortions, except those necessary to save the life of the pregnant woman. In more "liberal" versions, funding has been provided for abortions in situations of rape or incest.

88. *Maher v. Roe*, 432 U.S. 464, 496 (1977).

The Court considered the funding issue in several leading cases. It considered the constitutionality of the federal-funding ban in *Harris v. McRae*, 448 U.S. 297 (1980) and ruled on constitutional challenges to state laws limiting the availability of Medicaid funds in *Maher v. Roe*, 432 U.S. 464, 496 (1977) and *Beal v. Doe*, 432 U.S. 438, 446 (1977).

89. *Maher*, 432 U.S. at 476.

90. *Id.* at 495–96.

91. *Harris v. McRae*, 448 U.S. 297, 316 (1980).

92. *Maher*, 432 U.S. at 484. Justice Brennan dissenting, joined by justices Marshall and Blackmun.

93. *Webster v. Reproductive Health Services*, 492 U.S. 490 (1989)

94. *Id.* at 519–520. Chief Justice Rehnquist with justices White and Kennedy.

95. *Id.* at 538. Justice Scalia.

96. *Webster*, 492 U.S. at 541.

97. *Planned Parenthood of Southeastern Pennsylvania v. Casey*, 505 U.S. 833 (1992).

98. *Id.* at 846.

99. According to the Court, the test for determining whether it had the authority to overrule *Roe* was as follows: "we may enquire whether *Roe*'s central rule has been found unworkable; whether the rule's limitation on state power could be removed without serious inequity to those who have relied upon it.... whether the law's growth in the intervening years has left *Roe*'s central rule a doctrinal anachronism ... and whether *Roe*'s premise of fact has so far changed ... as to render its central holding somehow irrelevant or justifiable." *Casey*, 505 U.S. at 855.

Answering no to all of these considerations, the Court eloquently stated with respect to the reliance interest, "An entire generation has come of age free to assume Roe's concept of liberty in defining the capacity of women to act in society and to make reproductive decisions." *Id.* at 861–62. The Court concluded it was not free to overrule *Roe*.

100. *Id.* at 872.

101. Recall, also, that during the second trimester, the state's interest in the health of the pregnant woman becomes compelling, thus allowing states to enact valid health-related measures.

102. *Id.* at 876

103. *Id.* at 877.

104. *Id.* at 879.

105. *Id.* at 894–95.

106. *Id.* at 884 (emphasis added).

107. *Id.* at 885.

108. This law was brought to my attention by the NARAL Pro-Choice America Report *Who Decides? A State-by-State Review of Abortion and Reproductive Rights*, p. iii (2003). Available online at http:// www.naral.org/publications/whodecides2003.cfm.

109. Alan Guttmacher Institute, *An Overview of Abortion in America* (2003). Available online at http://www.agi-usa.org/pubs/ab_slides.html.

110. *Sternberg v. Carhart*, 530 U.S. 914, 939 (2000).

This case will be not the final word on the constitutionality of these bans, since antichoice activists are actively looking for ways around the Sternberg decision, such as through greater definitional clarity and the inclusion of narrowly worded health exceptions.

CHAPTER 2

1. *Planned Parenthood v. Danforth*, 428 U.S. 52 (1976).

2. *Bellotti v. Baird*, 443 U.S. 622 (1979).

3. For purposes of this historical discussion, distinctions will not generally be drawn between younger children and adolescents. However, as the subsequent discussion of *Bellotti* makes clear, developmental differences between these two groups are legally salient.

4. Elizabeth Pleck, *Domestic Tyranny: The Making of American Social Policy from Colonial Times to the Present*, p. 17 (1987).

5. Michael Grossberg, *Governing the Hearth: Law and the Family in Nineteenth-Century America*, p. 4 (1984).

This model of colonial family life was especially well-developed in the Puritan colonies of New England. *Id.* at 4.

For detail on regional variations in family structure, see Mary Ann Mason, *From Father's Property to Children's Rights* (1994). For additional information on the colonial family, see Pleck, supra note 4; *Planned Parenthood v. Danforth*, 428 U.S. 52 (1976).

6. Some historians have likened the relationship between father and child to that between owner and chattel or master and slave. However, Professor Mason notes that these comparisons fail to account for the responsibilities that fathers had for the support and education of their children. She thus argues that the master-servant relationship is a more appropriate comparison. Mason, supra note 5, at 7–10.

7. William Blackstone, *Commentaries on the Laws of England,* p. 372–73 (19th London ed. 1857).

8. Mason, supra note 5, at 12.

9. *Id.* supra note 5, at 11.

10. Viviana A. Zelizer, *Pricing the Priceless Child: The Changing Social Value of Children,* p. 21 (1985).

11. Many books and articles have been written on what historians have labeled the "cult of domesticity." Some of the classic works include: Mary P. Ryan, *Cradle of the Middle Class: The Family in Oneida County, New York, 1790–1865* (1981); Barbara Welter, *The Cult of True Womanhood, 1820–1860,* 18 American Quarterly 151 (1966); Carl N. Degler, *At Odds: Women and the Family in America from the Revolution to the Present* (1980); Nancy Cott, *Bonds of Womanhood: Women's Sphere in New England, 1780–1835,* p. 9 (1977).

12. Pleck, supra note 4, at 39.

13. *Id.*

14. Carl Degler, *At Odds: Women and the Family in American from the Revolution to the Present,* p. 74 (1980).

15. John Demos, "The Rise and Fall of Adolescence," at 98, in John Demos, *Past, Present and Personal: The Family and Life Course in American History* (1986).

Although beyond the scope of this text, it should be noted that there is a debate among family historians of the colonial era as to whether childhood was recognized as a distinct phase of life, or whether children were regarded more as "miniature adults." Demos is generally identified with the latter view.

16. During the Progressive Era (roughly the 1890s until around 1920), reformers responded to the social and economic dislocations caused by rapid industrialization and urbanization by turning to the state to enact sweeping social reforms. Their reform efforts were mainly directed toward the urban poor, including many newly arrived immigrants, who were crowded into tenements in the cities.

Many reformers acted out of genuine humanitarian impulses and a firm belief in the inevitable progress of humankind, while others were more likely motivated by a desire to control the "unseemly" masses and instill middle-class domestic norms in them. For a discussion of the "social benevolence" versus the "social control" perspectives, see Clay Gish, *Rescuing the "Waifs and Strays" of the City: The Western Emigration Program of the Children's Aid Society,* 33 J. of Social History 121 (1999). See also Pleck, supra note 4 at 74–75, and Mary E. Odem, *Delinquent Daughters: Protecting and Policing Adolescent Sexuality in the United States, 1885–1920* (1995).

17. Barry C. Feld, *Criminalizing Juvenile Justice, Rules of Procedure for the Juvenile Court,* 69 Minn. L. Rev. 141, 147 (1984).

18. Zelizer, supra note 10, at 72.

19. *Id*. at 3.

20. *In re Gault,* 387 U.S. 1, 15, citing Julian Mack, *The Juvenile Court,* 23 Harv. L. Rev. 104, 119–120 (1909).

21. Pleck, supra note 4, at 127.

22. *Gault,* 387 U.S. at 16.

23. Feld, *Criminalizing Juvenile Justice,* supra note 17, at 150.

24. Jessica Kulynych, *No Playing in the Public Sphere: Democratic Theory and the Exclusion of Children,* 27 Social Theory and Practice 231, 235–236 (2001)

25. Wendy Anton Fitzgerald, *Maturity, Difference, and Mystery,* 36 Arizona L. Rev. 11, 16 (1994).

26. 387 U.S. 1 (1967).

27. *Id*. at 18–19.

28. *Id*. at 13.

For further discussion of the juvenile justice system, see chapter 7.

29. 393 U.S. 503 (1969).

30. *Id*. at 511 (emphasis added). Note, however, that unlike in the abortion context, these cases did not involve a potential conflict between parent and child; accordingly, in identifying children as constitutional persons, the Court did not have to consider what would happen in a situation of competing views or interests—clearly, an important consideration in the abortion context.

31. Janet L. Dolgin, *The Fate of Children and the Parent-Child Relationship,* 61 Albany L.Rcv. 345, 373 and 377 (1997).

32. *Id*. at 392.

33. *Id*. at 393.

34. Gary B. Melton, *Toward "Personhood" for Adolescents: Autonomy and Privacy as Values in Public Policy,* 1983 American Psychologist 99. Many articles address these as well as other understandings of children's rights. For example, see Jessica Kulynych, supra note 24, *No Playing in the Public Sphere: Democratic Theory and the Exclusion of Children,* 27 Social Theory and Practice 231(2001); Janet Dolgin, supra note 31, *The Fate of Childhood: Legal Models of Children and the Parent-child Relationship,* 61 Albany L. Rev. 345 (1997); Bruce C. Hafen and Jonathan O. Hafen, *Abandoning Children to Their Autonomy: The United Nations Convention on the Rights of the Child,* 37 Harv. Int'l L.J. 449 (1996); Wendy Anton Fitzgerald, supra note 25, *Maturity, Difference, and Mystery,* 36 Arizona L. Rev. 11 (1994); Katherine Hunt Federle, *On the Road to Reconceiving Rights for Children: A Postfeminist Analysis of the Capacity Principle,* 42 DePaul L. Rev. 983 (1993); Martha

Minow, *Rights for the Next Generation: A Feminist Approach to Children's Rights,* 9 Harv. Women's L.J. 1 (1986); Hillary Rodham, *Children under the Law,* 43 Harv. Educ. Rev. 487(1973).

35. Martha Minow, *What Ever Happened to Children's Rights,* 80 Minn. L. Rev. 267, 274 (1995).

36. *Id.* at 282.

37. 430 U.S. 651 (1977).

38. 469 U.S. 325 (1985).

39. Additionally, as discussed in chapter 3, minors are treated as autonomous individuals for the purpose of making certain medical decisions.

40. *Planned Parenthood v. Danforth,* 428 U.S. 52 (1976).

41. *Bellotti v. Baird,* 443 U.S. 622 (1979).

The *Bellotti* case actually came before the Supreme Court twice. The first time, the Court sent the case back to the state court system so that the statute could be authoritatively interpreted under Massachusetts law. Our focus here is on the second *Bellotti* decision. The first decision will be discussed in greater detail in chapter 3.

For details on the entire course of litigation involving the Massachusetts parental consent law, see J. Shoshanna Ehrlich, *Journey Through the Courts; Minors, Abortion, and the Quest for Reproductive Fairness,* 10 Yale J.L. & Feminism 1 (1998).

42. *Danforth,* 428 U.S. at 74.

By this statement, it is clear that the Court simply assumes that minors possess the basic *Roe* right—that this is beyond question. It thus never addresses the issue head on.

43. *Danforth,* 428 U.S. at 76.

44. *Id.* at 103.

45. *Id.* at 71.

46. *Bellotti,* 443 U.S. at 643.

47. *Id.*

48. *Id.* at 634, quoting from the opinion of Justice Frankfurter, in *May v. Anderson,* 345 U.S. 528, 536 (1953).

49. *Id.* at 634. For a discussion regarding why the Court's reliance on these factors is misplaced, see J. Shoshanna Ehrlich and Jamie Ann Sabino, *A Minor's Right to Abortion—The Unconstitutionality of Parental Participation in Bypass Hearings,* 25 New Eng. L. Rev. 1185, 1189, n. 20 (1991).

50. *Id.*

51. *Id.* at 638.

52. *Id.* at 639, citing *Ginsberg v. New York,* 390 U.S. 629, 639, n. 18 (1969).

It should be noted that the authority the Court is referring to is not simply authority for its own sake, but is linked to the "growth of young people into mature, socially responsible citizens." *Id.* at 639.

53. Dolgin, supra note 31, at 374.

54. *Id.* at 355

55. *Id.* at 376.

56. *Bellotti*, 443 U.S. at 644–45. The Court noted that since the Massachusetts law provided for a court bypass, it would refer to the "alternative proceeding" in terms of a court hearing, but that this was not the only permissible option. *Id.* at 643, n. 22.

In his concurring opinion, Justice Stevens asserted that this aspect of the decision was advisory in nature and thus was not binding, since the court was no longer discussing an actual statute. *Id.* at 656 (Justice Stevens, joined by justices Brennan, Marshall, and Blackmun). However, regardless of whether Stevens' assertion is correct, the court has since made clear that *Bellotti* established the applicable legal standards against which consent laws must be evaluated. See, for example, *Ohio v. Akron Ctr. for Reproductive Health*, 497 U.S 502, 511–14 (1990); *City of Akron v. Akron Ctr. for Reproductive Health*, 462 U.S. 416, 439–40 (1983).

57. *Id.*, citing *Danforth*, 428 U.S at 74.

58. *Bellotti II*, 443 U.S. at 648.

59. *Id.* at 642.

60. *Id.* at 647. The Court also invalidated the law because, as interpreted by the Massachusetts Supreme Judicial Court, it allowed a judge to override the abortion decision of a mature minor based on the judge's independent determination that an abortion was not in the minor's best interest.

61. *Id.* at 648 (emphasis added).

62. This point was not lost on the concurring justices who characterized this aspect of the Court's opinion as "particularly troubling." *Id.* at 655 (concurring opinion of Justice Stevens, joined by justices Brennan, Marshall, and Blackmun).

CHAPTER 3

1. *Roe v. Wade*, 410 U.S. 113, 166 (1973).

It should be made clear at the outset that the point here is not to endorse the *Roe* Court's medicalized approach to abortion, but rather to challenge the integrity of the Court's reasoning in the cases involving minors. *Roe*'s characterization of abortion as primarily a medical choice has been subject to criticism on many grounds, including on the basis that it overemphasizes the role of the physician and ignores the dynamic relationship between reproductive control and gender equity. See, for example, Riva Siegal, *Reasoning from the Body: A Historical Perspective on Abortion Regulation and the Question of Equal Protection*, 44 Stan. L. Rev. 261 (1992).

2. Some commentators have suggested that the opinion's emphasis on the role of the doctor may reflect the fact that its author, Justice Harry Blackmun, had served as general counsel to the Mayo Clinic prior to his appointment to the Supreme Court. See Lawrence H. Tribe, *Abortion: The Clash of the Absolutes*, p. 13.

3. *Roe*, 410 U.S. at 153 (emphasis added).

4. *Id.* at 166.

There is a historic irony in the Court's celebration of the rights of physicians in light of the fact that our nation's restrictive abortion laws, such as the one invalidated in *Roe*, resulted, in large measure, from the nineteenth-century physicians' campaign to outlaw abortion (see chapter 2).

5. *Roe*, 410 U.S. at 166.

6. Anthony Szczygiel, *Beyond Informed Consent*, 21 Ohio N.U.L. Rev. 171, 185 (1994). *See also* Walter Wadlington, *Minors and Healthcare: The Age of Consent*, 11 Osgoode Hall L.J. 115 (1973).

7. Szczygiel, supra note 6, at 189.

8. *Canterbury v. Spence*, 464 F.2d 772, 781 (1972); cert. denied, 409 U.S. 1064 (1972).

9. For more detail on the doctrine of informed consent, see Roger B. Dworkin, *Getting What We Should from Doctors: Rethinking Patient Autonomy and the Doctor-Patient Relationship*, 13 Health Matrix 235 (2003); Barry Rosenfield, *Understanding Decision-Making with Regard to Clinical Research*, 30 Fordham Urb. L.J. 173 (2002); Grant H. Morris, *Dissing Disclosure: Just What the Doctor Ordered*, 44 Ariz. L. Rev. 313 (2002); Szczygiel, supra note 6.

10. Council of Scientific Affairs, American Medical Association, *Confidential Health Services for Adolescents*, 11 JAMA 1420 (1993) (quoting National Conference of Commissioners on Uniform State Laws, Uniform Health-Care Information Act, *Uniform Laws Annotated*, part L [St. Paul, MN: West Publishing Co., 1988]).

11. Abigail English, *Treating Adolescents: Legal and Ethical Considerations*, 74 Adolescent Med. 1097, 1103–1104 (1990). The Title X statute, 42 U.S.C. sec. 300 (a) (1982), and the accompanying confidentiality regulation, (42 C.F.R. 59.11, are available online at http:// www.opa.osophs.dhhs.gov/legislation.

12. Josephine Gittler, Mary Quigley-Rick, and Michael J. Saks, *Adolescent Health Care Decision Making: The Law and Public Policy* (working paper, The Carnegie Council on Adolescent Development, 1990).

13. *See* Angela Roddey Holder, *Legal Issues in Pediatrics and Adolescent Medicine*, p. 143 (2d. ed., Yale Univ. Press, 1985).

14. This view is embodied in the policy statements of the following organizations: The American Medical Association, see Council on Scientific Affairs, Am. Medical Ass'n, *Confidential Health Services for Adolescents*, 11 JAMA 1420 (1993); The American Public Health Association, see Am. Pub. Health Ass'n, *Adolescent Access to Comprehensive, Confidential Reproductive Care*, 81 Am. J. Pub. Health 241 (1991); The Society for Adolescent Medicine, see Society for Adolescent Med., *Position Statements on Reproductive Health Care for Adolescents*, 12 J. of Adolescent Health 657 (1991); The American College of Obstetricians and Gynecologists, see ACOG Educational Bulletin No. 249, *Confidentiality In Adolescent Health Care* (Aug. 1998); The American Academy of Pediatrics, see Committee on Adolescence, Am. Academy of Ped., *Counseling the Adolescent about Pregnancy Options*, 100 Pediatrics 938 (1998); and the American Academy of Family Physicians, see AAFP, *Statement of Policy on Adolescent Health Care* (2003), available online at http:// www.aafp.org.

15. See Carol A. Ford, Peter S. Bearman, and James Moody, *Foregone Health Care Among Adolescents*, 282 JAMA 2227 (1999); Carol A. Ford and Susan G. Millstein, *Delivery of Confidentiality Assurances to Adolescents by Primary Care Physicians*, 151 Archives Of Pediatrics & Adolescent Medicine 505 (1997); Carol A. Ford, Susan G. Millstein, Bonnie L. Halpern-Feisher, and Charles E. Irwin, Jr., *Influence of Physician Confidentiality*

Assurances on Adolescents' Willingness to Disclose Information and Seek Future Health Care: A Randomized Controlled Trial, 278 JAMA 1029 (1997).

16. Council on Scientific Affairs, Am. Med. Ass'n, supra note 14, at 1420; *see also* Ford et al., supra note 15, at 2232–33 (1999).

17. Council on Scientific Affairs, Am. Med. Ass'n, supra note 14, at 1420.

It should be noted that the growing trend is to involve adolescents in their own health-care decisions even in situations where parental consent is needed. As stated by the Committee on Bioethics of the American Academy of Pediatrics,

> Decision-making involving the health care of older children and adolescents should include, to the greatest extent feasible, the assent of the patient as well as the participation of the parents and the physician. Pediatricians should not necessarily treat children as rational, autonomous decision makers, but they should give serious consideration to each patient's developing capacities for participating in decision-making, including rationality and autonomy. If physicians recognize the importance of assent, they empower children to the extent of their capacity ... As children develop, they should gradually become the primary guardians of personal health and the primary partners in medical decision-making, assuming responsibility from their parents.

Committee of Bioethics, American Academy of Pediatrics, *Informed Consent, Parental Permission, and Assent on Pediatric Practice,* 95 Pediatrics 314, 315–16 (1995). *See also* Midwest Bioethics Center, Children's Rights Task Force, *Health Care Treatment Decision-Making Guidelines for Minors,* 11 Bioethics Forum A1 (1995).

18. In this regard, reference should be made to HIPAA (the Health Insurance Portability and Accountability Act)—the federal law that seeks to safeguard the privacy of a patient's health information and medical records. According to the HIPAA regulations, parents are the designated "personal representatives" of their minor children when they have the right to consent to their care. As personal representatives, parents possess the corollary rights of access to, in HIPAA language, their children's "personal health information."

However, HIPAA also includes several important exceptions to this parental-access rule. Information will be kept confidential and not shared with parents, absent the minor's express consent, under the following circumstances:

- A minor consents to a particular health-care service, and consent of a parent is not required under state or federal law, and the law expressly prohibits disclosure (if the law allows disclosure, or is silent, HIPAA vests discretion in the health care provider to determine whether or not to disclose);

- A minor has the legal right to obtain health care without parental consent, and the care is authorized by a recognized individual or a court (most notably in the case of abortion);

- A parent consents to a confidential relationship between his or her child and the health care provider;

- The health care provider determines that disclosure may endanger the minor.

See 45 C.F.R. Parts 160 and 164, available online at http://www.hhs.gov/ocr/hipaa.

The above discussion provides a very brief overview of a very complex law. For further detail, see Abigail English and Carol A. Ford, *The HIPAA privacy Rule and Adolescents: Legal Questions and Clinical Challenges,* 36 Perspectives on Sexual and Reproductive Health 12 (2004); Ann Maradiegue, *The Health Insurance Portability and Accountability Act and Adolescents,* 28 Pediatric Nursing 417 (2002); ACLU Reproductive Freedom Project, *Protecting Minors' Health Information Under the Federal Medical Privacy Regulations,* available online at http://www.aclu.org/ReproductiveRights.

19. The pattern may be different when mental health care is involved, when a provider may determine that therapeutic considerations militate against disclosure to the parent even if she or he is the party who has authorized the care. Thus, treatment considerations may take precedence over general rules regarding patterns of confidentiality. The author wishes to acknowledge the contribution of Jim Hilliard, counsel to the Massachusetts Psychiatric Association, who willingly gave of his time and expertise to discuss this issue with her.

20. 42 C.F.R. sec. 59.11.

21. James M. Morrissey, Adele D. Hoffman, and Jeffrey C. Thrope, *Consent and Confidentiality in the Health Care of Children and Adolescents: A Legal Guide,* p. 53 (1989).

22. Walter Wadlington, *Minors and Health Care: The Age of Consent,* 11 Osgoode Hall L. J. 115, 116 (1973). *See also* Morrisey, supra note 21, at 53.

23. Walter Wadlington, *Medical Decision Making for and by Children: Tensions Between Parent, State, and Child,* 1994 U. of Illinois L. Rev. 311, 323.

24. *Id.* at 314–15.

25. *Id.* at 319–23.

26. Angela Roddely Holder, *Legal Issues in Pediatrics and Adolescent Medicine,* p. 128 (2nd ed. 1985).

27. See H. Jeffrey Gottesfeld, *The Uncertain Status of the Emancipated Minor: Why We Need a Uniform Statutory Emancipation of Minors Act (USEMA),* 15 U.S.F.L. 473, 477–79 (1981) (also discussing the "first generation" of emancipation statutes, which, according to the author, were enacted primarily to reconcile the age of emancipation with the legal age of marriage). *See also* Wadlington, supra note 23, at 323; and Sanford N. Katz, William A. Schroeder, and Lawrence R. Sidman, *Emancipating Our Children: Coming of Legal Age in America,* 7 Fam. L. Q. 211 (1973).

28. 13 Del. C. sec. 710 (2001). It should, however, be noted that surgeons are required to notify parents of their intent to perform surgery, unless delay would pose a threat of death or there is a risk of serious injury.

In 1974 the statute was amended to exclude abortion from the self-consent provisions.

29. Angela Roddy Holder, *Minors' Right to Consent to Medical Care,* 257 JAMA 3400 (1987).

In general, the doctrine is less likely to be utilized where the treatment is highly risky or the underlying condition very serious *(Id.)* or where the treatment is undertaken for the benefit of a third party rather than the minor, such as in the case of organ donation. See Wadlington, supra note 22, at 119.

30. Ark. Code. Ann. sec. 20–9-602 (2004).

31. Of course, it is important to recognize that independence may be a response to parental neglect rather than a self-determined life course. See Carol Sanger and Eleanor Willemsen, *Minor Changes: Emancipating Minors in Modern Times*, 25 U. Mich. J.L. Reform 239 (1992).

32. Not all of these laws expressly prohibit disclosure to parents, which, of course, may well serve to defeat the underlying purpose of the law, since minors may not seek treatment if they know information may be disclosed to a parent.

33. Most of these laws were enacted before the AIDS epidemic. For a discussion about the different approaches states are taking with respect to whether minors can self-consent to the testing for and treatment of HIV-infection, see William Adams, *"But Do You Have To Tell My Parents?" The Dilemma For Minors Seeking HIV-Testing And Treatment*, 27 J. Marshall L. Rev. 493 (1994).

34. Pa. Stat. Tit. 50 sec. 7201(2004), discussed in Rhonda Gay Hartman, *Coming of Age: Devising Legislation for Adolescent Medical Decision-Making*, 28 Am. J.L. and Med. 409, 421 (2002).

35. *Id.*

36. 406 U.S. 205 (1972).

37. *Id.* at 212.

38. *Id.* at 242–246.

39. *Id.* at 247, note 3.

40. For some of the critiques of Piaget's stage theory, see chapter 7.

41. Merriam-Webster Online, http://www.m-w.com/ (accessed July 23, 2004).

42. This synthesis of Piaget's theory is drawn from Wallace J. Mlyniec, *A Judge's Dilemma: Assessing a Child's Capacity to Choose*, 640 Fordham L. Rev. 1873, 1880 (1996); and Elizabeth Cauffman and Lawrence Steinberg, *The Cognitive and Affective Influences on Adolescent Decision-Making*, 68 Temple L. Rev. 1763, 1768 (1995).

43. Courtney P. Gordon, *Adolescent Decision Making: A Broadly Based Theory and Its Application to the Prevention of Early Pregnancy*, 31 Adolescence 561, 563 (1996).

44. Mlyniec, supra note 42, at 1880.

45. Josephine Gittler, Mary Quigley-Rick, and Michael J. Saks, Adolescent Health Care Decision Making: The Law and Public Policy, p. 37 (working paper, the Carnegie Council on Adolescent Development, 1990). Many of the reviewed studies are summarized in this report. They are also reviewed in Mlyniec, supra note 42, at 1881–84.

46. The citation for this case is *Bellotti v. Baird*, 428 U.S 132, 149 (1976).

47. The plaintiffs raised a similar argument in the *Danforth* case, based on the fact that teens in Missouri were permitted to self-consent to "medical services for pregnancy (excluding abortion) venereal disease, and drug abuse." *Danforth*, 428 U.S. at 74. The plaintiffs also pointed out that "no other Missouri statute specifically requires the additional consent of a minor's parent for medical or surgical treatment." *Id.*

Although it struck down Missouri's parental-consent law because the law vested parents with veto power over their daughter's decision, the Court did not to address the illogic of this statutory scheme that gave teens choosing to carry to term greater decisional rights than teens choosing to abort. (The *Danforth* case is discussed in chapter 3.)

48. 1975 Mass. Acts 564, amending Mass. Gen. Laws ch. 112, sec. 12F.

Under this statute, minors are entitled to consent to their own medical care if they are married, widowed, or divorced; the parent of a child; a member of the armed forces; or living independently; additionally, minors who are or believe themselves to be pregnant, as well as those seeking diagnosis or treatment for diseases deemed dangerous to the public health, can self-consent to their own care. The law further provides that the relationship between the consenting minor and the physician is confidential in nature, except in cases of extreme risk to "life or limb."

49. *Bellotti*, 428 U.S. at 149.

The Court remanded the case because it believed that the federal trial court, which had invalidated the Massachusetts parental-consent law, in *Baird v. Bellotti*, 393 F. Supp. 847 (D. Mass. 1975), should have abstained from hearing the case until the statute had been interpreted under state-law principles. As the Court explained, abstention is appropriate where an unconstrued state statute is susceptible to a construction by the state judiciary "which might avoid in whole or in part the necessity for federal constitutional adjudication, or at least materially change the nature of the problem." *Bellotti*, 428 U.S. at 148, citing *Harrison v. NAACP*, 360 U.S. 167, 177 (1959). The Court thus vacated the *Bellotti* decision of the federal district court and ordered the lower court to develop a set of interpretive questions for the SJC. After the questions had been developed and answered, the district court again invalidated the statute, in *Baird v. Bellotti*, 450 F. Supp 997 (D. Mass 1978), resulting in the second *Bellotti* decision.

For a detailed discussion on the course of this litigation, see J. Shoshanna Ehrlich, *Journey Through the Courts: Minors, Abortion, and the Quest for Reproductive Freedom*, 10 Yale J. of Law and Feminism 1 (1998).

50. Bellotti, 428 U.S. at 148.

The Court's reliance on *Danforth* to justify distinguishing between consent requirements for abortion and other procedures is misplaced. In *Danforth*, the Court, in upholding record-keeping requirements for abortion that were not imposed on other medical procedures, made clear that this was acceptable only because these requirements did not have a "legally significant impact or consequence on the abortion decision or on the physician-patient relationship." *Danforth*, 428 U.S. at 81. Here, however, the distinction in consent requirements goes to the heart of both the abortion decision, since minors are not permitted to make this decision on their own, and the physician-patient relationship, since the doctor cannot act based on the consent of his or her patient.

51. In the course of interpreting the statute, the SJC also concluded that the state's common-law "mature-minor" rule no longer applied to abortion, having been superseded by the parental-consent law. See *Baird v. Attorney Gen.*, 360 N.E. 288 (Mass. 1977).

52. *Bellotti*, 443 U.S. at 638 (emphasis added and internal citations omitted).

This benign characterization obscures the fact that this law was sponsored by antichoice legislators as part of an omnibus antiabortion legislative package to "provide protection for the life of the unborn child." Otile McManus, *May I, Judge?* Boston Globe Magazine, p. 14 (1986).

53. *Bellotti*, 443 U.S. at 642.

In addition to carrying adult-like responsibilities, becoming a mother as a teenager has profound life consequences and is likely to negatively impact a young woman's future educational and economic opportunities, making it more likely that she will live in poverty. See, Cherly D. Hayes, ed., *Risking the Future: Adolescent Sexuality, Pregnancy, and Childbearing*, p.126–32 (1986).

However, also see Kristen Luker, *Dubious Conceptions: The Politics of Teenage Pregnancy* (1996), in which the author challenges the assumption that early childbearing causes poverty, arguing that poverty is likely to contribute to the decision to bear a child at an early age, thus inverting the traditional causal assumption.

54. Although this would be the result under Massachusetts law, in some states once a teen is a mother, she can self-consent to an abortion.

55. *Bellotti*, 443 U.S. at 634, 640.

56. For teens, abortion is eleven times safer than childbirth if performed before the 18th week of pregnancy. *Ask the Experts*, http:www.teen.wire.org (accessed July 23, 2004).

57. According to a public policy report issued by the Alan Guttmacher Institute in 2000, 34 states expressly permit a minor to make an adoption plan without parental knowledge or consent, and another 11 states do not distinguish between minors and adults, thus presumably also allowing a minor to act independently of her parents. Heather Boonstra and Elizabeth Nash, *Minors and the Right to Consent to Health Care*, 3 Guttmacher Report on Public Policy (2000), available online at http://www.guttmacher.org.

58. *Bellotti*, 443 U.S. at 640 (emphasis added).

Further suggesting that the Court is backing away from its earlier understanding of abortion as a medical decision, the Court goes on to question the ability of doctors, notably those at abortion clinics, to provide minors with "adequate counsel and support." *Id.* at 641, note 21 (quoting the concurring opinion of Justice Stewart in *Danforth*, 428 U.S. 91).

The Court also raises the concern that without the involvement of their parents, minors, unlike adult women, will not be able to "distinguish the competent and ethical from those that are incompetent or unethical." *Id.* Not surprisingly, the Court does not consider the fact that minors choosing to continue a pregnancy may be selecting their own doctors. Moreover, it fails to consider the fact that minors who seek and obtain judicial consent will also be doing the same.

59. 432 U.S. 464 (1977). See chapter 1 for a fuller discussion of the funding cases.

60. See chapter 1 for more on the *Casey* decision.

61. 450 U.S. 398 (1981).

62. *Id.* at 412.

63. *Id.* at 413.

As Justice Marshall remarked in his dissent (*Id.* at 444, note 38), this statement is indeed "baffling." Certainly, women carrying to term face decisions with profound "emotional and psychological consequences," such as whether to be tested and possibly treated for the AIDS virus, whether to undergo diagnostic tests, such as amniocentesis, or whether to submit to *in utero* surgery to correct fetal anomalies. These kinds of decisions suggest the possible range of difficult choices that pregnant women may be called upon to make that entail the balancing of risks to herself and the child she is carrying. See also Marshall, *Id.* at 1190, note 38.

64. *Matheson,* 450 U.S. at 413.

65. As we saw in chapter 2, the Court similarly ruled that the state's interest in encouraging childbirth justified denying Medicaid funding for abortions while covering the costs associated with childbirth.

One of the great ironies of these cases is that it seems hard to imagine that states were genuinely interested in encouraging teens and poor women to have babies, thus underscoring the point being made here—that the Court's support for these laws suggests an underlying discomfort with abortion.

This perception is subsequently born out by the *Casey* decision, in which, as we have seen, the Court abandoned *Roe's* trimester framework, allowing states to enact general abortion laws (meaning laws that apply to all women, and not just to poor women and teens) designed to persuade women to carry to term rather than abort, so long as the laws do not impose an "undue burden" on the right of choice.

66. *Hodgson v. Minnesota,* 497 U.S. 2926, 2944 (1990).

67. 497 U.S. 502 (1990).

68. *Id.* at 520 (emphasis added).

69. 505 U.S. 833 (1992).

70. *Id.* at 900–901 (emphasis added).

CHAPTER 4

1. The young women were referred to me by the attorneys who had represented them in the judicial-bypass hearings, in accordance with carefully developed selection and referral guidelines. Approval for this study, which required a rigorous review of all the measures intended to protect the confidentiality and well-being of the interviewed minors, was obtained from the Human Subjects Committee of the Institutional Review Board at the University of Massachusetts in Boston.

Given the difficulties inherent in the recruitment process, there was no way to guarantee a fully representative interview sample. However, the other primary component of the study generated a picture of the abortion-decision–making process of a representative sample through the coding and analysis of 490 counseling and referral interviews, which were conducted by the Planned Parenthood League of Massachusetts over a 12-month period. These counseling and referral interviews capture the experience of at least 90 percent of the minors who sought court authorization for an abortion during that 12-month period. The sociodemographic profile of the 26 young women I interviewed is remarkably similar to the profile of the representative sample of minors.

For a complete discussion of this study, including methodology and data limitations, see *Grounded in the Reality of Their Lives: Listening to Teens Who Make the Abortion Decision without Involving Their Parents,* 18 Berkeley Women's L.J. 61 (2003).

2. Mass. Gen. Laws ch. 112 sec. 12S. (The law was originally designated as section 12P of chapter 112. In 1977 it was redesignated section 12S, although no substantive changes were made.)

The law included an exception in cases of parental death or desertion, thus excusing a minor from having to contact a deceased or departed parent. If both parents were dead, or had deserted her, she was required to obtain the consent of her guardian or other adult legally responsible for her care. The law also contained an exception for married minors.

3. *Baird v. Bellotti*, 395 F. Supp. 847, 850 (D. Mass. 1975).

4. For a detailed analysis of the course of litigation in both state and federal court, see J. Shoshanna Ehrlich, *Journey Through the Courts: Minors, Abortion, and the Quest for Reproductive Fairness*, 10 Yale J.L. & Feminism 1 (1998).

5. *Planned Parenthood v. Attorney Gen.*, 677 N.E.2d 101, 105 (Mass. 1977), citing *Hodgson v. Minnesota*, 497 U.S. 417, 444 (1990). For further discussion of this decision, see Ehrlich, supra note 4.

6. *Planned Parenthood*, 677 N.E.2d at 105.

7. *Id.* at 108.

The Court's primary concern was the second parent requirement was unfair to the parent the minor had confided in: "the State has no legitimate interest in questioning one parent's judgment that notice to the other parent would not assist the minor or in presuming that the parent who has assumed parental duties is incompetent to make decisions regarding the health and welfare of the child." *Id.* at 107–108 (quoting *Hodgson*, 497 U.S. at 450).

8. See Theodore Joyce and Robert Kaestner, *State Reproductive Policies and Adolescent Pregnancy Resolution: The Case of Parental Involvement Laws*, 15 J. of Health Economics 579, 584 (1996).

9. Regarding some of the logistical difficulties that minors face, see Ehrlich, supra note 1, at 140; Leonard Berman, *Planned Parenthood v. Casey: Supreme Neglect for Unemancipated Minors' Abortion Rights*, 37 How. L.J. 577 (1994); and Patricia Donovan, *Judging Teenagers: How Minors Fare When They Seek Court-Authorized Abortions*, 15 Family Planning Perspectives 259 (1983).

10. This is intended as simply a thumbnail sketch of the process, and it is often considerably more complicated than presented here. For examples, some judges have idiosyncratic requirements, such as that the minor be less than a certain number of weeks pregnant, and will suspend a hearing in the middle if their particular requirements are not met. Some minors are in difficult situations that require careful planning. For example, if a minor is in state custody, permission may need to be obtained in order for her to be allowed to appear in court. Additionally, specific permission may need to be obtained in order for her to be allowed to appear without restraints, since appearing before a judge in handcuffs can intensify the anxiety and shame that many teens already feel in this situation.

11. As noted previously, in note 1, the sociodemographic profile of the young women I interviewed is very close to the representative sample's characteristics.

12. To safeguard privacy, some details have been slightly changed. Care has been taken to not make changes that would alter the meaning of what the interviewed women had to say. Also, all names used are pseudonyms chosen by the minors.

CHAPTER 5

1. Since my focus was on their abortion experiences, I did not specifically ask the young women I interviewed about contraceptive use, although a few spontaneously mentioned contraceptive failures, such as a broken condom.

About 80 percent of the pregnancies in teens under the age of 18 are unintended. Stanley K. Henshaw, *Unintended Pregnancy in the United States*, 30 FPP 24 (1998). Although teen pregnancy rates have actually fallen since the late 1950s, we still have a significantly higher teen-pregnancy rate and teen birthrate than other Western industrialized nations. See *Teen Pregnancy: Trends and Lessons Learned*, Issues in Brief, 2002 Series, No. 1, The Alan Guttmacher Institute, available online at http://www.agi-usa.org. See also U.S. Teenage Pregnancy Statistics, updated February 2004, available online at http://www.agi-usa.org.

2. Interview with Jill Casey.

3. Interview with Bianca Jones.

4. Interview with Miranda Roberts.

5. Interview with Stephanie Paul. Stephanie's concern about her family's response stems from her mother's abusive behavior and her isolation within her family.

6. Interview with Molly Moe.

7. Interview with Beth Smith.

8. There was some indication that Keiza felt some pressure from her boyfriend to abort, since he wanted to wait to have a baby until they were married. None of the other young women reported feeling any pressure to have an abortion.

9. Interview with Mary Jane.

10. Robert W. Blum and Michael D. Resnick, *Adolescent Sexual Decision-Making: Contraception, Pregnancy, Abortion, Motherhood*, 11 Pediatric Annals 797, 805 (1982).

11. Kristen Luker, *Dubois Conceptions: The Politics of Teen Pregnan* 154 (1996).

12. Blum and Resnick, supra note 10, at 801.

13. Katherine Schultz, *Constructing Failure, Narrating Success: Rethinking the "Problem" of Teen Pregnancy*, 103 Teachers College Record 582, 584 (2001).

14. Arlene T. Geronimus, *Teenage Childbearing and Personal Responsibility: An Alternative View*, 112 Political Science Quarterly 405 (1997), available at http://web7.infotrac.galegroup.com, at 10.

15. *Id.*

16. *Id.* at 10–11.

17. See Schultz, supra note 13, at 584. *See also* Cynthia Donaldson Connelly, *Hopefulness, Self-Esteem, and Perceived Social Support Among Pregnant and Nonpregnant Adolescents*, 20 Western J. of Nursing 195 (1995); and Hila J. Spear, A *Follow-up Case Study on Teenage Pregnancy: Havin' a Baby Isn't a Nightmare But It's Really Hard,"* 30 Pediatric Nursing 120 (2004) (This article includes a short, but thoughtful, review of some of the existing scholarship on this topic).

18. Interview with Jill Casey.

19. Interview with Amy Michaels.

20. Interview with Molly Moe.

21. Interview with Sandra Llonas.

22. Interview with Bianca Jones.

23. Interview with Miranda Roberts.

24. Interview with Sandra Kiwi.
This quote demonstrates how interconnected the reasons for aborting often were, since within this brief passage, one can see consideration of future plans, youthfulness, present circumstances, and the well-being of the child.

25. Interview with Anna Lynne Albano. This quote again illustrates how closely entwined the reasons for aborting are. Although the dominant motif here is Anna Lynne's desire to get her life back on track, which embodies an awareness that her present life circumstances were not compatible with parenthood, she is also expressing a concern for her future—fearing that a child would interfere with her goal of completing her education.

26. Interview with Kim Johnson.

27. Interview with Keisha Wood.

28. Interview with Taylor Jordan. As indicated by this quote, her reasons for choosing an abortion are closely intertwined.

29. Interview with Amy Michaels.

30. Interview with Jane Smith.

31. Interview with Beth Smith.

32. Interview with Beth Smith. Beth also made clear that having a child would interfere with her future plan to become an adolescent psychologist and work with troubled kids.

33. Interview with Jasmine Cruz. Jasmine's abortion decision was also based on the facts that the pregnancy was the result of a rape and that she was just starting a GED program.

34. Interview with Bianca Jones.

35. Interview with Mary Smith.

36. These minors also identified this as a reason for not discussing their abortion decision with a parent. Because fear figured more heavily into the noninvolvement decision, it will be discussed in greater detail in chapter 6.

37. Interview with Bianca Jones.

38. As will be discussed below, fear of disappointing a parent was an important consideration in the decision not to disclose pregnancy and abortion plans.

39. *Bellotti*, 443 U.S. at 634.

40. *Id.* at 640 (see chapter 3).

41. It should be noted that Piaget's work has been subject to a variety of criticisms. One important critique is that the stage model of development is too simplistic and that growth in cognitive maturity is domain-sensitive. Accordingly, rather than being constant across all domains, cognitive ability will vary from one situation to another, depending upon the contextual variables. See Rhonda Gay Hartman, *Adolescent Decisional Autonomy for Medical Care: Physicians Perceptions and Practices*, 8 U. of Chi L. School Roundtable 87 (2001).

Additionally, as will be discussed in detail in chapter 7, although not necessarily disagreeing with the findings regarding cognitive abilities, some influential development theorists argue that the cognitive approach is too narrow a lens within which to evaluate decisional competence because it fails to account for psychosocial factors, such as peer influence and attitudes toward risk that may impinge upon decisional capacity. Focusing mainly on the activities of juvenile offenders, these researchers believe that it is in the realm of "judgment" rather than cognitive processes that important differences in the decision-making abilities of adults and minors are likely to be found.

42. Wallace J. Mlyniec, *A Judge's Ethical Dilemma: Assessing a Child's Capacity to Choose*, 63 Fordham L. Rev. 1873, 1880 (1996), quoting R. Murray Thomas, *Comparing Theories of Child Development*, p. 1027 3rd ed. 1992).

43. Laurence Steinberg and Elizabeth Caufman, *Maturity of Judgment in Adolescence: Psychological Factors in Adolescent Decision Making*, 20 Law and Human Behavior 249, 262–63 (1996).

44. *Id.*

The other dimensions of perspective include the ability to "see both short-and long-term consequences ... to place one decision in the context of others." *Id.* at 263. Steinberg and Caufman also refer to this process as "decentration," since it entails the ability to "shift one's focus away from the center of a problem." *Id.*

45. The experts who testified at trial were Dr. Jane E. Hodgson, an associate professor at the University of Minnesota and the "author of numerous leading studies on first trimester abortions," and Dr. Carol Nadelson, an assistant professor of psychiatry at Harvard Medical School, a psychiatrist at a "major Boston Hospital" with several years of "extensive clinical experience" conducting evaluations of pregnant teens, and the author of numerous articles "relating to teenage sexuality, abortion and counseling in the medical literature."

Brief of the Appellees, p. 10–12, submitted to the U.S. Supreme Court in the case of *Bellotti v. Baird,* 443 U.S. 622 (1978).

46. *Zbaraz v. Hartigan*, 763 F.2d 1532 (7th Cir. 1985) aff'd sub nom. *Hartigan v. Zbaraz,* 484 U.S. 171 (1987).

47. Brief for Amicus Curiae, American Psychological Association, in Support of Appelles, 1987.

48. The court has relied upon social-science data to assist it "determine the content of law and policy and to exercise its judgment or discretion in determining what course of action to take" ever since the future associate justice of the United States Supreme Court Louis D. Brandeis submitted what is now referred to as a "Brandeis Brief " in the 1908 case of *Muller v. Oregon,* 208 U.S. 412. Kenneth Culp Davis, *Judicial Notice*, 55 Colum. L. Rev. 952 (1955). In his brief, Brandeis amassed all of the existing social-science literature to support his argument that protective labor laws would benefit women because they were more vulnerable than men due to their reproductive functions. The Court's decision was replete with references to his brief.

For more detail on the some of the issues involved in the Court's use of social-science data, see Ellie Margolis, *Beyond Brandeis: Exploring the Uses of Non-Legal Materials in Appellate Briefs*, 34 U.S.F.L. L. Rev. 197 (2000); George D. Marlow, *From Black Robes to White Lab Coats: The Ethical Implications of A Judge's Sua Sponte, Ex Parte Acquisition Of Social and Other Scientific Evidence during the Decision-Making Process*, 72 St. John's L. Rev. 291 (1998); and Peggy C. Davis, *"There Is a Book Out . . ."*: *An Analysis of Judicial Absorption of Legislative Facts*, 100 Harv. L. Rev. 1539 (1987).

In the abortion context, the *Casey* decision is a good example of how important social-science data can be in the decision-making process of the court. As illustrated by the following passage, the *Casey* Court relied upon multiple empirical studies documenting the pervasiveness and seriousness of domestic violence to affirm the factual findings of the trial court and invalidate Pennsylvania's spousal-notification requirement:

> These findings are supported by studies of domestic violence. The American Medical Association (AMA) has published a summary of the recent research in this field, which indicates that in an average 12-month period in this country, approximately two million women are the victims of severe assaults by their male partners. In a 1985 survey, women reported that nearly one of every eight husbands had assaulted their wives during the past year. The AMA views these figures as "marked underestimates," because the nature of these incidents discourages women from reporting them, and because surveys typically exclude the very poor, those who do not speak English well, and women who are homeless or in institutions or hospitals when the survey is conducted. According to the AMA, "researchers on family violence agree that the true incidence of partner violence is probably *double* the above estimates; or four million severely assaulted women per year. Studies on prevalence suggest that from one-fifth to one-third of all women will be physically assaulted by a partner or ex-partner during their lifetime." AMA Council on Scientific Affairs, Violence Against Women 7 (1991) (emphasis in original). Thus on an average day in the United States, nearly 11,000 women are severely assaulted by their male partners. Many of these incidents involve sexual assault. *Id.*, at 3–4; Shields & Hanneke, Battered Wives' Reactions to Marital Rape, in The Dark Side of Families: Current Family Violence Research 131, 144 (D. Finkelhor, R. Gelles, G. Hataling, & M. Straus eds. 1983). In families where wifebeating takes place, moreover, child abuse is often present as well. Violence Against Women, *supra*, at 12.

> Other studies fill in the rest of this troubling picture. Physical violence is only the most visible form of abuse. Psychological abuse, particularly forced social and economic isolation of women, is also common. L. Walker, The Battered Woman Syndrome 27–28 (1984). Many victims of domestic violence remain with their abusers, perhaps because they perceive no superior alternative. Herbert, Silver, & Ellard, Coping with an Abusive Relationship: I. How and Why do Women Stay?, 53 J. Marriage & the Family 311 (1991). Many abused women who find temporary refuge in shelters return to their husbands, in large part because they have no other source of income. Aguirre, Why Do They Return? Abused Wives in Shelters, 30 J. Nat. Assn. of Social Workers 350, 352 (1985). Returning to one's abuser can be dangerous. Recent Federal Bureau of Investigation statistics disclose that 8.8 percent of all homicide victims in the United States are killed by their spouses. Mercy & Saltzman, Fatal Violence Among Spouses in the United States, 1976–85,

79 Am. J.Public Health 595 (1989). Thirty percent of female homicide victims are killed by their male partners. Domestic Violence: Terrorism in the Home, Hearing before the Subcommittee on Children, Family, Drugs and Alcoholism of the Senate Committee on Labor and Human Resources, 101st Cong., 2d Sess., 3 (1990).

. . . The vast majority of women notify their male partners of their decision to obtain an abortion. In many cases in which married women do not notify their husbands, the pregnancy is the result of an extramarital affair. Where the husband is the father, the primary reason women do not notify their husbands is that the husband and wife are experiencing marital difficulties, often accompanied by incidents of violence. Ryan & Plutzer, When Married Women Have Abortions: Spousal Notification and Marital Interaction, 51 J. Marriage & the Family 41, 44 (1989).

49. Preston A. Britner, Suzanne J. LaFleur, and Amy J. Whitehead, *Evaluating Juveniles' Competence to Make Abortion Decisions: How Social Science Can Inform the Law*, 5 U. of Chi L. School Roundtable 35 (1998); *see also* Josephine Gittler, Mary Quigley-Rick, and Michael J. Saks, *Adolescent Health Care Decision Making: The Law and Public Policy*, p. 37 (working paper, The Carnegie Council on Adolescent Development, 1990); Mlyniec, supra note 42, at 1882; and Elizabeth Cauffman and Lawrence Steinberg, *The Cognitive and Affective Influences on Adolescent Decision-Making*, 68 Temple L. Rev. 1763 (1995). However, some contemporary development theorists, although not necessarily disagreeing with the findings regarding cognitive abilities, argue that the cognitive approach is too narrow for evaluating decisional competence because it fails to account for psychosocial factors that may impinge upon the decision-making abilities. Focusing mainly on the activities of juvenile offenders, these researchers believe that it is in the realm of "judgment" rather than cognitive processes that important differences in the decision-making abilities of adults and minors are likely to be found. However, as discussed in chapter 7, most of this research has been done in a very different context, and thus is not directly applicable to the abortion decision.

50. See Catherine C. Lewis, *A Comparison of Minors' and Adults' Pregnancy Decisions*, 50 Amer. J. of Orthopsychiatry 446 (1980).

According to Lewis, the young women in her study tended to focus more on "external" considerations, such as the reaction of their families or the fear of fetal deformity, as reasons for choosing abortion in contrast to the more self-directed considerations of the adults, such as an inability to care for the child. She theorized that the "existence of a convenient external 'excuse' may 'short-circuit' the thinking of the younger adolescent, allowing her to avoid full consideration of the implications of immediate childbearing." *Id.* at 450. However, she also suggested that this externalization could reflect the fact that young women have less objective control over their lives and are, in fact, more constrained by external considerations.

In contrast to Lewis' results, the young women I interviewed were not focused on external considerations; moreover, the majority of them mentioned concern for the child as one of the reasons for choosing abortion.

51. Bruce Ambuel and Julian Rappaport, *Developmental Trends in Adolescents' Psychological Competence to Consent to Abortion,* 16 Law and Human Behavior 129, 149 (1992).

52. *Id.*

In another study on volition, researchers presented children, adolescents, and young adults with hypothetical vignettes involving a range of medical problems and asked them to choose the best treatment option based on the information provided. The vignettes were then repeated with varying degrees of parental influence inserted into the narrative in order to evaluate the extent to which this pressure would affect their view as to the best course of treatment.

The researchers found that adolescents approached medical decisions with the same "quality of intentionality" that is displayed by young adults, particularly with respect to the more serious of the medical dilemmas that they were presented with. David G. Sherer, *The Capacities of Minors to Exercise Voluntariness in Medical Treatment Decisions,* 15 Law and Human Behavior 431 (1991).

53. Ambuel and Rappaport, supra note 51, at 145.

54. *Bellotti II,* 443 U.S. at 640 (emphasis added).

55. Steinberg and Cauffman, supra note 43, at 266.

56. Blum and Resnick, supra note 10, at 804.

57. In fact, Blum and Resnick found that "aborters had the most developed future time perspective," whereas teen mothers "had the last developed conceptualization of the future." *Id.* at 801.

58. Interview with Jill Casey.

59. Robert W. Blum and Michael D. Resnick, *Adolescent Sexual Decision-Making: Contraception, Pregnancy Abortion, Motherhood,* 11 Pediatric Annals 797, 804 (1982).

60. Of course, because of the small sample size, no definitive conclusions can be drawn about the relationships between age, life circumstances, and the incorporation of future plans into the decision-making process.

61. Interview with Mary Jane.

It is worth noting that Mary Jane's future plan was not articulated as a freestanding goal, as it was for the non-mothers who were planning to go to college. The non-mothers could imagine a future that was not bogged down by the weight of their present circumstances. In contrast, for Mary Jane, her future goal was enmeshed in the complexities of her current life. Although no less important to her, her vision of her future was more precarious—more vulnerable to disruption.

62. Interview with Kim Johnson.

63. Interview with Keisha Wood.

64. Stephanie did not think her mother would hit her if she was pregnant, but given her family history, she was afraid of emotional abuse and isolation within her family.

65. Interview with Jane Smith; for Jane, being "straight" meant being on the right path in life and was not a reference to sexual orientation.

66. The same cannot be said for the fourth 14-year-old—Sandra Kiwi—to mention future plans as a reason for abortion. However, her future plan to join her mother who had

abandoned her in infancy was, in fact, no less reflective of a desire to begin building an adult life than the education and career plans identified by the other minors.

67. Interview with Monique White.

68. Interview with Teresa Clark.

69. Interview with Teresa Clark.

70. Interview with Taylor Jordan.

71. According to Blum and Resnick, in addition to requiring a personal sense of the future, a future orientation also requires a belief that the future is attainable. Hence, in the absence of hope, a minor, even if she possesses the requisite cognitive ability, may not incorporate a future orientation into her decision-making process. Blum and Resnick, supra note 10, at 805.

72. Although most of the young women had steady boyfriends, a few had become pregnant through a casual encounter, and two reported having become pregnant as a result of a rape.

73. Fear of disclosure has been identified as a barrier to help-seeking behavior in adolescents. See Kimberly A. Schonert-Reichl and Jennifer R. Muller, *Correlates of Help-Seeking in Adolescence*, 25 J. of Youth and Adolescence 705 (1996).

74. Virtually all of the young women (98 percent) in the larger sample of Massachusetts minors spoke with at least one other person about their abortion decision, with a mean number of 3.14 persons consulted. About 90 percent of these young women spoke with at least one adult; if friends and boyfriends over the age of 18 are excluded from the universe of adult contacts, the percentage drops to 70. Regarding this component of the Massachusetts abortion study, see chapter 4, note 1, and J. Shoshanna Ehrlich, *Grounded in the Reality of Their Lives: Young Women Who Make the Abortion Decision without Parental Involvement,* 18 Berkeley Women's L.J. 61, 91–100 (2003). For other studies, see Stanley Henshaw and Kathleen Kost, *Parental Involvement in Minors' Abortion Decisions,* 24 Family Planning Perspectives 198 (1992) (finding that 81 percent of minors involved at least one adult in the abortion decision-making process). Michael D. Resnick, Linda H. Bearinger, Patricia Stark, and Robert Wm. Blum, *Patterns of Consolation Among Adolescent Minors Obtaining an Abortion,* 1994 American J. of Orthopsychiatry 310 (1994) (finding that 75 percent of minors involved at least one adult)

75. Ehrlich, supra note 74, at 99; Resnick et al., supra note 75, at 314; Henshaw and Kost, supra note 75, at 205.

76. In the larger Massachusetts sample, almost 60 percent of the young women spoke with a professional, compared to about 25 percent who turned to an adult relative. For further detail, see Ehrlich, supra note 74, at 98–100. Henshaw and Kost likewise found that professionals were the most important source of adult support for teens who did not involve their parents. Henshaw and Kost, supra note 75, at 205.

77. Ehrlich, supra note 74, at 99–100 and 160.

78. Laurie S. Zabin, Marilyn B. Hirsch, Mark R. Emerson, and Elizabeth Raymond, *To Whom Do Inner-City Minors Talk About Their Pregnancies? Adolescents' Communication with Parents and Parent Surrogates,* 24 Family Planning Perspectives 148 (1992). *See also* Vickey

Howell Pierson, *Missouri's Parental Consent Law and Teen Pregnancy Outcomes*, 22 Women & Health 47, 55 (1995).

79.   Peggy C. Giordano, Stephen A. Cernkovich, and Alfred DeMaris, *The Family and Peer Relations of Black Adolescents*, 55 J. of Marriage and the Family 277, 280. It should be noted that this study did not focus on abortion. Rather, it focused on the importance of taking "race/ethnicity into account in building theories about adolescent development, and in understanding how social networks influence important outcome." *Id.* at 277. More specifically, the authors tested the hypothesis that the presumed shift in adolescent attachment from family to peer group was not automatically applicable to black teens in light of the "historically and culturally unique experiences of black youths." *Id.* at 280.

80.   *Id.*

81.   Steinberg and Cauffman, supra note 43, at 254.

82.   Catherine C. Lewis, *Minors' Competence to Consent to Abortion*, 42 American Psychologist 84, 86 (1987).

83.   A number of researchers have suggested a direct link between experience and decisional competence. According to Lewis, any differences that exist in the decision-making performance of adults and minors may, rather than reflecting distinctions in cognitive ability, instead be attributable to the "circumscribed role of adolescents in family and society." Lewis, supra note 82, at 87.

In a similar vein, Ambuel and Rappaport recommend that we recognize that decisional competence is "the outcome of a complex social process" and develop procedures for "obtaining informed consent that create competence by empowering minors as decision makers." Ambuel and Rappaport, supra note 51, at 150.

84.   Schonert-Reichl and Muller, supra note 3, p 707.

85.   Cauffman and Steinberg, supra note 49, at 1775.

86.   Lewis, supra note 82, at 86.

87.   Ambuel and Rappaport, supra note 51, at 146.

CHAPTER 6

1.   Depending upon the study, the rate of disclosure is generally between 45 and 65 percent, regardless of whether a parental-involvement law is in effect. See Michael D. Resnick, Linda H. Bearinger, Patricia Stark, and Robert Wm. Blum, *Patterns of Consultation among Adolescent Minors Obtaining an Abortion*, Amer. J. Orthopsychiatry 64 (1994); Stanley K. Henshaw and Kathryn Kost, *Parental Involvement in Minors' Abortion Decisions*, 24 Family Planning Perspectives 196 (1992); Robert Wm Blum, Michael D. Resnick, and Trisha Stark, *Factors Associated with the Use of Court Bypass by Minors to Obtain Abortions*, 22 Family Planning Perspectives 158 (1990); and Aida Torres, Jacqueline Darroth Forrest, and Susan Eisman, *Telling Parents: Clinic Policies and Adolescents' Use of Family Planning and Abortion Services*, 12 Family Planning Perspectives 284, 291 (1980).

2.   Minors in this group include Anna Lynne Albano (mother); Jill Casey (both parents); Theresa Clark (both parents); Kathleen Johnson (mother), Bianca Jones (father); Taylor Jordan (mother); Sandra Llonas (mother);

Molly Moe (both parents); Beth Smith (father); Dion Smith (mother); Mary Smith (both parents); Mary Souza (mother); and Monique White (mother).

3. Interview with Molly Moe. For further detail, see discussion.

4. Interview with Anna Lynne Albano.

5. Interview with Taylor Jordan.

6. Minors in this group include Corey Adams, Angel Cavanaugh, Jasmine Cruz, Kathleen Johnson, Kim Johnson, Sandra Kiwi, Amy Michaels, Stephanie Paul, Miranda Roberts, Melissa Silver, Jane Smith, Keiza Smith, and Keisha Wood.

7. Interview with Mary Souza.

8. Interview with Stephanie Paul.

9. Interview with Corey Adams.

10. These fathers were generally living apart from their families. Some were in another state, others were in another country, and some were in jail. No conclusion should be drawn from this discussion about whether teen daughters tend to have worse relationships with their fathers than they do with their mothers, as this was not an intended focus of the interviews.

11. Interview with Sandra Llonas. Although Sandra did not have what she considered to be a relationship with her father, she did have some regular contact with him, unlike some of the other minors. She described him as "cool" and always making "sexual jokes."

12. Interview with Stephanie Paul.

13. Interview with Monique White.

14. Interview with Sandra Kiwi.

15. Interview with Miranda Roberts.

16. Both Miranda and Taylor were born to immigrant parents, and both linked their parents' negative views toward sex with the cultural outlook of their home cultures. This is simply noted here. There is no attempt to correlate parental views to racial or cultural backgrounds.

17. As discussed in the text, Mary's father also filed a delinquency petition in court when he learned she was sexually active.

18. Interview with Jill Casey.

19. Interview with Beth Smith.

20. See James Jaccard, Patricia J. Dittus, and Vivian V. Gordon, *Parent-Adolescent Congruency in Reports of Adolescent Sexual Behavior and in Communications about Sexual Behavior,* 69 Child Development 247 (1998); Kim S. Miller, Beth A. Kotchick, Shannon Dorsey, Rex Forehand, and Anissa Y. Ham, *Family Communication about Sex: What Are Parents Saying and Are Their Adolescents Listening?* 30 Family Planning Perspectives 218 (1998); Bruce M. King and Joann Lorusso, *Discussions in the Home about Sex: Different Recollections by Parents and Children,* 23 J. of Sex and Marital Therapy 52 (1997).

21. King and Lorusso, supra note 20, at 58.

22. See Jaccard et al., supra note 20, at 188. However, in one study only 35 percent of males (compared to 62 percent of the females) reported that their mothers had talked to them about sexual matters. *Id.* at 188.

23. Henry J. Kaiser Family Foundation, *Communication: A Series of National Surveys of Teens about Sex* (2002). However, according to survey results, although 50 percent of the

young men had discussed condom use with a parent, only 35 had discussed other forms of birth control with them.

24. Interview with Melissa Silver.

25. Although the department has the legal authority to do so, the policy of DSS is not to consent to abortions for minors in their custody.

26. It is not clear whether her mother knew that Jasmine's pregnancy was the result of a rape.

27. Henshaw and Kost, supra note 1, at 202–203.

28. Blum, Resnick, and Stark, supra note 1, at 160.

29. Proportionally, these results are quite similar to those from the larger representative sample of minors (see chapter 4, note 1).

30. Interview with Stephanie Paul.

31. As mentioned in the section entitled "Talking About Sexuality," the only conversation Mary had had with her father about sex consisted of him calling her a whore.

32. Interview with Angel Cavanaugh.

33. A considerably smaller percentage of the minors in the larger representative sample gave this as a reason for nondisclosure. Although the reason for this is not entirely clear, it may well reflect the fact that the interviews gave the young women more of an opportunity to reflect upon their lives in a more complete manner. (See Chapter 4, footnote 1).

34. Interview with Jill Casey.

35. When Mary uses the word "choice" here, she is referring to the voluntary nature of the sexual encounter, not to becoming pregnant.

36. Interview with Molly Moe.

37. Interview with Sandra Llonas.

38. Interview with Corey Adams. Recall that Corey was one of the minors whose parents found out about her abortion—her father's abusive response is described earlier.

39. This is a significantly higher percentage than in the larger sample, where fewer than 10 percent of the minors mentioned this as a reason. Like with concern for the relationship, this may say something about the different methodologies employed, with the interview allowing for a more reflective response, or it may say something about a possible difference between the two samples.

However, in his nationally representative sample, Henshaw found that "twenty-five percent of the minors who had not told their parents and 12 % of those who had not told their father said that their parent was already under too much stress. The most common sources of stress mentioned for both mothers and fathers were related to family, work, finances and health." Henshaw and Kost, supra note 1, at 203.

40. Interview with Mary Smith.

41. Interview with Anna Lynne Albano.

42. Interview with Monique White.

43. Interview with Beth Smith.

44. Interview with Molly Moe.

45. Interview with Monique White.

46. Interview with Amy Michaels.

47. Interview with Corey Adams.

48. A similar percentage of the minors in the representative sample gave this as a reason for nondisclosure.

49. Interview with Beth Smith.

50. Interview with Jane Smith.

51. Interview with Keiza Smith.

52. Interview with Molly Moe.

53. Interview with Monique White.

54. See J. Shoshanna Ehrlich, *Grounded in the Reality of Their Lives: Listening to Teens Who Made the Abortion Decision without Parental Involvement*, 18 Berkeley Women's L. J. 63 (2003).

55. *Hodgson v. Minnesota*, 497 U.S. 417 (1990).

56. *Id.*, at 439–440, quoting the findings of the district court.

57. Suellyn Scarneccia and Julie Kunce Field, *Judging Girls: Decision Making in Parental Consent to Abortion Cases*, 3 Mich. J. Gender & L. 75, 96–97 (1995).

58. James Jaccard, Patricia J. Dittus, and Vivian V. Gordon, supra note 20, at 257.

59. *Id.*

60. Carol Gilligan, *Remapping the Moral Domain: New Images of Self in Relationship*, in Carol Gilligan, Janie Victoria Ward, and Jean Mclean Taylor, eds., *Mapping the Moral Domain* (1988).

61. Lance L. Weinmann and Nora Newcombe, *Relational Aspects of Identity: Late Adolescents' Perceptions of Their Relationships with Parents*, 50 J. of Child Psychology 357, 357–58 (1990).

62. Mary S. Griffin-Carlson and Paula J. Schwanenflugel, *Adolescent Abortion and Parental Notification: Evidence for the Importance of Family Functioning on the Perceived Quality of Parental Involvement in U.S. Families*, 39 J. of Child Psychology/Psychiatry 705, 726 (1998).

63. Doreen Rosenthal, Teresa Senserrick, and Shirley Feldman, *A Typology Approach to Describing Parents as Communicators about Sexuality*, 30 Archives of Sexual Behavior 463, 464 (2001).

64. *The Parent Gap: Teen Pregnancy and Parental Influence*, http://www.teenpregnancy. org.

65. Laurence Steinberg and Elizabeth Caufmann, *Maturity of Judgment in Adolescence: Psychological Factors in Adolescent Decision Making*, 20 Law and Human Behavior 249, 262–63 (1996).

66. Griffin-Carlson, supra note 62, at 543, 549. *See also* Nancy E. Alder, Emily J. Ozer, and Jeanne Tschann, *Abortion among Adolescents*, 2003 American Psychologist 211, 214; Mary S. Griffin-Carlson and Kathleen J. Mackinn, *Parental Consent: Factors Influencing Adolescent Disclosure Regarding Abortion*, 28 Adolescence 1 (1993); Laurie S. Zabin, Marilyn B. Hirsch, Mark R. Emerson, and Elizabeth Raymond, *To Whom Do Inner-City Minors Talk about Their Pregnancies? Adolescents' Communication with Parents and Parent Surrogates*, 24 Family Planning Perspectives 148 (1992); and Resnick et al., supra note 1, at 314.

67. Aida Torres, Jacqueline Darroch Forrest, and Susan Eisman, *Telling Parents: Clinic Policies and Adolescents Use of Family Planning and Abortion Services*, 12 Family Planning Perspectives 282, 289 (1980).

68. Interview with Mary Souza.

69. Interview with Jill Casey.

70. Interview with Monique White.

71. Interview with Miranda Roberts.

72. Interview with Amy Michaels.

73. Interview with Melissa Silver.

74. Interview with Taylor Jordan.

75. Interview with Jill Casey.

76. Interview with Beth Smith.

77. Interview with Mary Jane.

78. Interview with Beth Smith.

79. Interview with Mary Smith.

80. Interview with Mary Souza.

81. Interview with Jill Casey.

82. Interview with Beth Smith.

83. Interview with Angel Cavanaugh.

84. Interview with Corey Adams.

85. Interview with Teresa Clark.

86. *Hodgson v. Minnesota*, 497 U.S. 417, 442. (1990). *See also Planned Parenthood League of Massachusetts v. Attorney General*, 677 N.E. 2d 101, 106 (1997); and *American Academy of Pediatrics v. Lungren*, 940 P.2d 797 (Cal. 1997).

87. *Id.* at 442.

88. *Id.* at 443.

89. *Id.* at 442.

90. See Helena Silverstein and Leanne Speitel, *"Honey: I Have No Idea": Court Readiness to Handle Petitions to Waive Parental Consent for Abortion*, 88 Iowa L. Rev. 75 (2002) (focusing on the courts in Alabama); Helena Silverstein, *Road Closed: Evaluating the Judicial Bypass Provision of the Pennsylvania Abortion Control Act*, 24 Law & Social Inquiry 73 (1999); Melissa Jacobs, *Are Courts Prepared to Handle Judicial Bypass Proceedings?* Human Rights Magazine (2005) (focusing on the courts in Texas), available online at http://www.abanet.org.

91. *In re B.S.*, 74 P.3d 285 (Ariz. Ct. App. 2003).

92. Helena Silverstein, *In the Matter of Anonymous, A Minor: Fetal Representation in Hearings to Waive Parental Consent for Abortion*, 11 Cornell J.L. Pub. Pol'y 69 (2001).

93. Helena Silverstein, *Religious Establishment in Hearings to Waive Parental Consent for Abortion*, 7 U. PA J. Const. L 473 (2004).

94. As quoted in Silverstein, supra note 92, at 82–83.

95. *Id.* at 84, quoting the order of the trial court judge.

96. *In re Jane Doe*, 566 N.E. 2d 1181 (Ohio 1991).

97. *Id.* at 1188 (Douglas dissenting). Note that some states have altered the second step of the two-tiered inquiry from a consideration of whether the abortion is in the minor's best interest to one of whether parental notification is in her best interest.

98. *In re Jane Doe,* 19 S.W. 346 (Tex. 2000). The denial was upheld by the Texas appeals court but was ultimately reversed by the state's high court.

99. *Id.* at 360–61.

100. *Ex Parte Anonymous,* 803 So. 2d 542, 546 (Ala. 2001).

101. *Id.*

102. *Id.* at 548.

103. As quoted in Patricia Donovan, *Judging Teenagers: How Minors Fare When They Seek Court-Authorized Abortion,* 15 Family Planning Perspectives 259, 267 (1983). *See also* M. C. Crosby and Abigail English, *Mandatory Parental Involvement Judicial Bypass Laws: Do They Promote Adolescents' Health?* 12 J. of Adolescent Health 143 (1991).

CHAPTER 7

1. *Planned Parenthood of Southeastern Pennsylvania v. Casey,* 505 U.S. 833 (1992).

2. *Id.* at 877. As discussed in Chapter 1, the regulation may not impose an "undue burden" on the woman's right to terminate her pregnancy.

3. Donald L. Beschle, *The Juvenile Justice Counterrevolution: Responding to the Cognitive Dissonance in the Law's View of the Decision-Making Capacity of Minors,* 48 Emory L. J. 65, 68 (1999).

4. *Id.* at 85.

5. *Id.* at 68.

6. I leave it to the conservatives to reconcile their own positions on these issues.

7. Almost all states set the age of majority at age 18, although a few states set it at 19.

The use of 18 as the age of majority is a relatively recent occurrence. At common law, the age of majority was 21, apparently due to the fact that "in the Middle Ages, most men were presumed capable of carrying armor at this age." Elizabeth Scott, *The Legal Construction of Adolescence,* 29 Hofstra L. Rev. 547, 559 (2000).

This downward shift in the age of majority from 21 to 18 is attributable to the passage of the 26th Amendment, which lowered the age at which citizens have a right to vote in federal and state elections to 18. In turn, the passage of this amendment is generally attributable to the turmoil of the Vietnam War era, when the inherent unfairness of asking young men between the ages of 18 and 21 to risk their lives for their country while denying them the vote galvanized a demand for lowering the voting age to 18. *Id.* at 564. In addition to this political reality, the senate committee that recommended passage of the amendment also grounded its support for the age reduction in developmental truths, recognizing that by age 18, young people are "mentally and emotionally capable of full participation in our democratic form of government." *Id.* (citing the Senate Comm. On the Judiciary, Lowering the Voting Age to 18, S. Rep. No. 92–26, at 6).

8. Laurence Steinberg and Robert G. Schwartz, *Developmental Psychology Goes To Court*, in Thomas Grisso and Robert G. Schwartz, eds., *Youth on Trial: A Developmental Perspective on Juvenile Justice*, p. 23 (2000).

9. *Danforth v. Missouri*, 428 U.S. 52, 74 (1976).

10. Scott, supra note 7, at 548. Scott's concept of boundary-shifting is a very helpful way to think about the legal status of adolescents. I am indebted to her for this conceptualization of adolescent rights.

11. *Id.*

12. *Id.* at 577.

13. *Tinker v. Des Moines*, 393 U.S. 503 (1969).

14. *Id.* at 11, dissenting opinion of Justice Black.

15. Of course, this means that one's position on the wearing of armbands would be highly unstable, since an armband is actually a stand-in for views on the issue being protested.

16. Barry C. Feld, *The Transformation of the Juvenile Court*, 75 Minn. L. Rev. 691, 694 (1991).

17. *In re Gault*, 387 U.S 1,16 (1967).

18. Mary E. Odom, *Delinquent Daughters: Protecting and Policing Adolescent Female Sexuality in the United States*, 1885–1920, pp. 99–100 (1995).

19. *Id.* at 147.

20. *Gault*, 387 U.S. at 15.

21. Barry C. Feld, *Criminalizing Juvenile Justice: Rules of Procedure for the Juvenile Court*, 69 Minn. L. Rev. 141, 149 (1984).

22. *Id.* 151.

23. *Id.* at 150.

24. *Gault*, 387 U.S. at 18–19.

25. *In re Winship*, 397 U.S. 358 (1979).

26. *Breed v. Jones*, 421 U.S. 517 (1975).

27. *McKeiver v. Pennsylvania* 403 U.S. 528, 545 (1971).

28. *Id.*

29. *Id.*

30. Elizabeth S. Scott and Thomas Grisso, *The Evolution of Adolescence: A Developmental Perspective on Juvenile Justice Reform*, 88 J. of L. & Criminology 137,146–48 (1997). *See also* C. Antoinette Clarke, *The Baby and the Bathwater: Adolescent Offending and Punitive Juvenile Justice Reform*, 53 Kan. L. Rev. 659 (2005).

31. Richard E. Redding, *Juveniles Transferred to Criminal Court: Legal Reform Proposals Based on Social Science Research*, 1997 Utah L. Rev. 709, 711–13.

32. *Id.* at 713.

33. Paul J. McNulty, *Natural Born Killers? Preventing the Coming Explosion of Teenage Crime*, 71 Policy Rev. 84 (1995).

34. For more detail on these reforms, see Thomas Grisso, *The Competence of Adolescents as Trial Defendants*, 3 Psych. Pub. Pol. and Law 3 (1997); Redding, supra note 31; and Beschle, supra note 3.

35. Michelle Cotton, *Back With a Vengeance: The Resilience of Retribution as an Articulated Purpose of Criminal Punishment*, 37 Am. Crim. L. Rev. 1313, 1318 (2000).

36. Edward Rubin, *Model Penal Code: Sentencing: Just Say No to Retribution*, 7 Buff. Crim. L. R. 17, 29 (2003).

37. Although efforts toward adult rehabilitation were not marked by the same degree of optimism regarding the inherent malleability of the individual who had "gone wrong," rehabilitation was also a primary goal of punishment in the adult criminal system during most of the twentieth century. However, paralleling changes in the juvenile court system, over the last quarter of the twentieth century, retribution moved to the fore as part of the effort to crack down on crime. For more detail, see Cotton, supra note 35, and Rubin, supra note 36.

38. Scott and Grisso, supra note 30, at 151.

39. *Id.* at 149.

It should, however, be noted that in 2005, the United States Supreme Court held that the execution of offenders who were older than 15 but younger than 18 at the time the offense was committed is cruel and unusual punishment under the Eighth Amendment. *Roper v. Simmons*, 5434 U.S. 551 (2005). Previously, the Court had ruled that it violated the Eighth Amendment to execute offenders who were under the age of 16 at the time of the offense (*Thompson v. Oklahoma*, 487 U.S. 815 [1998]), while upholding the right of states to execute offenders who were 16 or 17 year old at the crime was committed (*Stanford v. Kentucky*, 492 U.S. 361 [1989]).

It is not clear what impact, if any, this decision will have on the trend to treat juvenile offenders like adults. On the one hand, the Court was quite clear that due to their youth, juveniles are less calpable than adults and that because juveniles are still in the process of solidifying their identity, "it is less supportable to conclude that even a heinous crime committed by a juvenile is evidence of irretrievably depraved character" (*Id.* at 1196), which suggests that there may be limits on how far a state may go in treating juveniles like adults. On the other hand, the Court was also clear that the death penalty raises unique considerations since it is limited to "those offenders who commit 'a narrow category of the most serious crimes' and whose extreme culpability makes them 'the most deserving of execution,' " (*Id.* at 1196, citing *Atkins v. Virginia*, 536 U.S. 304, 319 [2002]), thus limiting the applicability of the reasoning of this case to other aspects of the criminal process.

40. This is the term that Donald L. Beschle uses to describe the tension that is generated when the extension of autonomy rights to teens "in a wide-range of non-criminal matters" bumps up against the idea that "in the criminal sphere, paternalism is still appropriate." Beschle, supra note 3, at 68.

41. Laurence Steinberg and Elizabeth S. Scott, *Less Guilt by Reason of Adolescence: Developmental Immaturity, Diminished Responsibility and the Juvenile Death Penalty*, 53 American Psychologist 1009, 1010 (2003).

These experts include, but certainly are not limited to, Elizabeth Cauffman, Thomas Grisso, Elizabeth S. Scott, and Laurence Steinberg. The works of these and many other influential thinkers in this field are included in Thomas Grisso and Robert G. Schwartz, eds., *Youth on Trial: A Developmental Perspective on Juvenile Justice* (2000).

42. Elizabeth Cauffman and Laurence Steinberg, *The Cognitive and Affective Influences on Adolescent Decision-Making*, 68 Temple L. Rev. 1763, 1768. However, some concerns have been raised about the reliability of these studies, such as, for example, that they may involve hypothetical rather than real decision-making situations. *Id.* at 1770.

43. Laurence Steinberg and Elizabeth Cauffman, *Maturity of Judgment in Adolescence: Psychosocial Factors in Adolescent Decision Making*, 20 Law & Hum. Behav. 249, 250 (1996).

44. See generally the essays included in *Youth on Trial*, supra note 41.

45. Elizabeth Caufmann et al., *Justice for Juveniles: New Perspectives on Adolescents' Competence and Culpability*, 18 Quinnipiac L. Rev. 403, 412–13 (1999).

46. Scott and Grisso, supra note 30, at 161–62.

There is a direct link between competence and culpability, and those who are not competent are generally regarded as less blameworthy than those who are. In classical criminal theory, the adult criminal actor is regarded as a rational actor who freely chooses to engage in criminal activity. Punishment is likewise considered a reasoned response that respects the wrongdoer's "choice to create his own moral regime and to live with its consequences." Beschle, supra note 3, at 95.

The competence to stand trial actually consists of two distinct competencies—the competence to assist counsel, which is "a threshold concept that refers to the defendant's capacity to grasp the meaning of the legal procedure and to participate in it with counsel," Grisso, supra note 34, at 9, and "decisional competence," which refers to the "capacity to engage in reasoning processes and to make judgments with input from counsel." *Id.* Grisso develops these concepts in greater detail in his article.

47. Scott, supra note 7, at 592–93.

48. Scott and Grisso, supra note 30, at 175. For some of the policy implications of this position, see *Id.* at 183–90; Grisso, supra note 34, at 23–27; Joseph P. Allen and Claudia Worrell Allen, *Getting the Elephant Out of the Closet: Applying Developmental Perspective to the Disposition (Not Just the Assessment) of Juvenile Offenders*, 6 Va. J. Soc. Pol'y & L. 419 (1999); and Vance L. Cowden and Geoffrey R. McKee, *Competency to Stand Trial in Juvenile Delinquency Proceedings: Cognitive Maturity and the Attorney-Client Relationship*, 33 U. of Louisville J. of Fam. L. 629, 658–59 (1995).

49. Steinberg and Scott, supra note 41, at 1010.

50. Caufmann et al., supra note 45, at 407.

51. *Roe*, 410 U.S. at 163.

52. See chapter 5.

53. Jeffrey Fagan, *Contexts of Choice by Adolescents in Criminal Events*, in *Youth on Trial*, supra note 41, at 389.

54. *Id.* at 379. In particular, Fagan is focused here on robbery.

55. However, it should be noted that although these factors may not be not particularly salient in the abortion context, they may be relevant with respect to the underlying

decision to engage in sexual intercourse; thus, for instance, a girl may decide to have sex because she is pressured into it by her boyfriend.

56. Catherine C. Lewis, *Minors' Competence to Consent to Abortion*, 42 Am. Psychologist 84 (1967).

57. See David G. Sherer, *The Capacities of Minors to Exercise Voluntariness in Medical Treatment Decisions*, 15 Law & Hum. Behav. 431, 444 (1991); and Bruce Ambuel and Julian Rappaport, *Developmental Trends in Adolescents' Psychological and Legal Competence to Consent to Abortion*, 16 Law & Hum. Behav. 129 (1992).

58. Franklin E. Zimring, *Penal Proportionality for the Young Offender: Notes on Immaturity, Capacity, and Diminished Responsibility*, in *Youth on Trial*, supra note 41, at 280–81.

59. *Id.* at 281.

60. Fagan, supra note 53, at 374.

61. Scott and Grisso, supra note 30, at 164.

62. Steinberg and Cauffman, supra note 43, at 258.

63. Cauffman and Steinberg, supra note 42, at 1772–1773.

64. *Id.* at 1773; Scott and Grisso, supra note 30, at 164.

65. Mary Beckman, *Crime, Culpability and the Adolescent Brain*, 305 Science Magazine 599 (2004), available online at http://www.deathpenaltyinfo.org.

66. Steinberg and Cauffman, supra note 43, at 266.

67. Robert W. Blum and Michael D. Resnick, *Adolescent Sexual Decision-Making: Contraception, Pregnancy, Abortion, Motherhood*, 11 Pediatric Annals 797, 804 (1982).

68. Grisso, supra note 34, at 21.

69. Scott and Grisso, supra note 30, at 167.

70. *Determinants of Adolescent Sexual Behavior and Decision Making*, in Cheryl D. Hayes, ed., *Risking the Future: Adolescent Sexuality, Pregnancy, and Childbearing*, p. 112 (1987).

71. Kristen Luker, *Dubious Conceptions: The Politics of Teenage Pregnancy*, p. 154 (1996) (emphasis added).

72. Blum and Resnick, supra note 67, at 805. However, as discussed in chapter 5, this dichotomized view of young women has recently been challenged by some researchers as reflecting a middle-class bias. Rather than seeing childbearing as representing a sense of hopelessness and despair, researchers assert that it may be a rational response to a young woman's life circumstances that gives her a sense of purpose and future direction.

73. National Mental Health Association, *Prevalence of Mental Health Disorders among Children in the Juvenile Justice System*, http:///www.nmha.org/children.justjuv/prevelence.cfm (accessed January 11, 2003).

74. Alan E. Kazdin, *Adolescent Development, Mental Disorders, and Decision Making of Delinquent Youths*, in *Youth on Trial*, supra note 41, at 40. *See also* Thomas Grisso, *Dealing with Juveniles' Competence to Stand Trial: What We Need to Know*, 18 Quinnipiac L. Rev. 371, 379 (1999).

75. Kazdin, supra note 74, at 56.

76. Thomas Grisso, *Dealing with Juveniles' Competence to Stand Trial: What We Need to Know*, 18 Quinnipiac L. Rev. 371, 379–80 (1999).

77. Grisso, supra note 34, at 11–12 (comparing his results to those of Gary Melton).

78. Grisso, supra note 76, at 380.

CONCLUSION

1. These states include Connecticut, Colorado, Delaware, Iowa, Maine, Maryland, North Carolina, Ohio, South Carolina, West Virginia, and Wisconsin.

Resources

BOOKS

Demos, John, *Past, Present and Personal: The Family and Life Course in American History* (New York: Oxford University Press, 1986).

Ginsburg, Faye D., *Contested Lives: The Abortion Debate in An American Community* (Berkeley: University of California Press, 1989).

Gordon, Linda, *Women's Body, Women's Right: A Social History of Abortion in America* (New York: Penguin, 1977).

Grisso, Thomas, and Robert G. Schwartz, eds., *Youth on Trial: A Developmental Perspective on Juvenile Justice* (Chicago: University of Chicago Press, 2000).

Grossberg, Michael, *Governing the Hearth: Law and the Family in Nineteenth-Century America* (Chapel Hill: University of North Carolina Press, 1984)

Hayes, Cheryl D., ed., *Risking the Future: Adolescent Sexuality, Pregnancy, and Childbearing* (Washington, D.C.: National Academy Press, 1986).

Holder, Angela Roddey, *Legal Issues in Pediatrics and Adolescent Medicine* (2nd ed., New Haven: Yale University Press, 1985).

Lader, Lawrence, *Abortion* (Boston: Beacon Press, 1979).

Luker, Kristen, *Abortion: The Politics of Motherhood* (Berkeley: University of California Press, 1984).

Luker, Kristen, *Dubious Conceptions: The Politics of Teenage Pregnancy* (Cambridge: Harvard University Press, 1996).

Mason, Mary Ann, *From Fathers' Property to Children's Rights* (New York: Columbia University Press, 1994).

Mohr, James C., *Abortion in America: The Origins and Evolution of a National Policy, 1800–1900* (New York: Oxford University Press, 1978).

Odom, Mary E., *Delinquent Daughters: Protecting and Policing Adolescent Female Sexuality in the United States, 1885–1920* (Chapel Hill: University of North Carolina Press, 1995).

Pleck, Elizabeth, *Domestic Tyranny: The Making of American Social Policy from Colonial Times to the Present* (New York: Oxford University Press, 1987).

Regan, Leslie J., *When Abortion Was a Crime: Women, Medicine, and Law in the United States, 1867–1973* (Berkeley: University of California Press, 1997).

Starr, Paul, *The Social Transformation of American Medicine: The Rise of a Sovereign Profession and the Making of a Vast Industry* (New York: Basic Book, 1984).

Tribe, Lawrence H., *Abortion: The Clash of Absolutes* (New York: W.W. Norton & Co., 1982).

ARTICLES

Ambuel, Bruce, and Julian Rappaport, *Developmental Trends in Adolescents' Psychological Competence to Consent to Abortion*, 16 Law & Hum. Behav. 129 (1992).

Beschle, Donald L. *The Juvenile Justice Counterrevolution: Responding to the Cognitive Dissonance in the Law's View of the Decision-Making Capacity of Minors*, 48 Emory L.J. 65 (1999).

Blum, Robert W., and Michael D. Resnick, *Adolescent Sexual Decision-Making: Contraception, Pregnancy, Abortion, Motherhood*, 11 Pediatric Annals 797 (1982).

Blum, Robert W., Michael D. Resnick, and Trisha Stark, *Factors Associated with the Use of Court Bypass by Minors to Obtain Abortions*, 22 Family Planning Perspectives 158 (1990).

Cauffman, Elizabeth, and Lawrence Steinberg, *The Cognitive and Affective Influences on Adolescent Decision-Making*, 68 Temple L. Rev. 1763 (1995).

Connelly, Cynthia Donaldson, *Hopefulness, Self-Esteem, and Perceived Social Support among Pregnant and Nonpregnant Adolescents*, 20 Western J. of Nursing 195 (1995).

Council on Scientific Affairs, American Medical Association, *Confidential Health Services for Adolescents*, 11 JAMA 1420 (1993).

Dolgin, Janet, *The Fate of Childhood: Legal Models of Children and the Parent-Child Relationship*, 61 Albany L. Rev. 345 (1997).

Donovan, Patricia, *Judging Teenagers: How Minors Fare When They Seek Court-Authorized Abortions*, 15 Family Planning Perspectives 259 (1983).

Ehrlich, J. Shoshanna, *Journey through the Courts: Minors, Abortion, and the Quest for Reproductive Fairness*, 10 Yale J.L. & Feminism 1 (1998).

Ehrlich, J. Shoshanna, *Grounded in the Reality of Their Lives: Listening to Teens Who Make the Abortion Decision without Involving Their Parents*, 18 Berkeley Women's L.J. 61 (2003).

Ehrlich, J. Shoshanna, and Jamie Ann Sabino, *A Minor's Right to Abortion: The Unconstitutionality of Parental Participation in Bypass Hearings*, 25 New Eng. L. Rev. 1185, 1189 (1991).

English, Abigail, *Treating Adolescents: Legal and Ethical Considerations*, 74 Adolescent Med. 1097 (1990).

Feld, Barry C., *Criminalizing Juvenile Justice: Rules of Procedure for the Juvenile Court*, 69 Minn. L. Rev. 141 (1984).

Ford, Carol A., Peter S. Bearman, and James Moody, *Foregone Health Care among Adolescents*, 282 JAMA 2227 (1999).

Ford, Carol A., and Susan G. Millstein, *Delivery of Confidentiality Assurances to Adolescents by Primary Care Physicians*, 151 Archives Of Pediatrics & Adolescent Medicine 505 (1997).

Ford, Carol A., Susan G. Millstein, Bonnie L. Halpern-Feisher, and Charles E. Irwin Jr., *Influence of Physician Confidentiality Assurances on Adolescents' Willingness to Disclose Information and Seek Future Health Care: A Randomized Controlled Trial*, 278 JAMA 1029 (1997).

Geronimus, Arlene T., *Teenage Childbearing and Personal Responsibility: An Alternative View*, 112 Political Science Quarterly 405 (1997).

Gottesfeld, H. Jeffrey, *The Uncertain Status of the Emancipated Minor: Why We Need a Uniform Statutory Emancipation of Minors Act (USEMA)*, 15 U.S.F.L. 47 (1981).

Griffin-Carlson, Mary S., and Paula J. Schwanenflugel, *Adolescent Abortion and Parental Notification: Evidence for the Importance of Family Functioning on the Perceived Quality of Parental Involvement in U.S. Families*, 39 J. of Child Psychology/Psychiatry 543, 549 (1998).

Griffin-Carlson, Mary S., and Kathleen J. Mackinn, *Parental Consent: Factors Influencing Adolescent Disclosure Regarding Abortion*, 28 Adolescence 1 (1993).

Hartman, Rhonda Gay, *Coming of Age: Devising Legislation for Adolescent Medical Decision-Making*, 28 Am. J.L. and Med. 409 (2002).

Hartman, Rhonda Gay, *Adolescent Decisional Autonomy for Medical Care: Physicians Perceptions and Practices*, 8 U of Chi L. School Roundtable 87 (2001).

Henshaw, Stanley K., *Unintended Pregnancy in the United States*, 30 FPP 24 (1998).

Henshaw, Stanley, and Kathleen Kost, *Parental Involvement in Minors' Abortion Decisions*, 24 Family Planning Perspectives 198 (1992).

Holder, Angela Roddy, *Minors' Right to Consent to Medical Care*, 257 JAMA 3400 (1987).

Jaccard, James, Patricia J. Dittus, and Vivian V. Gordon, *Parent-Adolescent Congruency in Reports of Adolescent Sexual Behavior and in Communications about Sexual Behavior*, 69 Child Development 247 (1998).

King, Bruce M., and Joann Lorusso, *Discussions in the Home about Sex: Different Recollections by Parents and Children*, 23 J. of Sex and Marital Therapy 52 (1997).

Lewis, Catherine C., *A Comparison of Minors' and Adults' Pregnancy Decisions*, 50 Amer. J. of Orthopsychiatry 446 (1980).

Lewis, Catherine C., *Minors' Competence to Consent to Abortion*, 42 American Psychologist 84 (1987).

Melton, Gary M., *Toward "Personhood" for Adolescents: Autonomy and Privacy as Values in Public Policy*, 1983 American Psychologist 99.

Mlyniec, Wallace J., *A Judge's Dilemma: Assessing a Child's Capacity to Choose*, 640 Fordham L. Rev. 1873 (1996).

Resnick, Michael D., Linda H. Bearinger, Patricia Stark, and Robert Wm. Blum, *Patterns of Consolation among Adolescent Minors Obtaining an Abortion*, 1994 American J. of Orthopsychiatry 310.

Schonert-Reichl, Kimberly A., and Jennifer R. Muller, *Correlates of Help-Seeking in Adolescence*, 25 J. of Youth and Adolescence 705 (1996).

Schultz, Katherine, *Constructing Failure, Narrating Success: Rethinking the "Problem" of Teen Pregnancy*, 103 Teachers College Record 582 (2001).

Scott, Elizabeth, *The Legal Construction of Adolescence*, 29 Hofstra L. Rev. 547, 559 (2000).

Scott, Elizabeth, and Thomas Grisso, *The Evolution of Adolescence: A Developmental Perspective on Juvenile Justice Reform*, 88 J. of L. & Criminology 137, 146–48 (1997).

Sherer, David G, *The Capacities of Minors to Exercise Voluntariness in Medical Treatment Decisions*, 15 Law & Hum. Behav. 431 (1991).

Siegal, Riva, *Reasoning from the Body: A Historical Perspective on Abortion Regulation and Questions of Equal Protection*, 44 Stan. L. Rev. 261 (1992).

Silverstein, Helena, and Leanne Speitel, *"Honey, I Have No Idea": Court Readiness to Handle Petitions to Waive Parental Consent for Abortion*, 88 Iowa L. Rev. 75 (2002).

Silverstein, Helena, *Road Closed: Evaluating the Judicial Bypass Provision of the Pennsylvania Abortion Control Act*, 24 Law & Social Inquiry 73 (1999).

Silverstein, Helena, *In the Matter of Anonymous, a Minor: Fetal Representation in Hearings to Waive Parental Consent for Abortion*, 11 Cornell J.L. Pub. Pol'y 69 (2001).

Steinberg, Laurence, and Elizabeth Caufmann, *Maturity of Judgment in Adolescence: Psychological Factors in Adolescent Decision Making*, 20 Law & Hum. Behav. 249 (1996).

Torres, Aida, Jacqueline Darroth Forrest, and Susan Eisman, *Telling Parents: Clinic Policies and Adolescents' Use of Family Planning and Abortion Services*, 12 Family Planning Perspectives 284 (1980).

Wadlington, Walter, *Minors and Health Care: The Age of Consent*, 11 Osgoode Hall L.J. 115, 116 (1973).

Wadlington, Walter, *Medical Decision Making for and by Children: Tensions between Parent, State, and Child*, 1994 U. of Illinois L. Rev. 311.

Zabin, Laurie S., Marilyn B. Hirsch, Mark R. Emerson, and Elizabeth Raymond, *To Whom Do Inner-City Minors Talk about Their Pregnancies? Adolescents' Communication with Parents and Parent Surrogates*, 24 Family Planning Perspectives 148 (1992).

CASES

Akron v. Akron Center for Reproductive Health, Inc., 462 U.S. 416 (1983).

Bellotti v. Baird, 443 U.S. 622 (1979).

Harris v. McRae, 448 U.S. 297 (1980).

In Re Gault, 387 U.S 1 (1967).

Planned Parenthood of Central Missouri v. Danforth, 428 U.S. 52 (1976).

Planned Parenthood of Southeastern Pennsylvania v. Casey, 505 U.S. 833 (1992).

Roe v. Wade, 410 U.S. 113 (1973).

Thornburgh v. American College of Obstetricians and Gynecologists, 476 U.S. 747 (1986).

Webster v. Reproductive Health Services, 492 U.S. 490 (1989).

Wisconsin v. Yoder, 406 U.S. 205 (1972).

OTHER

ACLU Reproductive Freedom Project, *Parental Notice Laws: Their Catastrophic Impact on Teenagers' Right to Abortion* 3 (1986).

Donovan, Patricia, *Our Daughters' Decisions*, The Alan Guttmacher Institute (1992).

Gittler, Josephine, Mary Quigley-Rick, and Michael J. Saks, *Adolescent Health Care Decision Making: The Law and Public Policy* (working paper, The Carnegie Council on Adolescent Development, 1990).

NARAL Pro-Choice America, *Who Decides? A State-By-State Review of Abortion and Reproductive Rights* 2003, available online at http://www.naral.org/publications/whodecides2003.cfm.

Index

About the Author

J. Shoshanna Ehrlich is an associate professor in the Legal Studies program at the University of Massachusetts–Boston's College of Public and Community Service. This book draws upon several previously published articles, as follows:

J. Shoshanna Ehrlich, *Minors as Medical Decision Makers: The Pretextual Reasoning of the Court in the Abortion Cases*, 7 Michigan J. of Gender & Law 66 (2000).

J. Shoshanna Ehrlich, *Grounded in the Reality of Their Lives: Listening to Teens Who Make the Abortion Decision without Involving Their Parents*, 18 Berkeley Women's L. J. 61 (2003).

J. Shoshanna Ehrlich, *Shifting Boundaries, Abortion, Criminal Culpability and the Indeterminate Legal Status of Adolescents*, 18 Wisconsin Women's L. Journal 77 (2003).